P. H. SOLOMON

An Arrow Against the Wind

ARCHER'S
AIM PRESS

First published by Archer's Aim Press 2022

Copyright © 2022 by P. H. Solomon

All rights reserved. No part of this publication may be reproduced, stored or transmitted in any form or by any means, electronic, mechanical, photocopying, recording, scanning, or otherwise without written permission from the publisher. It is illegal to copy this book, post it to a website, or distribute it by any other means without permission.

This novel is entirely a work of fiction. The names, characters and incidents portrayed in it are the work of the author's imagination. Any resemblance to actual persons, living or dead, events or localities is entirely coincidental.

P. H. Solomon asserts the moral right to be identified as the author of this work.

P. H. Solomon has no responsibility for the persistence or accuracy of URLs for external or third-party Internet Websites referred to in this publication and does not guarantee that any content on such Websites is, or will remain, accurate or appropriate.

Designations used by companies to distinguish their products are often claimed as trademarks. All brand names and product names used in this book and on its cover are trade names, service marks, trademarks and registered trademarks of their respective owners. The publishers and the book are not associated with any product or vendor mentioned in this book. None of the companies referenced within the book have endorsed the book.

An Arrow Against the Wind is a work of fiction. Names, characters, places, and incidents either are the product of the author's imagination or are used fictitiously. Any resemblance to actual persons on the cover or in the text of the book, living or dead, events or locales is entirely coincidental.

Copyright 2017 by P. H. Solomon, Second Edition 2017

Excerpt for An Arrow Against the Wind Copyright 2015 by P. H. Solomon

All maps are the property of the author, Copyright 2015 by P. H. Solomon

This eBook is licensed for your personal enjoyment only. This eBook may not be re-sold or given away to other people. If you would like to share this book with another person, please purchase an additional copy for each recipient. If you're reading this book and did not purchase it, or it was not purchased for your use only, then please return to your favorite eBook retailer and purchase your own copy. Thank you for respecting the hard work of this author.

This book contains an excerpt from the forthcoming title The White Arrow by P. H. Solomon. This excerpt has been formatted for this book only and may not reflect the final content for the forthcoming edition.

Hardcover ISBN: 979-8720106591

Cover image licensed/commissioned through/by Chris Rawlins. Special thanks also goes to Chris Rawlins whose artistic vision produced such excellent cover art.

Second edition

ISBN: 979-8-72-010659-1

This book was professionally typeset on Reedsy.
Find out more at reedsy.com

Dedication

To my daughter who has been a thoughtful, avid reader and without whom there would be no Spark. Thank you for your helpful suggestions

Contents

Acknowledgement	iii
Maps	1
CHAPTER ONE	3
CHAPTER TWO	16
CHAPTER THREE	31
CHAPTER FOUR	46
CHAPTER FIVE	58
CHAPTER SIX	71
CHAPTER SEVEN	90
CHAPTER EIGHT	109
CHAPTER NINE	120
CHAPTER TEN	127
CHAPTER ELEVEN	139
CHAPTER TWELVE	146
CHAPTER THIRTEEN	165
CHAPTER FOURTEEN	187
CHAPTER FIFTEEN	197
CHAPTER SIXTEEN	203
CHAPTER SEVENTEEN	213
CHAPTER EIGHTEEN	224
CHAPTER NINETEEN	229
CHAPTER TWENTY	237
CHAPTER TWENTY-ONE	250
CHAPTER TWENTY-TWO	265
EPILOGUE	279
About the Author	289

Also by P. H. Solomon

Acknowledgement

Beta Readers:

The following is a list of my beta readers. They are a bright group and were so generous with their time and feedback: Carolyn Smith, Lyn Smith, Katherine King.

I want to especially offer my thanks to my editor, Jessica Barnes, without whom I wouldn't have made it this far. Jessica, you are truly a gem of an editor and you've taught me a great deal through your work.

Other Books by P. H. Solomon:
The Bow of Hart Saga:
Trading Knives (prequel novella)
What Is Needed (prequel novella)
The Bow of Destiny
An Arrow Against the Wind
The White Arrow

Thank you for reading this book. Upon finishing, if you liked this book, please click here and leave a few kind words about it.

Also, if you enjoy reading my work, you can subscribe to my newsletter for more information about my other books, fun updates about the series, and news about upcoming releases. Click here to subscribe and receive a gift. Read on about the next book in the series.

Maps

Northeast Denaria
From the Sigoth Range to Dragon's Maw

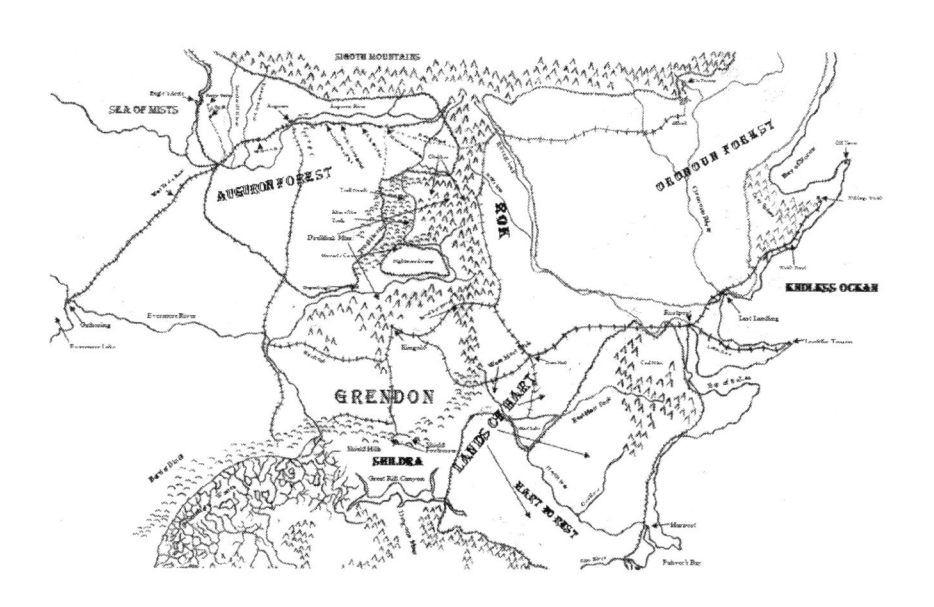

Central Drelkhaz Region

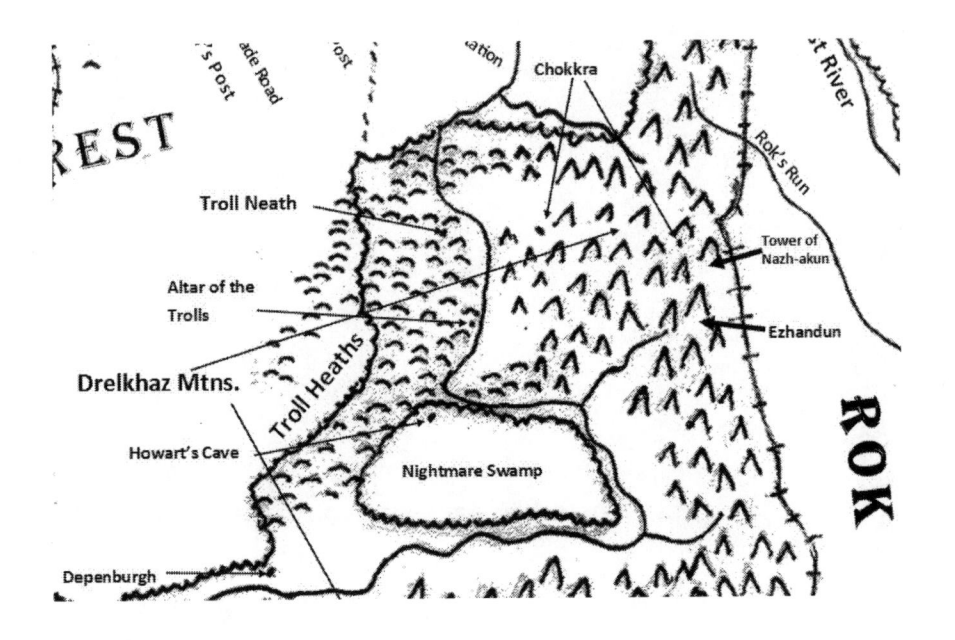

AN ARROW AGAINST THE WIND

CHAPTER ONE

The stone door *boomed* shut with the finality of a sarcophagus lid over a tomb. The echoing memory jolted Limbreth from her inner numbness by the morning fire. Athson was trapped inside Chokkra. Fear—she knew its feel now since the Banshee—rose like a bubble within her and lodged as a blocked sob in her chest. Limbreth closed her eyes. She'd almost opened her vein with a knife but for the death-grip. She picked up the travel-bread she'd dropped and stared at it. If she could only find him. But was Athson even alive after the door to Tordug's hidden rooms slammed shut?

Gweld's cloak flapped in the wind like crow's wings beside her and drew her attention from her glum thoughts. She watched the elf shoulder his pack. "What do you think? Could we find him?"

The elf crossed his arms and scanned the peaks that rose above the little stand of cedar where they camped in the mountains. He sighed a plume of breath. "I wouldn't know where to look, Limbreth. We'll just have to trust Makwi to get them out."

Hastra stirred and stood with her pack in hand. She patted Limbreth's shoulder. "They'll make it out. I'm that certain of Eloch's will."

Limbreth pushed Hastra's hand away and scowled at the Withling. The old woman had let it happen. "Really? Like when you believed the Bow of Hart was in Chokkra with Corgren? They're trapped in a huge den of trolls with Corgren like Athson's father, and all you can say is that you're right? I should have gone with Athson." At least she would have been with him.

Hastra recoiled from Limbreth as if stung by bees. Her gaze shifted to Tordug and Gweld, then back to Limbreth. "I was not for rescuing Ath, but Eloch's sending was clear to me. Survival depended on those three going alone if it was to be done. No others. I don't know why, but I do know they will make it."

"Well, now they're trapped and probably lost. I don't see how you are correct." Limbreth scrambled to her feet and shouldered her gear. To the dry wastes with respect for Withlings. She didn't regret her angry tone.

Tordug approached her with his bushy brow furrowed. "Limbreth, I think Makwi will get them out. We'll go to several shelters and try to meet them at some point."

She crossed her arms and swallowed the rising sob in her throat. "Shelters? Meet them?" She flailed an arm toward the path they'd traveled out of Tordug's little vale when they'd left his hidden apartments. "They're stuck in Chokkra. We need to figure out how to find them."

Tordug raised his hands as if to halt Limbreth in her tracks. "Gell, I understand how you feel. But it's a task beyond us and blaming Hastra does no good. She didn't set that trap! We must trust that Makwi can do it. We should believe that Hastra is right about Eloch's foresight. She's been correct on many things. Makwi's gotten out of tight spots before."

Limbreth wheeled away and wiped a sudden tear from her cheek. Her response came in a muted, husky tone. "So we're to abandon Ralda and Makwi and—and Athson?" Her shoulders sagged. She couldn't abandon him. Any of them. "And where do we go? If we find them at all? Where do we go?" She wheeled toward Hastra. The Bow of Hart hung over all of them, and they'd found nothing of it. "Where do we search?"

Hastra touched her midsection, and a pained expression flashed across her face. "I'll admit I don't have that direction. Yet."

"But you're correct about sending the others into a trap?"

"Athson chose it. I merely expressed what I know to be Eloch's own truth of the matter. I can't know what's not given. I knew nothing of that trap at the door."

Limbreth walked away through the surrounding cedars. This was wrong.

CHAPTER ONE

Hastra led them with no straight answers. No wonder Athson distrusted her. Had Limbreth been blind to her manipulations all along? Was the Withling just after the bow no matter what happened? She wiped her cheeks with her gloved hands and sniffed.

"So where are we going, Tordug?" Gweld asked, back at the fire.

Silence followed for a moment before Tordug cleared his throat. "Uh, we'll take a path to a high road and follow it south. We'll try to find the others. Makwi knows where to look for us. If we get far enough without them, we'll stop and wait."

Limbreth rolled her eyes toward the puffy clouds drifting among the mountain peaks. They were just to wait? She wanted to scream, but her breath felt short for some reason, and her heart lurched in her chest. Fear. She hated it.

"Speaking of traveling, I think it's time we go." Tordug sounded closer. "Limbreth, will you come? There's little chance of going back the other way and finding them. We'll more likely find trolls waiting."

She nodded over her shoulder. "Yeah, coming. I'll catch up in a minute."

Where else could she go? Athson wasn't with her, so she had to try to find him with the others. No matter how crazed it seemed. Tordug had planned for it with Makwi.

Weakness weighted her limbs, but she paused at the dregs of the fire. Wisps of smoke rose from under the snow kicked on the coals by Tordug. Leaving felt like giving up. But she wasn't. Limbreth trudged after the others and left the snow-doused fire behind as they departed the isolated vale. She fell behind no matter her efforts to keep up with her companions, and Gweld often waited for her. At least the elf would help her find Athson, wherever he was. If he still lived.

~ ~ ~ ~ ~ ~ ~

Ralda shifted, and Athson slammed into rock. He grunted. The giant kept running. Spark loped at Ralda's heels.

Athson blinked again. He squeezed his eyelids shut. It was easier in the dark just now. His father was gone. Athson's breath caught in his throat as he exhaled.

Ath's shout echoes in Athson's ears, "Run, Athson!"

"I am." No, Ralda ran. Where? His father was with Corgren. "Go back. Ath."

Ralda ran on.

A spray of pebbles and larger rocks pelted them. Hadn't the giant heard him? No, he couldn't with all that noise. Athson turned his head and glimpsed a dark beard waving at him. Makwi? He was here too? Of course! Athson shut his eyes again as the crash of stone and Ralda's movement faded.

Athson runs in the dark. Trolls howl as they thunder like an avalanche after him through the underbrush. Clawed paws snag and tear his clothing. Firelight fades. Heavy footfalls of trolls pound near, their huffing punctuated with grunts and snorts.

He turns and rushes back toward the gorge, the Funnel, near the troll camp. More trolls search the night, and others call for help. A kobold appears in front of him, and he runs into it. They fall hard, and the creature squeals as Athson grunts and kicks the creature in the face. Athson scurries off its back and rushes on. Where can he hide?

Deeper darkness yawns at his feet. He slides to a stop but not soon enough. He goes over the edge and rolls on a steep slope. Below, at the sheer edge, Athson's legs go over, and he grasps wildly for any handhold.

Trolls point at him and howl as he slides over the edge. He falls and screams. As he goes, his father's sword spins gleaming out of the darkness.

~ ~ ~ ~ ~ ~ ~

The rumble of collapsing stone faded to groans and squeals from the mass of surrounding rock. Ath half-gagged, half-coughed dust and grit from his throat. "Hello?" His hoarse whisper echoed ahead. An open passage. He checked his limbs by feel. Cuts and bruises, but nothing broken.

Ath crawled, but his chain pulled taut. His hands fumbled along the metal links. Who had held his chain last? Was it a buried troll? He felt around for a stone with a rough edge and enough weight to break the metal.

His hand passed over an object. Ath touched it. Rough edges, cold metal with teeth. His heart thudded. A piece of a file. He grinned. With this, he

CHAPTER ONE

could escape.

Ath started scratching a link, his movement fast. He should make it quick, lest trolls come searching. Where could he go in this place? Where was a door? The questions slowed his fervor against the hard, thick chain.

Someone groaned.

Ath paused. He hid his short file in a pocket, a vast treasure. His hands trailed back along the chain. A large chunk of rock lay on it, and he slid it away with effort. He continued on along the chain. Rock fell near him. Ath cringed and covered his head with his arms. Silence settled around him. Just settling rock. Still, best not to linger longer than necessary.

He searched along the length of his chain. He touched a hand and drew back with a gasp. He touched it again. It was warm and felt human. Ath sat back with a groan. "Corgren!" He coughed, and it sounded like a shout in the silence of the tunnel. Ath trembled a moment, frozen in place.

Key! Did Corgren have it? He scrambled to the wizard and went through his pockets. Nothing. Ath pounded his leg with a fist. After a few moments, his frustration ended. So, it would be the file or nothing. He reached for his pocket.

Corgren groaned.

Ath froze again. If the wizard woke, he would take Ath's prize. Then what? Ath felt around for a heavy rock. He'd have to kill Corgren and then use the file. He felt for the wizard's bald head and lifted the rock with both hands.

Rock tumbled in the blocked passage as the corridor quaked.

The file might take too long. Ath's face contorted with the effort of holding the rock. If it took too long, he might be buried. He grunted. Who cared if Corgren died?

Athson's voice, now a man's voice, flickered in his memory. Defiance. Had he survived? If so, he'd need Ath's help.

Ath needed to escape Chokkra, and someone needed to lead him out. He needed the file—and Corgren—to escape. How, he didn't know, other than that they had used him against Athson. He'd use the file little by little and break loose at the best opportunity. Preferably when Corgren took him to

7

bully Athson again to get the Bow of Hart. He tossed the rock aside, his arms trembling. He'd help Athson at the right opportunity, and that would come in time.

He searched Corgren for broken limbs and found nothing but a bloody knot on his head. Ath dragged Corgren away from the rock, out of the choking dust. The chain clinked with his movements. He progressed with the arduous proficiency of a blind man. He felt for obstacles, lest he fall, until the occasional sound of settling rock faded.

Corgren coughed and groaned. He rolled over in Ath's grasp.

"What are you doing? Where am I?" Corgren shoved Ath weakly away.

Ath stepped back. "There was a collapse. I pulled you away."

Corgren hissed in pain. "That's a nasty blow." He went still and then pulled Ath close. "Why did you save me?" A trembling grasp reached for Ath's throat. "You tried to kill me. This head wound."

Ath struggled with Corgren. "Please, no! It's the chain. We're attached. I don't think the trolls survived." He waved his hand in a vague approximation of the collapse.

Corgren's grasp loosened. A weak laugh echoed in the tunnel. "I suppose you want some thanks, some reward?"

Ath scrambled away. "No. It was just that rock kept falling around us."

He heard Corgren rise with prolonged grunts. He pulled on the chain. "Well, since you want to live, come along."

Ath followed. He squeezed the file in his pocket. He'd be ready if the time came. He shook his head. *When* it came. He coughed to cover a laugh. The file blazed like a candle of hope in his mind. *When...*

~ ~ ~ ~ ~ ~ ~

Fire roared at Athson when he opened his eyes. He flinched and hissed in pain. Corgren's spell—no, a campfire. He groaned and sat up, or tried to. He flinched at his stinging hands and fell onto his back. Athson focused on the firelight. Definitely not wizard's fire. He groaned again. Stars wheeled into place over him with a roll of his eyes. He took a ragged breath. Where was his father? Still in Chokkra? Buried? Athson turned his head, touched his nose with a tender finger, and found dried blood. Salve covered his

CHAPTER ONE

hands. "What's going on? Where is he?" He barely sounded like himself with this croaking voice.

Someone poked the fire. Athson squinted into the light and guessed aloud, "Makwi?"

"So you are awake, then." The dwarf's voice rumbled but fluttered with weariness. His arm was in a sling. "Ralda's around, be back anytime."

"No, my father."

"Who knows after that cave-in." Makwi shrugged and winced. "Sorry, lad. Barely made it ourselves, many thanks to Ralda."

"I need to know." Athson forced himself into a sitting position. His head spun, and he leaned against a rock. They camped among boulders, and the touch of frigid wind brushed his hair and rustled needles among the squat pines surrounding them. "What happened?" His voice was hoarse, and his lips felt chapped beneath more salve.

"I don't know for sure. Ralda got us out. He went hunting down the valley before dark." The dwarf's face wrinkled into a worried frown as he turned to look into the night for the giant. "It is dangerous this close to Chokkra, but we have little choice. I doubt they will follow. Ralda says the gate is blocked. We're settled at an old watch-post off one of the connecting walks to the mountain roads leading south."

Athson thought back. He had dived to block the magic fireball from the wizard. What else that had happened escaped his memory after those moments. He closed his eyes, and the image of his father's sword in the night whirled through his spinning head. That had never happened. The memories of that night on the Funnel flooded him. They were all from a fit. Even though he'd had the sword.

His eyes flicked open. He didn't have the sword. That was why he'd had the fit. He touched the scabbard at his hip. Empty. "Where is it?"

"You want more salve? Water?" Makwi pointed with his good hand. "That salve will help. We'll put more on later."

Makwi tossed him a skin of water with a hiss of pain over his shoulder. Athson found a way to drink through the discomfort in his hands. But he gasped after a few gulps and trembled at the flash of troll shadows bouncing off the surrounding boulders, chasing him from the past. He focused on his boots and took ragged breaths.

Athson took stock of his hands, which were red with burns on the back. Burns from the wizard's attack. He flexed his fingers, but they were swollen. He looked at the dwarf, who seemed to be in pain and tired or dazed, judging by his lack of energy. But the sword—he needed it. "Where is it?" He searched his memory for what had happened.

Makwi didn't answer. His head slumped on his chest, and a soft snore escaped his lips.

Athson gingerly felt the throb on his head. He winced. A lump on the left side, and that eye was blurred when he closed the right one. The dwarf bore a few bruises too. Athson chuckled at their ragged appearance, but it passed his lips as a grunt. "We are a pair. The trolls could take us easily." The shadows dancing in their camp crept toward him.

Makwi stirred. "Eh, what? I think we could give them some trouble if needed." He offered a dour grin. But the dwarf's eyes said otherwise.

Athson doubted he could rise to his feet now. Where was his sword and bow? He glanced around and found them propped against a boulder alongside Makwi's ax. "Makwi, my sword. Can you give it to me? I don't think I can stand."

The dwarf fought the pain in his shoulder and struggled to his feet.

A big shadow loomed out of the darkness between a pair of rocks.

Makwi snatched his ax.

Athson scrambled back against the rock at his back. Those remembered shadows looked too real. He reached for his wolf-head dagger. At least he had that, and his palms weren't burned.

Ralda stepped out of the shadows, his broad face and bulbous nose smudged with grime. He chuckled, a sound that echoed among the rocks. "Not troll!" His gaze shifted to Athson. "Awake. Good. Fear you hurt bad." The giant slung a field-cleaned deer carcass from his shoulder to the ground and proceeded with cooking preparations.

Makwi set his ax by his pack and blanket. Then the dwarf retrieved Athson's sword and bow.

CHAPTER ONE

Athson took the weapons and laid the bow aside. He held the sword a moment, and his head spun less. He glanced around their little encampment. The shadows from the firelight on the surrounding rock wriggled. All normal now. Not trolls at all. Athson sighed. What a relief. Just the remnants of walls with two old doorways.

He sat up with a struggle, and his head resumed spinning. So that was the injury. He touched the lump on his head. But now he saw Spark. The mountain hound panted by the fire. He shut his eyes for long moments, and the confusion of old memories faded. The sword had never followed him over the ledge that night. It broke instead. He tightened and loosened his grip on the sword with a wince and exhaled. He'd had a fit when Ralda carried him from Chokkra. And just now. Some. That was certain. But the sword helped. Maybe there would be none of the side effects with it now.

Soon enough venison cooked over the fire, and Makwi watched Ralda turn it with a fixed gaze. Makwi cleared his throat. "What happened? After Corgren's fireball?"

Ralda motioned for Makwi to turn the meat. The giant squatted by Athson and began wrapping cloth around his head. "Take sword." Ralda touched the hilt where Athson hugged it to his chest. "Break chain. Leave." The giant paused in bandaging Athson's head and motioned to them with several hand signs. "Take on shoulders, run. Gates crushed." He smacked his big hands together. "Rock fall on me." He tapped his chest. "Hide in crack. All stop. I find this place." He thrust a thumb at Makwi. "He show me come here, good camp." The giant ended with a few more wiggles of his fingers and brushed dark strands of his hair over his shoulder.

"Of course! The blessed sword broke the spelled chains on the gate." Makwi grimaced at his shoulder. "Even my dwarf-steel ax couldn't do that. Small wonder I'm injured, then."

Athson wobbled to his feet and gave what bow he could to the giant, as did the dwarf. The giant's face flushed in the firelight, but he thanked them for their politeness. It was then that Athson noticed the big man had a few bruises from falling rock and a few seared spots on his face and his arms. Athson almost fell over, and Ralda steadied him as he sat again.

The giant waved a hand in Athson's face. "You see good?"

Athson pointed to his left eye, the same side of his head as the bump. "This one's blurry, but that binding helps some. What of my father and the wizard?" His father, he had seen him! After all these years! It had been a bitter sight. That disheveled, dirty figure standing beside the wizard with a tattered cloth over his eyes. Athson looked at the fire and squeezed his eyes shut. The sight remained. He clenched his jaw, winced at the pain in his head, and rubbed the side of his face.

Ralda went back to the fire and checked Makwi's sling. "No see what happen. Maybe die. Yes? Not good. Sorry, Athson."

Athson sighed. "Not your fault, Ralda. There wasn't much we could do." Was his father really dead? He needed confirmation—somehow. He lowered his head, and tears stung his eyes. He should have sought his father long ago. But how could Athson have known he was alive or where to look?

When the venison was cooked, they ate. Athson had to hold his portions gingerly in his burned hands after letting them cool. Afterward, he let the giant bathe his hands in cold water at Makwi's direction and apply more salve when they were dry. The icy water from a spring Ralda had found felt good on his hands, and Athson resolved he would soak them himself when he could walk. The giant's touch on his hand was painful, though, and he winced twice.

Makwi handed him an herb. "Take this. It'll help the pain. It'll put you to sleep too, at least for a while."

Athson hesitated. He didn't want more herbs messing with his perception. "That's all?"

"All I know. Just chew a while." Makwi took some himself, chewed it several times, and shoved it into a ball in his cheek.

Athson shifted his gaze to Spark, but the mountain hound lay still. The sight of Spark comforted him. But solid sleep sounded good even if for just a while. He shoved the dried leaves in his mouth with a grimace of pain in his head and chewed them on the right side of his mouth. His eyes soon blinked, and he slid into his blanket and let the sleep cover his mind.

~ ~ ~ ~ ~ ~ ~

CHAPTER ONE

An arrow streaks past Athson's head, and light snaps off in the bowl of surrounding stone. Darkness swallows him in an instant, and his anger drains with a breath. Why is he angry? Someone moves beside him. Athson turns, and it's Gweld.

He seems disappointed. "I just missed him?"

"Missed who? You mean the arrow?"

And then they are walking through the night among trees.

Gweld turns to him. "Athson, you must go for the bow, and you will find him then."

"Find who?" They walk on the path in the night, and Gweld is gone.

Out of the night so thick Athson thinks he's choking, light gleams, welcoming him as if from a long journey. He steps forward, and there's a table and chairs, the former set with bread and wine. He's hungry and moves forward and voice speaks, "Eat. It's all here for you." Athson whirls and there is the trader with his floppy hat and another man he doesn't know, both beckoning him to sit.

Athson steps toward the table and he's suddenly on a high, windswept ledge beneath a cloudy sky. The eagle screams out of his past, and Athson crouches. He looks up, and Limbreth sails past him on the wind, her face intent like an eagle, like the one with Zelma at Eagle's Aerie. She flies by with another eagle's cry shrill in his ears.

Athson turns and darkness surrounds him again. A chain clinks, and someone grunts. Light flashes by a hand being pulled by a chain. The dim light shines along an arm to a hook-nosed face. Athson gasps at Corgren's face, pale as death. The chain drags the wizard past Athson. He looks along the length of chain and sees a silhouette. The figure turns, and Athson sees him in the dim flash of light like distant lightning. The haggard, blind face of his father grimaces as he pulls Corgren away, and the flicker ends like a dying flame.

~ ~ ~ ~ ~ ~ ~

Athson stirred from sleep beside the low embers of the fire. Ralda and Makwi snored in exhausted sleep nearby. Wind whistled softly like a lullaby past their camp, but cold lay among them like a merciless blanket as the stars spread above.

He rolled onto his side, thankful for merely a dull ache in his head. His father was alive. Athson struggled to his hands and knees, and his head spun.

He should get up, go find him.

He placed his hands on the boulder beside him and pushed himself to his feet but stood doubled over. He held his head until the spinning sensation stopped. Almost. If he could only stand, he'd go find his father.

He would now. *Go now.*

Athson reached for his sword on the ground and almost fell. He leaned heavily against the boulder, and his head grazed the rock. Pain shot through him afresh, and nausea rose from his stomach. On the second try, Athson grasped his sword and then fumbled with it until it slid into the sheath.

Athson stretched a hand toward his pack, on which his quiver and bow lay. His finger snagged the pack, and he half dragged it and half stepped toward it. Athson opened the pack and searched for the inheritance – his inheritance. He found it, untied the bowstring and read the note afresh through his blurry vision. He shut his eyes and remembered his dream from the night at Eagle's Aerie when it all started with this familial inheritance.

A silhouette kneels and rocks, dark against the fire beyond it. It was Zelma, Hastra's sister, and a Withling too. He knew that now. *Her uneven voice chants:*

"The bow shall be hidden from heart..."

Zelma feeds wood into the fire. Sparks snap from the coals and whirl amid the orange-blue tongues. An arc forms in the smoke and fades into the stars.

"The eagle will guide the heir..."

An eagle's scream pierces the night wind.

"The bow shall be found at need..."

Zelma's wrinkled hands tie a wad of cloth with string - a bowstring. This inheritance.

"And the arrow shall Eloch prepare."

A shooting star streaks across the horizon and drags Athson's attention from the crouching figure before the popping fire.

The eagle screams again - louder and nearer.

Athson shuddered out of the dream as he opened his eyes. He squinted.

CHAPTER ONE

The wrapping was a banner. For what? He re-wrapped it all and tied the string anew. It didn't matter now. He had to find his father. He shoved the inheritance into the pack and worked it onto his shoulders with the quiver, then leaned on the boulder again. After a slow rise to his feet with the bow, Athson staggered past Ralda and somehow missed tripping over the giant.

He leaned against a natural wall of stone and stumbled along the path out of the old dwarven watch-station. Beneath the light of the stars, he came to a paved walk of stone with a wall running along the edge, past which the night yawned. The walk stretched into the night to his left and right. Athson stood like a reed, shifting with the wind as his breath plumed in his face with the cold. Which way? His body leaned right, and he followed with a stagger.

Spark padded by Athson's side. "That's right, Spark. We'll do what we should've done all along. I'm going to find my father." He steadied himself against the mountainside rising from the path and wobbled away.

CHAPTER TWO

Wind moaned down the mountainside beyond the shelter door. Magdronu, disguised as Gweld the elven ranger, sat on the rough floor and pretended to meditate. He yearned to sail on the raucous wind and hunt. But his ultimate prey lay beyond his reach—for now.

He sent the summons again over his magical connection. *'Corgren!'* There were no more scheduled meetings now that Corgren wore his Ring of Summoning again after his return to Chokkra. Magdronu-as-Gweld suppressed the urge to pace the cramped confines of the shelter. Stacked stone and wooden roofs. The stone-rats built pathetic little nests for traveling away from their grandly carved nests and villages in the mountains. He exhaled slowly and stayed in character, since the others were close by.

Not even Paugren had answered since Magdronu had sent Corgren's brother in search of the wizard. It boded some ill fortune. Probably Eloch's doing again. He drew Athson like a moth to flame, but Eloch thwarted each attempted trap. Magdronu-as-Gweld shifted slightly. No one ignored his summons lightly. Not even his most trustworthy servants. For hundreds of years, he had groomed his two wizards, and they always performed faithfully.

Magdronu waited in silence. The others murmured their concerns beside the low fire. Huddling before the pitiful heat. His own heat warmed him even in the cold. But he needed not wrath at this moment. Just information.

Corgren and his brother, Paugren understood Magdronu's goals. Thwart

CHAPTER TWO

Eloch's prophecy against his rise by taking the Bow of Hart from this old traitorous Hartian family. But one of the family needed to give it willingly. Magdronu-as-Gweld inhaled and exhaled in his "meditation". One of Magdronu's hallowed grounds–the Funnel or a high place in these, the Drelkhaz Mountains–would serve best. Manipulation of the young ranger was best and Magdronu-as-Gweld could do it. Trust was important and built over a long time. Until then, Magdronu maintained his disguise to the very moment the bow entered his possession. He clasped his elven hands. Then he'd grow his power and throw off this accursed dragon's form forced on him by Eloch. Magdronu-as-Gweld shifted his position. But did they have Athson in hand? The delay threw doubt amid his plans.

Another sending, this time to the brother. *'Paugren!'*

A day of traveling afoot for this tiny nest of minuscule warmth. He'd rather they slept in the cold. But the poor things required shelter. Weak and worthy only to serve and be consumed. He sniffed. Their worry fed his senses, and it tasted delicious.

'Master, I answer.'

Magdronu almost shouted, almost jumped to his elven-disguised feet and clapped his hands. He almost roared an answer along the magical connection. *'Paugren, what news?'* And what was this? The taste of anger, tinged with—disloyalty? Questioning? He sent a rumble of displeasure from his inner core along the magic spell. A face hove into view, Corgren's likeness with hair and a face shaved bare.

Paugren cringed and strove to keep his balance under the weight of the communication spell. *'M-master, I have searched long and found my brother with this slave. They were caught in a cave-in that killed his squads at the gate. I've brought them away, but we know nothing of the ranger. I'll heal Corgren of his injuries after we're done.'*

'The ranger yet lives.' Magdronu had felt that much over the familial curse, as with the father, blind though he was. He ignored the conversation around him in the shelter. *'What happened at the gate?'* Eloch—it had to be his doing.

'Corgren used a fire spell that struck a blade blessed by our enemy. The collision set off the collapse in the old hall.' Paugren wobbled on his legs.

Satisfaction rose in Magdronu. Let Paugren feel the force of his presence and remember his place. Disloyalty, indeed! *So Athson has escaped or is trapped somehow. Likely the former, knowing Eloch.* He must counter this move, and quickly. He needed to apply pressure once they met Athson. Magdronu-as-Gweld inhaled and exhaled in the slow exercise of an elf. Too bad Limbreth traveled with him and not Athson. Magdronu almost laughed—indeed, he let a rumble of mirth flow along the magic. *'Do what you must for Corgren. I must have control of the Bane. It will cause pain.'*

Magdronu reached along the thread of magic from him to the Bane. *'Master, wait. He shrieks! I've not healed him!'*

The disloyalty grew to rebellion along the communication spell. Magdronu rumbled his anger at Eloch, at his own cursed dragon's form, at Paugren's doubts, at Corgren's mishandled spell. He still had to teach them lessons after all these centuries. No servant was to be trusted—ever. *'He will live!'* Magdronu pulled and released the thread of magic several times. Let them learn consequences. He tugged a final time at the thread to the Bane and snapped it from Corgren. *'Return to Rok and send more sacrifices. Await my instructions. These events change my plans.'* He snapped the thread of communing magic. He imagined Paugren collapsing like the stone in Chokkra. Lessons. The brothers would serve him well or die.

Magdronu-as-Gweld opened his eyes. But for now, focus on the moment and what to do after that poorly constructed dwarf-rat nest that collapsed. Magdronu-as-Gweld flicked a quick, hard glare, unobserved, at Tordug. He scooted toward the fire and pretended to warm his hands before he took his portion of food. Now to find Athson and exert control. He raised his cup of water to pale-faced Limbreth with a nod of welcome. She wasn't well in these heights, frail thing. But she'd feel worse if his plan worked. Leverage was all he needed. Magdronu-as-Gweld almost laughed—almost.

~ ~ ~ ~ ~ ~ ~

Hastra picked at the haunch of mountain goat going cold in her hands. Her aches from walking dulled as she stared into the waving flames and the smoke drifting past her face toward the shelter's cunningly devised hole. Her eyelids flickered as she drifted like the smoke into her state of

CHAPTER TWO

meditation. Eloch had been gracious with food. Eloch had given what was needed. Perhaps her prayers would bring answers. Hastra inhaled and slowly exhaled.

Tordug stirred and drew her attention. The dwarf touched Limbreth's shoulder. "Can you breathe better now?"

Limbreth answered with a silent exaggerated series of nods.

Hastra turned back to the fire and her thoughts. Best not to frown at Limbreth. If only she could regain Limbreth's trust. Imagine refusing a Withling's blessing for her short breath in these heights. She grunted at the unnecessary refusal and covered her disapproval by warming her hands at the fire. A glance at Limbreth told Hastra she wasn't well. Good thing there weren't any trolls close. Limbreth had lagged behind all day and arrived well after dark at the shelter. She'd even made Tordug go back for her and reel her in like a fish. Hastra grunted and frowned, then held her meat over the fire. Best not to stir up more animosity from Limbreth when she needed encouragement. Hastra picked warm meat from the bone and ate it.

"That goat goes down well after a long day walking." Gweld motioned to Hastra's share of the meal.

"Mmm. A good shot. What is needed…" Hastra brushed hair from her face.

Gweld and Tordug intoned together, "Is given."

Limbreth just nibbled her food, her face pale in the firelight. Her gaze flicked toward Hastra and back to her hands. "Is given." Her whisper sounded lifeless, or thankless.

"So, will you tell us where we're going next?" The elf adjusted his cloak and one of several old woolen blankets they'd found in this shelter.

Hastra cocked her head, inhaled, and closed her eyes for several moments. When she opened her eyes, she shifted her gaze among her companions in turn. "That is a question for Tordug, who's been rather quiet about our destination." She cleared her throat and arched a single eyebrow at the old dwarf-lord.

Tordug opened his mouth in answer.

"Not where we're to meet the others. Where do we seek the bow?" Gweld touched his own bow in emphasis of his meaning.

Hastra slouched, aware of Limbreth's keen stare in her direction. The girl worried about the wrong things. She didn't believe Hastra's certainty of Athson's safety. But then, Hastra knew hardships loomed, though Eloch withheld her from revealing such things. Such insights were hard to bear in silence, but Hastra knew the price of speaking out of turn—no matter the consequences otherwise. "I do not know that yet, but it shall be given in time. For now, we need to find the others, make for this village, and obtain supplies and better winter gear." She nodded at Tordug.

The dwarf shifted his gaze toward his feet, then glanced at Hastra again as he frowned.

Hastra picked at her meat again. Tordug's uncertainty told her everything. He wasn't certain they'd get much help because of him, his loss of honor among his people. A hardship for him, possibly shared with them. "But that too shall be given as needed."

Tordug's shoulders relaxed and he genuflected to Hastra. His dwarven response indicated his trust in her.

Limbreth shifted her gaze between them, catching the dwarven response. Understanding drifted across her expression. It wasn't as simple as walking into a remote dwarven settlement and getting help at a word from their leader. The young Grendonese woman frowned.

Hastra leaned against the stacked-stone wall behind her, and the cold sucked the warmth from her body. She quivered, but not at the cold touch at her back. Even she would see hardship in the coming weeks, maybe worse. "But come, tell us our path, Tordug. Perhaps Eloch will show me something from your words to help us."

Finding the Bow of Hart was a prophecy she little doubted. She touched her recovered book where it was written. The result weighed on her, as it had for long years. Not even Gweld understood her burden of several centuries, the unction that drove her. She hated the loss of her youth and her order and bore it all with less patience over the years. It was no excuse to show Athson her frayed patience, or act in a peremptory fashion. She'd made her mistakes too over the years, not to mention since meeting the

CHAPTER TWO

Archer in Auguron City. *Make it right.* That was one clear unction. With Athson. She shifted her eyes toward Limbreth again. And with Limbreth, if possible. Hastra regretted losing her trust. Even though she often failed at relating with people, Eloch remained gracious. She sighed. Why did it feel like she'd failed with more than people?

Tordug cleared his throat and tossed more wood on the fire as it burned low. "I suppose I may as well tell you where we're going. You don't know the way without a dwarf anyway, and we're well away from the dangers of Chokkra."

Hastra leaned toward the fire and warmth. "But not from hardship, I'll warrant. Always something ahead, good and hard alike. But each new day is a blessing of Eloch, and the hardship is but a small thing compared to what is given." She wasn't fond of hardship, regardless. But she'd made that choice at Withling's Watch. She shuddered at the memory of all the blood that day. Hardship had stalked her days since that day she had died on Corgren's blade and come back.

~~~~~~~

Tordug swept his hands to indicate the shelter to his companions. "We'll visit several more shelters like this one and meet Makwi and the others at one. We'll leave indication we've been at each, just as Makwi will if they reach them before us. If necessary, we—or they—will wait at the last point, the Tower of Nazh-akun."

He paused and swallowed the lump rising in his throat. His people despised him now—or near enough—for the fall of Chokkra and their hardships. The shame weighed on his shoulders like a mountain. Even here, within the stacked-stone walls where no dwarf accompanied them, his failure cut-off his honor. But with help, he could win back some of it. He glanced between Limbreth and Hastra. A chance amid his weakness. If only he could reveal it to them.

Gweld checked his taut bowstring. "And where to after that? Or will the tower hold enough supplies for us?"

Tordug's face twitched. *Never reveal your weakness, even to friends.* A code of survival for the dishonored, lest he be held in lower esteem yet. "There might be more than here but not all that we need. Any dwarves patrolling this region of the mountains likely wouldn't stay there long."

Limbreth huffed with her short breath. "Why wouldn't they linger?"

Tordug withheld a harsh word to the ax-maid. She should receive the Withling's blessing and breathe. "Because Rokans patrol these mountains too. It is rumored in the west that they capture our people and use them for sacrifice to the dragon." His lips twitched. For his people's sake, he'd make his appeal. He motioned open-handed to Gweld. "We'll go farther, to a settlement named Ezhandun. There we'll seek assistance, should they agree to even speak with us."

Limbreth swallowed water hard and avoided choking.

Tordug turned to her. She was confused and lacked understanding. A quick glance at Hastra told him she understood.

"Why wouldn't they speak with us? You're their lord." Limbreth's voice sounded like wind through reeds, and she took deep gasps.

A sigh escaped Tordug's lips. He ground his teeth a moment and then threw his proverbial dice for all to see. "Because I'm accounted very low in honor, ax-maid, after the fall of Chokkra."

"But surely there is some appeal we can make? You've taught me how to ask for help." Limbreth shifted her gaze between Tordug and Hastra.

Tordug pursed his lips. She was still perplexed by dwarven custom. That needed changing along this trek. He nodded. "There is a way." He pointed to Limbreth and Hastra in turn. "But I'll need your help and the Withling's. And Makwi's if—" If Makwi still lived. But surely he did, if Athson did, according to Hastra. He fixed the Withling with a steady gaze, and she nodded affirmation to his questioning glance. He'd take that over nothing. "The honor you three have among dwarves will raise my standing and get us what we need."

Limbreth managed to whisper, "I see."

Tordug pointed toward Limbreth. "But there is much you yet need to learn. You need your strength instead of this high-mountain sickness. It can linger for days. You need to take the blessing if you're to learn as a dwarf, as an ax-maid, and—"

CHAPTER TWO

Limbreth struggled to her feet and wobbled out of the shelter, into the cold night.

Hastra motioned to Limbreth's weapons. "Take your sw—"

Limbreth cut her eyes at Hastra the moment she shut the door behind her.

Tordug spread his hands to Hastra. "Can you do nothing? We will need her learning all she can."

Hastra shook her head with a grimace.

Gweld moved to stand. "I'll go speak with her."

Hastra motioned to the elf to sit as she held Tordug's attention. "No, Gweld. I think Tordug must speak to her. She's angry with me, but she'll listen to a mentor."

Gweld settled back and raised his hands. "Fair enough, Withling." He offered her an elven gesture of honor.

Tordug grunted as he gathered himself to stand. "She's right, Gweld. It should be me for now."

Hastra motioned for Tordug to sit. "But give her a few moments in the cold with short breath. Maybe she'll start thinking some."

Tordug stood anyway, strolled to the door, and waited. "A few moments might clear her head." Or she'd faint over the side of the trail wall and he'd lose his chance to regain some of his honor. He shook his head. Showing up with a Withling and an ax-maid with death-grip should be enough for a festival. Not counting the support of his champion. If Makwi did indeed live. Tordug stroked the braids in his beard and squeezed one large knot. If only he could remove that sign of failure to all. He ducked out the door without checking for Hastra's approval. He needed Limbreth to remove the dishonorable knot.

~ ~ ~ ~ ~ ~ ~

Limbreth stood with the murmur of her companions' voices muffled beyond the door and the rush of mountain wind. Rain pelted her rain-cloak. Not so soft a sound as it had seemed within the shelter. Regret weighed on her mind over her rudeness throughout the day. She shouldn't have brushed Hastra and Tordug aside like that. But they let Athson walk into a trap. Limbreth pulled the cloak close, fastened the stays, and trudged down the short crack in the mountain where the shelter lay nestled out of the wind and away from the dwarven road.

She felt her way across the road to the wall and grasped the rough top edge. The wind fingered her cloak. Limbreth turned left, northward. Athson was off somewhere in the mountains, likely on a different road. It could be higher or lower than this one. Her lower lip trembled. These roads seldom intersected, as she recollected their day of travel on them. Nothing to do but wait and walk until they met. If they lived. If they'd escaped Chokkra.

Limbreth paced on the road. And Tordug expected her to learn dwarven ways. She did regret walking out on the conversation and Trodug's pleas. But Hastra had left Athson and the others stranded. It was an empty conversation. Nothing mattered without him on this quest. Hastra didn't care about him, only about that precious prophecy and the Bow of Hart. She kicked a stray stone, bent to feel around for it, grasped it, and threw it into empty night beyond the roadside wall.

The cold rain suddenly ended. Deep inside her, a wild wail of despair lurked. Food tasted like ash these last few days. The others made plans, talked like Athson and the others were on a walk through flowery fields or something, while Limbreth labored with the inadequate breaths that left her weak.

Her anger and impatience wilted. She half-turned for the shelter. She'd better apologize. She hesitated and stepped back to the wall, lifting her face to the constant mountain wind. Only a few hard raindrops fell now. She'd go in a moment.

The weather muffled her thoughts, and only one thing crept through her—where was Athson? She wanted more than anything to see him, to feel his lips kissing hers. Limbreth imagined his hand caressing her cheek. Silly thoughts. Things she'd never allowed herself in Grendon. Or on the long trek this far. That door had closed him away from her, and emptiness had flooded her since. She should let her hair out of its braid. She closed her eyes at the thought of Athson stroking her hair.

Limbreth sighed audibly. She was away from the others, so there was no one to hear. This waiting for word from Athson—and the others—weighed on her so heavily that she stepped back from the protective wall lest she be pulled over. But the heaviness dulled her thoughts more than any sadness she had ever known—even the sorrow of her disagreements with her father.

A sob escaped her mouth suddenly. She put a hand over her mouth lest a desperate wail also escape. That sadness lingered like an old wound, like the ache from the arrow in her left arm. She'd followed the Withling from home because of anger, and now she stood in the cold, angered by the old woman. Adventure was one reason she'd left, but fighting with her father was another. That wound lingered, yes. Being princess of the realm of Grendon bored her, along with all the suitors who took a fancy to her flashing eyes and pretty smile. They faked their interest for a chance at power, a chance they'd ascend with her if something happened to her older siblings. She knew history, and it had happened. They didn't want her, and she had angered her father, who had a realm bigger than her stubborn scruples.

Another sob racked her body as Limbreth thought of the times her father had held her in his lap and comforted her when she was sad or tickled her into squirming fits of laughter when she was playful. Childhood had been lost with responsibility. Limbreth looked up at a sudden spray of rain that washed away her tears.

She jumped as someone touched her elbow. Her heart beat faster than ever with the mountain sickness. "Tordug," she breathed as her heart surged. "I did not hear you." She swayed with dizziness and braced herself with a sudden grasp at the elder dwarf's shoulder.

"You have not heard much these last days." He handed her the pair of swords she had left inside the shelter. "You left these even though the Withling suggested you take them."

Limbreth looked sidelong at the dwarf as she took the belt and swords. The same concern reflected in the light of the fire within their refuge now glinted in the dwarf-lord's eyes.

"Thank you." She hugged the weapons close.

He stood silent beside her for a moment.

"Where are the others?" Her whisper sounded like the murmuring wind. Lack of breath. Her chest rose and fell in an effort for more air. "Where are they? South of us, or north? Higher up or lower?" She searched the impenetrable night with her gaze.

"We left farther south of them, I should think. We're on a middle road, so they might be lower than us for now." Tordug laid a sympathetic hand on her arm and spoke with as much kindness as a gruff-voiced dwarf could. "They will be well. Makwi will see to that. The boy is safe, Hastra knows this. Don't fret, ax-maid."

Limbreth shrugged. "I can't help myself. I don't know why I can't." But she did know and avoided eye contact with the dwarf, lest he see it too.

"Every ax-maid I have known of would give her life for her man. You are no different. You wish to be near and share the danger with him."

The dwarf spoke according to his culture, and Limbreth just gazed at him in the dim light of his glow-moss lantern. Were all dwarves insane? Share in the danger? But she did want that. *Crazy, Limbreth.* She did not deny it. Instead she embraced the openness of her affection, and it lent her sudden warmth. Limbreth flashed a faint smile at the dwarf's kind words, dwarf-like though they might be. Tordug's words rang true, though. She could not deny them any longer. She wished to share Athson's life—and his dangers.

"Thank you again." She bobbed her head and touched her forehead—a dwarven gesture.

Tordug's face broadened into a grin for a moment only and then hardened. He cleared his throat. "Now, about what I was saying inside. I only—"

Limbreth looked at her boots and glanced up Tordug. He was so like a father. "I was coming to apologize. I'll—I'll learn what you need."

Tordug's face softened again. "I know it's hard with him gone, but you must do what you can to help now and later. That's what you can do while he's gone—anytime you're separated. I'll teach you formal requests and responses. I can show you how to gain respect with just a joke among warriors."

Limbreth nodded. Yes, she'd help Athson as much she could—and the

CHAPTER TWO

others. She could, she knew it.

"And the best start you can make is the Withling's blessing."

They locked eyes. Tordug didn't look away. Neither did Limbreth. Her jaw clenched, and her lips quivered at a negative response, but she pushed that down. She was only hurting herself. It was the least she could do for Athson, Tordug, and the others. Her chest heaved for breath to speak. She forced the words out in a whisper. "I'll do it."

They turned for the shelter, but Tordug suddenly pushed past her roughly. "Who goes there in the dark?"

Limbreth wheeled. A shadow loomed to the north up the walk.

The Withling gave a warning shout from within the shelter. Firelight cast dim light along the crack at the road. Hastra scrambled out the door.

The shadow, whoever it was, was gone in an instant, faded back into the rain-soaked gloom.

Hastra scurried onto the road without her cloak. "Did you see it?"

"Someone was back up the walk." Tordug pointed a stubby finger into the darkness.

"That was not a someone, but a something." The Withling glanced with narrowed eyes in the direction indicated for any sign of the vanished figure. "That cursed spirit haunts our tracks."

"The Bane? It's not after Athson?" Limbreth reached for a sword as the dwarf turned to usher the Withling back into the shelter.

Gweld met them halfway to the shelter door, his elven long-knife drawn and casting a glint in Limbreth's eye.

"Apparently not." Hastra stopped short upon entering the chamber with her jaw firmly set. "But why us? Why now?"

~~~~~~~

Athson trudged along the dwarven walk. Either Spark leaned against him often or he leaned into the mountain-side of the path. He clattered with loose legs down steps. His arms flailed. *Can't stop.* His head spun, and the ache arrived with greater intensity than in the encampment. His shoulder and pack scraped along the rock face. *Whoa!* He tipped forward. *Keep those feet moving.* He misjudged a step with his blurred vision, veered toward the low wall, and toppled toward it.

Spark lunged under him, but Athson fell over the mountain hound and rolled on his arms and knees. His bow, hanging from his shoulder, slapped him in the face. He fetched up against the wall, the wind knocked from his lungs a moment. He rubbed his head. It ached like a dozen trolls had pounded on it. He shook his head to clear his vision and the pain. *Don't do that again.* He held his head like it might fall off and wobbled like a drunk dwarf after one of their festivals—whatever it was they celebrated. He'd seen Chokkrans and traders from elsewhere drunk in Auguron City. He'd have to ask Makwi sometime, sometime, what they celebrated. He'd never seen a drunk elf. Why weren't elves ever drunk? He rested his head against the wall.

He shook awake at the pain in his head and blinked at his blurred vision. *Won't go away.* His vision cleared, and he winced at the light around him. Daylight? When had that happened? Was it dark when he fell? He couldn't remember.

Spark sat in front of him and panted, looking up. The mountain hound woofed.

"Hey there, Spark. Did I sleep?" He reached for the top of the wall and attempted to pull himself to his feet. "Want me to get moving, eh?"

The dog grabbed a sleeve with his teeth and pulled Athson over.

"Hey, stop that! I have enough trouble without you doing that!" He tried again, farther from the wall this time. He staggered into a low crouch and leaned for the wall.

Spark snagged his pack again with his teeth.

Athson fell away from the wall. "Stop it, or I'll never get up!" More trolls pounded at his head. Maybe a few bugbears with clubs. His stomach fluttered, and darkness swirled in his vision. "Got to find father."

Spark barked, ears up, and wagged his tail.

"I know, I'm trying. Just help me and stop pulling me over."

The mountain hound trotted toward the mountain side of the road. He wagged his tail and woofed again.

"Ok, I'm coming. Just stand still, will you?" Athson braced himself on

CHAPTER TWO

Spark's back and got halfway to his feet before the dog walked off. Athson followed as the dog angled toward the rock face, away from the roadside wall. "Hey, cut it out!"

The dog kept walking at a steady pace, directly at the mountain-face.

Athson followed as he steadied himself again Spark as his pack leaned the other way. Somehow, they arrived at the rock face, where Athson pulled himself into a slouch and adjusted his pack. His head spun and ached even more. Maybe it was a couple ogres pounding away in there. He staggered along and grabbed several handholds on the mountainside.

He glanced back and almost fell.

Spark lunged up and nudged him steady.

Athson frowned at the mountain hound and then at the retaining wall on the other side of the dwarven walk. It wasn't even waist-high. "Oh, you've been trying to keep me from tumbling over that." He grabbed the mountainside again as a chill ran along his spine. His foggy thinking. Without Spark, he would've gone over the side. He patted Spark. "Sorry, old boy. Good dog."

Spark licked his hand.

Athson held his hand up to his face. It wasn't wet. Of course, it wasn't. He took a few steps and grabbed the rock face. *Gotta find father—somehow, somewhere.*

He stumbled along the road and lost track of time. He remembered falling a few times, getting back up. Twice he came to his senses with Spark lying beside him on the walk. Both times he got up and strode along the path. He had to find his father.

Athson paused, his breath coming in ragged gasps. He drank some water. Had he been winded like this all along?

Something moved in his blurred vision back the way he'd come. Someone cloaked in black moved toward him. Athson backed away. The Bane. He fumbled his sword out of its sheath.

He blinked, and it was gone. He turned in an unsteady circle. Nothing there. He touched his aching head where Ralda's bandage still wrapped the lump. He must be seeing things. Couldn't be a fit if he had the sword in hand. A small smudge of blood decorated his hand where he'd touched the bandage. Great. He took a deep breath but didn't get enough air. "Come on, Spark." He headed off again. He should keep his right hand on the mountain.

Sound reached Athson's ears after a while. He squinted back the way he'd come. Two figures raced toward him. Trolls! A small one and a big one, maybe one of those ogres pounding on his head. He touched his forehead. He couldn't let them catch him. He staggered away, looking over his shoulder more than once. Each time the trolls had closed the distance. They shouted and mocked him in their rough way. His sword was in his hand. Good. He was ready for them. He didn't think he'd be able to draw from the sheath fast enough otherwise. Athson wobbled farther on the dwarven highway.

"Athson!"

He turned toward the call. It was Ralda and Makwi! Where had they been? "Makwi! Watch out! There are trolls back there."

He staggered as he waved his sword toward the trolls. He almost fell, catching himself with a lunge for the wall.

Spark woofed and darted between him and the roadside wall.

Suddenly, Athson leaned out over clear air. His shallow breath caught in this throat. He tipped farther over the wall.

A hand grasped Athson's arm.

His sword slipped from his grasp and spun away down the mountainside.

CHAPTER THREE

Ralda grinned. "Got you!"

Athson gasped. "My sword!" He swayed like grass in the wind away from the wall. But he wanted to see.

Makwi swore. The dwarf leaned over the wall and visored his eyes. "There! It's balanced on a ledge, blade out."

Ralda looked over the side with a groan.

Athson leaned in the giant's grasp and held his thick forearm like he might fall. And he just might. The sword glinted in the sunlight. Athson winced and squinted at the flash of light off the blade. A sunny day? He hadn't noticed. The blade waved in the wind and threatened to slide off the ledge.

He sighed. "I'll get it." He swung a leg over the wall.

Spark grabbed his pant leg in his teeth. Ralda hauled him away from the edge.

Makwi rounded on Athson, his cheeks puffed. "Crazy ranger! You can barely walk, let alone make that climb! I'll have to do it." He started to remove his pack with a grunt and a wince.

Ralda put his hand on Makwi's chest. "No, you fall. I go."

Makwi paused with his pack half off and gave the giant a sidelong squint. "You have experience climbing? On a mountainside?"

Ralda shook his head and then nodded. "Climb in mountains. Hunt with brother, Kralda. Many time." The giant swallowed hard. "I go."

Athson pulled free of Ralda. "You can't. You might fall. Really, just lower me with a rope." He'd just dangle and get the sword. If he didn't fumble it away. He steadied himself against the giant. He could do it with a rope. Really.

"Sorry, no rope with us. It's Ralda or we go the long way to collect it when—or if—it falls on the lower road." Makwi puffed his cheeks again. "Besides, you don't even have your breath for these heights yet."

Athson grabbed his head. Definitely ogres pounding in there. Which reminded him. "Where did those trolls go?"

Makwi and Ralda glanced at each other before Makwi spoke, "That was us. You're seeing things with that lump on your head. Probably shouldn't be on your feet, either."

Athson laughed. Seeing things. *His head must be bad.* "I'm barely there now." He knew that much at the moment.

Ralda shrugged out of his pack and set it against the mountainside.

Makwi went with Ralda to the low wall but cast a glance at Athson. "Just where were you going on your own?"

The giant clambered over the side, his big hands grasping the top of the wall.

Athson leaned back against rock and slid into a squat. "After my father."

Spark sat with his face in Athson's like the dog was guarding him.

"Crazy thing, when he's likely—" Makwi sidestepped away from the giant. "I'll keep watch and tell you when you're close." The dwarf glanced over his shoulder at Athson. "Sorry, it's just that that's not good thinking. Though I guess you aren't well just now." The dwarf leaned over. "No, over the other way if you can find a hold. Yes, there's a ledge just under your foot, Ralda." He raised his hand to Athson and glanced at him. "You just stay there."

Athson chuckled. "I don't think Spark will let me go anywhere."

Makwi frowned at Athson. "What?"

"Never mind."

Makwi turned back to Ralda. "Big as you are, you're almost there."

Athson crawled past Spark. "Come with me, dog. I need to see this." He got to the wall and peeked over.

Makwi gasped. "No! Don't put your foot there. You'll kick it off!"

Ralda slid his foot to the very end of the ledge. He shoved his fist into a

CHAPTER THREE

crack and leaned precariously toward the sword with his other hand.

Makwi pitched his voice into a softer, lower shout. "Ralda! Don't move!"

Athson squinted at the giant. "What? Why?"

Makwi pointed below Ralda. "There's Rokans on the lower road. They might spot him!"

Ralda nodded.

The dwarf pulled Athson back, his last sight of Ralda frozen in place, straining for the sword, but unmoving. Surely Ralda had seen them. But what if he slipped? Athson gulped and stared into Makwi's strained face. Ralda couldn't move, and he might fall. Athson's stomach rolled over.

~ ~ ~ ~ ~ ~ ~

Limbreth paused with Tordug and Hastra by Gweld.

"What was it?" The ranger glanced from one to the other.

"That Bane has followed us." Hastra headed back to the shelter. "We'll need a close watch." She sighed. "And there's only four of us." She paused at the door and eyed Limbreth, opened her mouth to speak, shook her head, and ducked inside.

Limbreth followed the Withling with the others.

Hastra threw wood on the fire as Tordug shut the door against the cold. "Well, best get some sleep. We've an early start or we—we won't find the others."

Limbreth cut her eyes at Tordug and cleared her throat. "About that, making it to the next stop and finding the others…" She was still angry with Hastra, but this was for Athson. "I'll take that blessing now."

Hastra approached Limbreth. The Withling peered at her with teary eyes. "I've meant no harm. Just doing what I must. Not easy sometimes, you know."

Limbreth nodded. What to say to an apology from a Withling?

Hastra then blessed Limbreth. The litany of her prayer lasted several minutes while the others remained respectfully quiet.

Her heart slowed, and Limbreth took deeper and deeper breaths. It was like a weight she'd been carrying was gone. She took a final deep breath, and Hastra released her hands and turned away to her things. "Thank you,

Withling Hastra. This ax-maid is grateful."

The old woman patted Limbreth's hand. "What is needed is given, Limbreth. You are welcome."

Limbreth glanced at Tordug.

The old dwarf beamed a smile of approval at her through his beard. He coughed once. "We will need an early start. But everyone have a care. That Bane is onto us here."

"My thoughts exactly, Tordug." Hastra pulled her blanket up to her chin as she lay down.

"I will keep a sharp eye," Gweld said, and Limbreth felt certain he would. "I'll check outside." The elf stepped out into the night to check the walk. He returned several minutes later, satisfied nothing was there after hearing only the patter of rain and seeing the fog roll by the door. He took up his station by the door.

Tordug stoked the fire against the cold. "Stay alert, Gweld. That thing was there and gone in an instant." He poked at the fire. "Wouldn't be surprised if there was snow in the morning too."

Limbreth's troubles tried to peck at her thoughts as she lay with her head on her pack. But her eyes drooped, and the crows of her angst faded.

Hastra awakened Limbreth much later, and she rubbed her eyes, surprised at how soundly she had slept. Breathing right helped. She sat out her watch, and nothing stirred her attention but her thoughts. Limbreth sifted through her emotions and thoughts with a clear head. The Withling was rarely wrong, so she would trust her assertions about Athson and the others for now. Nothing else she could do otherwise. Anything done was done already. *Don't let the worry hang like the memory of the Banshee.* She rubbed the wrist she'd almost cut open that night under the influence of that underworld creature.

In those uncertain moments that troubled her heart, sudden dread seized Limbreth, and she shrank from the door. The nape of her neck stirred with chill sensation, and she quaked. The light from the fire dimmed, though it burned readily on the wood just recently added. Her breath plumed in a thick mist. She slipped a sword loose. Even Hastra was restless under her

CHAPTER THREE

blanket.

But as quickly as the sense of unease arrived, it faded. Limbreth caught her breath anew. Hastra stilled in her sleep, and the fire flared to its original brightness. Limbreth peeked from the doorway. Nothing. Not even rain now. Just mist. Fitful wind rose along the mountain, the shelter roof shuddered a moment, and she closed the door.

When they readied their departure before the dawn, Limbreth paused as she ate her breakfast. "On my watch, a chill of dread entered my mind and this shelter. I saw nothing outside though, and the chill went away."

"That was likely the cold and weariness." Gweld yawned. "The air in these mountains is different, and the cold is noticeable."

"It is indeed cold." Tordug frowned, though, and stroked his beard. "We do not have the gear for this travel, so we should be on our way soon and travel as late as possible or risk being caught in worse weather. But I think Limbreth's report should not be ignored. We did see this Bane last night. I have been in these mountains all my life and never felt such things on the coldest of nights, even when I knew a bear was near. What do you say, Hastra?"

The old woman looked up from adjusting the contents of her pack with a creased brow. "My dreams were unsettled by something dark and grasping. Perhaps next time you should wake me, Limbreth?"

By the firmness in Hastra's voice Limbreth knew the Withling expected a wiser response next time she sensed something wrong. *Be on your toes—for yourself and Athson.* "Sure, probably should have anyway. Just didn't want to wake you for nothing." Limbreth shoved the last of her food in her mouth and stood with her pack.

"Better to wake me than something worse than a chill enter our shelter."

Limbreth saluted acknowledgment dwarf-style and settled her pack on her shoulders in just the right way to allow her access to her swords.

They set out just a few minutes later, but Limbreth was still working to adjust her cloak, tugging it about under her straps and making sure her hood was not on the hilts of her weapons at her shoulders. Darkness and mist shrouded them on the mountainside. Limbreth doubted it would grow very light anytime soon.

"Be careful of the walks," Tordug warned them. "Rainstorms like last night leave thin ice, and we do not have the best boots for this time of year."

Limbreth stepped warily along, but they went as swiftly as they could anyway. They all slipped a few times, only to catch their balance with flailing arms—a feat more difficult with a pack, Limbreth noticed.

Ahead, Tordug grumbled, and she sometimes caught bits of it. "Get caught in snow if we're not fast enough."

The sun rose but the mist clung to the mountain like a gray blanket. They held their comments to few with the poor visibility, since trolls or Rokans might lurk on these mountain roads. Tordug advised them, "Trolls probably won't be this far from Chokkra, but Rokans do travel the roads as we head farther south. Leastways, that's what I've heard from reports back west over the mountains."

As the sun finally rose higher, the fog lifted, and their sight improved. But they came to portions of the dwarven highway in disrepair. The protective sidewall bore gaps where rock had broken away, while scree from falling rock littered the walkway or holes cratered the rock so that the going was slower for a while. Tordug grumbled more, and his mustache drooped. "Such disrepair, but they're still solid underfoot."

Limbreth walked alongside the dwarf. "It is remarkable." She found her energy restored and smiled into the growing daylight. Best to make the most of the sunlight rather than worry. She avoided a patch of ice with restored ease. Much better traveling today. The others were right. But a thought returned to her. "Why don't all of you suffer from the mountain sickness?"

Tordug blew out his mustache in a plume of breath. "Dwarves are born to these heights as much as to tunnels. It takes us little time to adjust."

Limbreth glanced at Gweld, who shrugged. "I don't think elves are much affected by it. I've traveled other mountains in the past without ill effects."

"And you, Withling? I assume it's some blessing of Eloch?"

Hastra rubbed her upper abdomen as she did at times, just below her sternum. She frowned, though. "You might say that."

CHAPTER THREE

The morning drew on, and the sun rode higher, burning the clouds away. The mass of last night's storm slipped away southeast of them. Any worry about ice eased out of their minds with the sun's brightness. Tordug waved them on to a faster pace. "We must hurry lest we're caught in a colder storm and risk freezing. We don't normally travel these roads with so few provisions laid into the shelters. Few dwarves do much this far north these days. Perhaps we'll find plenty at the Tower of Nazh-akun."

Limbreth peered beyond the road's edge after the sky cleared so that only lazy white clouds drifted by above and below their position. At times the haze cleared so that she could see hints of distant lands and the arms of the mountains stretching into valleys covered in green foliage or stubborn mist. Amazing views. If only Athson shared this with her. She lowered her head and missed him all the more. But it was a good view. She raised her head and made the best of it. She dodged another patch of ice extending from the shadow of the retaining wall.

After a while, the events of the previous night drew their attention along their back-trail, where the walkway wound among the folds and shoulders of the mountain. The Bane might lurk back there. Gweld stayed ahead ten paces, so she ranged backward at times in case something tracked them. But nothing ever caught her attention and, later that afternoon, fog settled around them. Then Limbreth felt a chill creep down her neck. *Like last night.* She paused and peered through the gathering mist. Unease grew in her mind. Limbreth shuddered and hurried after her companions. She pitched her voice low. "Hastra, do you feel that chill? It's not just the cold."

Hastra's face bore a taut expression. "It's come closer in this gloom. Tordug, let's hurry on, but stand ready, everyone."

Soon after, they passed a shelter, a small, dark pile of stacked stone. Tordug pressed on past it without pause.

Limbreth glanced at the misty sky. Daylight was fading. So soon! "Shouldn't we stop here?"

Tordug quickened his pace with a shake of his head. "No, we can yet make the next one. It's earlier than you think, and I fear snow stalks us from the north as well as…"

The dwarf's words trailed into silence, but Limbreth knew what he avoided mentioning. The Bane. They might beat the snow, but not the Bane. It followed them. She whispered to herself, "Why does it follow?"

Hastra patted her arm. "We don't know for now, but we must do as Tordug urges. I feel it in my bones and my, uh, heart."

The day wore on, and an hour passed. The afternoon sun waned further and all too soon. Shadows gathered over wide steps that led mostly down. Tordug clamored down the stair, almost heedless of ice. "There's a shelter likely farther along if we can find it. It was too soon to stop at that last one and we needed to lengthen our progress today." He glanced meaningfully at Limbreth and then shook his lantern of water and glow-moss. "Not frozen, so that's good. I fear we'll be in the dark a while."

Limbreth bit her lower lip. Her foolish anger and stubbornness. She'd held them up yesterday. She quickened her pace after the dwarf, who gained the end of the stair and trotted off, passing Gweld. The shelter an hour or more back loomed with sudden welcome against an all too early night on a cloudy mountainside with the Bane haunting their steps. Limbreth frowned. That shelter—there had been no door. No wonder Tordug gambled they could reach the next one. She quickened her pace.

The creeping chill ran along her spine. Limbreth shivered and glanced behind them but saw nothing in the murk. She tugged at Hastra's sleeve. "The Bane is near again."

"Yes, I fear it prefers the night." The old woman lifted a squint-eyed glance up the cliff in apparent concern. "It matters not why it follows, though, I suppose. I'll deal with it as best I can with what is given."

"Perhaps it thinks it will follow us to Athson?"

The Withling shrugged. "Perhaps it is. But we must remain wary of it." She called for Tordug to speak with her.

The dwarf fell back but did not stop. "Withling, we must keep going. We will be late in the night as it is and will have to carry the lantern exposed to any unfriendly eyes."

"It's not that. The Bane is near. Limbreth thinks it's following us to get at Athson. Still, we must have a care."

CHAPTER THREE

Tordug glanced up to the rocks above and along their back-trail with narrow eyes. Then with a nod to the Withling, the dwarf stepped forward. "Gweld, look out from our rear. Hastra says that Bane is near."

The elf fell back, and Tordug took the lead with his lantern ready.

Hastra snagged Gweld's sleeve. "Don't fight it. Just let us know if you see it. I'll do the rest if needed."

Gweld nodded and fell farther behind. "Limbreth, you up for a little scouting with me?"

"Uh, I doubt she's got your experience." Hastra grabbed Limbreth's arm. "Let her help this old lady on the icy path."

Limbreth leaned close. "What's that all about?"

Hastra's answer was pitched to a whisper. "You are the only one I can guess it may be after among us. It may just be following like you say, or it may have other motives. I've been thinking and believe it nearly entered the shelter last night. According to what you said."

"Me? Why me?"

"Same reason as following us. To get to Athson. And the bow."

Worry for Athson danced across her mind, but Limbreth suppressed the thoughts. No good worrying now, Bane or not. She reached up to a sword hilt to check it against being caught on her pack strap or cloak. Satisfied her weapons were ready to her hands, Limbreth jogged after the dwarf with Hastra a step behind.

Soon enough Tordug opened the shutters on the lantern for light.

The damp air grew cold against Limbreth's skin, but the odd chill grasped her back beneath her cloak and pack in spite of her exertion. They pushed on as night gripped the mountainside and slowed only for the areas of disrepair. "How far to the next shelter?" They were usually hours apart. She chewed her lower lip again.

"A ways yet. They are less than a day because of weather but far enough to make a good trek of it. Good places to build them were used, so it can vary, but this is closer than farther, if I remember right." Tordug held the light higher as they scrambled up icy steps.

Soon after Limbreth asked her question, the first whistling gusts of wind rushed out of the night. It rose stiff from the north and pushed Limbreth along for a few moments. But when the current wavered about, it threatened to drag her toward the crumbling safety wall. Limbreth leaned into the wind and fought her way back toward the mountain side of the walk. She stumbled through a hole and then over loose stone in a scrambling effort that jarred a knee and hip awkwardly. The wind let up, and she staggered into the rock face with another grunt. The others staggered as well, and Limbreth heard the lantern clang on the rock.

Tordug cried out, held the lantern gingerly, and checked it for damage.

Whether they were just weary or stunned or both, they halted a few moments, then set out again. The wind pulled and pushed them along with little pause. Was this like walking on a ship in high swells? The wind caught her unawares, and she staggered hard into the safety wall. Empty blackness spread beneath her. She thrust herself away from the black maw. Her belly flopped. Nice views earlier but death now. In that instant, a single snowflake fell past as hands yanked her farther from the edge, lest the wind force her back again. "Thanks!" It was Gweld and Hastra. Her shout flew away on the wind.

Tordug returned from forging ahead, unaware of Limbreth's danger, and checked on them all. He grimaced in the blue light of moss and raised his voice, "Stay close! We might make it before the moss and water freeze!"

Limbreth followed the dwarf with the others. No wonder dwarven voices boomed. He yelled through the gale with ease.

They hustled along together and held fast against the mountainside as best they could. Limbreth battled the gusts and forgot the other danger of the Bane. She ground her teeth. This must end soon! She pulled her hood lower against the wind.

"Stop!" Tordug raised his hand for a halt, though even his voice was lost in the wind.

Limbreth slouched against the mountainside. *We're forced to spend the night in this weather?* She slumped further in a gust. Just dreadful. A few flakes of snow whipped past her eyes in the light. She squinted. Was the light dimmer?

CHAPTER THREE

The familiar chill crept up her neck again, and Hastra shot her a glance. The Bane now? It had been waiting?

Tordug plunged into deeper shadow, and the lantern lit a narrow crevice. Limbreth and the others shambled after the dwarf into a break in the cliff face.

Limbreth sighed as they left the brunt of the wind behind on the exposed road. Good thing Ralda wasn't with them. He would never have squeezed in here. She twisted her shoulders, and her pack dragged against the rock. Within the cleft, they followed a smooth path. This was dwarf work. But she glimpsed little except Tordug's silhouette ahead in the light of the lantern. The walls widened, and then Limbreth saw the stone piled into a shelter as Tordug pushed past an old door and ducked into the square opening. Limbreth glanced to the shelter roof as she scrambled closer along the path after Hastra and saw the remains of a chimney built into the natural wall of the cleft. Maybe the draw on the hearth still worked. Then she ducked into the shelter after Hastra.

Within the shelter, a low ceiling lay over a dry chamber, both in decent repair. Wood lay beside the hearth in decent supply. Tordug soon lit a fire that crackled with a cheeriness that warmed Limbreth's mind far more than the shelter's interior. She laid aside her oiled cloak and rubbed her arms. Much better than the blustery road. She'd never felt wind like that. She found some hardtack and warmed it near the fire.

"Dwarves have been here recently." Tordug pointed to the firewood and a newer beam in the roof. "Not only is the wood fresh, but the chimney has been repaired, as well as the roof and that beam replaced. So some are making it this far north."

Limbreth shut her eyes in sudden weariness. Good for the dwarves. Their care proved the greatest of boons this night. They piled their gear across the opening to block the wind. Soon warmth grew in the shelter.

Gweld cooked up some of their remaining rations into a soup. "We will need food soon and our water is low," he said. The elf's gray eyes cut to Tordug with expectation.

"There should be a cistern nearby." Tordug swallowed some soup. "Likely to be frozen, but we can check it in the morning. We travel for some days yet, but maybe we can gather some dried stores at other shelters along the way. We can start checking shelters tomorrow. If dwarves have been here, then..." He trailed off as the wind howled outside.

Limbreth wiped her mouth from the last of her soup. "Do you think it will snow much?"

The old dwarf shrugged. "I do not know, ax-maid. I feel snow in my bones, but this seems only a wind storm to me. This storm sweeps east, so who knows how long it will last. We must hurry tomorrow. Our way will go lower, so we can avoid snow better, and winter food can be found."

Weariness dragged them all into silence for several minutes.

The dwarf stirred at last. "Conserve your hardtack." He shifted his firm gaze to each of them until they all acknowledged his wishes. Then Tordug stowed his bowl and spoon and rolled into his blanket.

Gweld said nothing further but moved to squat by the door for his watch.

Limbreth gazed at her companions as the light from the fire played across their faces. They were friends now, she decided. She lay down under her blanket. Hastra sat still as she stared into the flames. The Withling's eyes shifted toward Limbreth, but the old woman neither said anything nor gave any facial expression that indicated what she was thinking. Limbreth rolled over and shut her eyes.

Now Limbreth allowed herself to consider Athson. She wished she had—could—tell him what bothered her. It was not his absence or the affliction of her morose feelings. *Tolerate your failure.* She shrugged inwardly. But not fear. She hated that—could not tolerate it. She wasn't the master of it like she'd thought in Auguron. That was an age ago. She'd never known fear before then, not really. Not even when she and Athson met the Bane. But the echo of the slammed door in Chokkra haunted her. It left her shut away and helpless. Limbreth bit her lower lip and sniffed. *Find something else to think of.* She rolled back over and stared into the fire. Her breathing slowed. Her eyes fluttered, then closed, and her thoughts wandered into dreams.

When Hastra awakened her to watch, Limbreth yawned. So soon? Only minutes had passed, surely. Another long day loomed beyond her watch. *So tired. Needed more than that.* She dragged herself to her feet.

Hastra spoke at Limbreth's ear. "No Bane. Not since we came here."

Limbreth nodded and rubbed her eyes. Too much to hope they'd lost it. The old woman was soon asleep and left Limbreth yawning in the dim light of the low fire. But soon enough everyone stirred and stowed blankets while readying to leave.

"No waiting to eat. Do that while we walk." Tordug shooed them out the door. The dwarf checked the cistern when they exited the shelter but found it broken open and dry. He shrugged over the discovery but he said nothing. If there was nothing at the next shelter, they would soon be in trouble or have to collect snow and melt it over a fire.

They pushed through the crevice out onto the road while it was still dark, but the clouds had blown away. Late stars wheeled overhead. Tordug spared only a little water for the lantern's glow-moss, since the sun would rise soon enough.

Limbreth winced at the wind. "My face feels burned."

"It's the wind. I've a salve for that in my pack. We'll get it when we stop. Time to move now, so cover your face up to your eyes, gell." Tordug hustled them along the road.

But the break was a long time coming, so she bore the discomfort for several hours under a spare cloth she'd had tucked deep in her hood. Limbreth's stomach rumbled often. *Ignore it and conserve food for the evening.*

They finally found a shelter and paused at the working cistern for fresh water. Then Tordug tended Limbreth's face as well as the others'. "It's far too early to stop. We'll push on." The dwarf had them moving in moments. "We need to reach lower walks if possible. We'll have a better chance against any snow. Got lucky last night."

Hastra raised her eyes from ice on the walk. "What is needed is given, Tordug."

"That it is, Withling, for whatever reason."

Not long after their break, the wind battered them through a natural cut in the shoulder of the mountain. Beyond the crevice, they arrived at a fork in the road. The old dwarf led them down the lower choice.

Limbreth searched for the Bane on their back-trail often but noted dark clouds to the north. *That storm grows quickly. Tordug checks it often.* She hustled after the dwarf. *Forget the Bane for now.*

"Snow will catch us yet." Tordug frowned.

Hastra grunted and picked up her pace beside Limbreth.

Not long after Tordug's comment, the outriders of the dark clouds overtook them around mid-afternoon. Cold poured over them, and fat raindrops pelted them for a while. Ahead of them, the clouds stretched over the blue sky, and behind them the wind howled warning of worse to come. They raced the storm to the shelter Tordug had set as their goal.

Limbreth spied spare, windblown evergreens amid the roll of storm clouds on the lower slopes. *Those are much closer now. Will it be enough?* Her gut knotted with doubt. *It'll snow, but how much and how long?* She trotted after Tordug when Hastra passed her. They all risked a bad fall on the rain-slicked walk.

The rain turned to snow and slowed their progress as the walk became more treacherous under their feet. They slipped more than once, most frequently when they scrambled through areas in disrepair. As daylight faded into early dusk, the snow swirled in their faces. Sleet also fell with the snow, and both stung Limbreth's chapped cheeks when they were blown into her face. She pulled the cover over her face.

They trudged miserably through the snow, but they found the shelter sooner than Limbreth expected. She sighed through her makeshift mask. The early start with few delays had done the trick, and none too soon. She ducked after Hastra into as snug a shelter as they had found, and Tordug soon had their fire lit.

He kept the fire low and by its light they found a small store of dried food to supplement their remaining rations. They were cheered by a warm meal and even some hot tea, and felt some measure of comfort against the snowstorm. As the wind whistled, Limbreth thought she had never been so glad for a fire and a meal. The others' faces reflected the same relief.

But they were weary, and after treating their faces against the effects of

CHAPTER THREE

the biting wind, everyone turned to their blankets for sleep. Gweld took up the first watch.

Limbreth lay beneath her blanket. She grunted to herself. She'd hardly thought of Athson all day. The weather race had taken all of her attention. She sighed in weariness. Sleep overtook her without further thought.

The touch of a cold hand drew Limbreth out of the depths of slumber. Her watch already? But her eyes only fluttered open and shut. Hastra said nothing. That touch—it was far colder than the weather. It crept deep into her sluggish thoughts and along her spine.

Limbreth groaned and turned her head. Her eyes flared wide at the sight of a black hand. It grasped her arm. Her jaw worked, but she uttered not a sound. Her heart slammed in her throat, and her chest heaved. The Bane dragged her toward the door where Gweld squatted.

The figure of the Bane swallowed all the light in the small space even though the fire still burned well. Limbreth found some strength and flopped as the Bane pulled her to the door's threshold and then ducked out.

Limbreth's lungs strained to utter any noise. It was a spell! She fought for a sound and croaked a whimper. The Bane pulled her right arm out the door.

Why wouldn't Gweld do anything?

Limbreth fumbled with her free hand and snagged the rock edge of the doorway. The Bane yanked at her arm. Her breath came in gasps but made no viable sound.

She drew the deepest of breaths and mustered all her strength, which passed her lips in a feeble whisper: "Help." Not enough to wake anyone. *You're on your own.* Gweld never moved.

The Bane yanked her torso into the blizzard outside. Her hand grasped the doorway fast and her left arm locked in pain. A groan escaped her lips.

CHAPTER FOUR

Athson crouched face-to-face with Makwi. The dwarf's expression was tense. Athson shifted his stance and made to peek over the wall. "Where are they?"

Makwi held him back. "Not yet. Ralda's a big enough sight to spot as it is. Let's not tip those Rokans with movement."

"He might fall."

"He might. Either way, there's nothing we can do from here."

Athson watched Spark. Makwi was right. He rubbed his temple, but the pain remained. "While we're here, have you got more of that herb?"

"Yeah, keeping it close to hand." He fished in his pocket and drew out a parchment packet. "But this will make you sleep too, so don't take it now."

The ogres still pounded Athson's head. He leaned against the wall. "What about just a little? Will that help the pain?"

Makwi chewed the inside of his cheek and stroked his beard. "Just a pinch then. But you already stumble like a drunk, so have a care." He held out some pain herb.

Athson pinched the sparest he dared, put it on his tongue, and drank some water. Anything to ease the pain.

Makwi patted Athson's arm. "Stay down. I'll check." He rose with care, grasped the top edge of the wall with one hand, and peered over. His voice erupted in a loud hiss. "What are you doing? They'll spot you."

Ralda's voice answered from beyond the wall. "They go. No see. Come back. Here." The sword hilt appeared over the edge of the wall.

CHAPTER FOUR

Makwi snared it and handed the weapon to Athson.

Ralda scrambled over the wall and they waited for him to don his pack. "We go now?"

Makwi tugged his beard. "We're on one of the lowest roads. That one comes from the lowlands and turns several times until it crosses this one. They've as far to go as us—maybe. We better push on to avoid them. I'd wait, but the others are farther south already." The dwarf shifted his gaze to Ralda. "Sorry there's no rest after that climb."

Ralda shrugged. "Ready go now."

Athson got his sword sheathed and set out with the dwarf and giant. His headache faded, and his mind cleared. What had he been doing? He'd almost gotten himself killed. But his energy soon faded, and then he yawned. He fell behind his companions, and Spark walked slowly on his left. Ralda and Makwi turned back for him. The giant took Athson's pack and carried it.

Makwi supported Athson as best he could with his own sore shoulder. "You probably shouldn't even be on your feet yet. We need to get to Hastra."

They pushed forward at the best pace Athson could manage. They soon spotted the intersection in the distance beyond a turn in the road at the fold of a mountain. They hustled for the turn, where Makwi peeked around and observed the crossing roads.

Athson held his breath. Two other roads crossed here as well. There were too many places to hide. He touched his sword hilt. Too many cracks and boulders. The dwarves chose this place well for bringing several roads together.

They waited but neither saw nor heard anything of the Rokans. They crept forward in what shadow and the cover of the retaining wall was available.

Makwi gathered them close. "They should have passed by now. There's nothing for it but to go on. I can go myself."

Ralda laid his big hand on Makwi's good shoulder. "We all go."

Makwi nodded and led them away, and they closed on the intersection. They crossed with a rush.

Athson touched his forehead. *Should've sent Spark ahead.* The mountain hound's ear flicked to alertness.

Shouts rang in the heights ahead as well as above and below their road. Weapons clattered, and a several whistles blew. Ralda groaned and hefted his staff. Makwi fumbled with his ax. Athson snatched his sword from its scabbard.

Rokans sprang from their trap.

~ ~ ~ ~ ~ ~ ~

Things would not go well. Of that, Corgren was sure. His gut knotted. The pain of the Bane's stripped spell throbbed within his head. He'd been too rash with the Dragon's fire at Chokkra's gates. But he couldn't have known about the power of the blessed sword. But the way his master had taken over the Bane remained a none–too–subtle lesson—and message. *Redouble your efforts.* His legs wobbled. *Barely on your feet after two days—even with Paugren's help. Now this.* The summons flashed pale blue in his ring. Meeting with Paugren in Rok. Did it blink faster with urgency or anger? Corgren set his jaw. He must face his Master regardless.

Corgren stepped from his room in Chokkra and raised his hand toward the chain leashing his years-long prisoner. "Ha o-tou navuras." The magic, which bound the chain like a lock to the stone wall, released, and he caught it. He yanked the chain, and the blind prisoner stumbled to his feet. "Come, we travel." Corgren watched Ath's hands with a squint. Had he secreted something in his boot? Without a word, he forced the boot from Ath's foot and felt inside it. *Nothing there.* "Put it back on." He shoved the boot into his prisoner's fumbling hands. "Be quick! You waste my time."

Ath knelt and worked his foot into the boot, stood and stamped it to fit.

With a shrug, Corgren turned away. Suspicion was necessary with prisoners like this. This one might seem hopeless, but he had backbone. Corgren stroked his short beard. He wasn't about to leave this prisoner alone. Ath might have saved him, but there was a reason.

Corgren lifted his hand again and spoke the dragon's tongue for their transport. "Sa na-a-va cor-a-Rok khee zhan tu-avath." Light from the few torches and the shadows of the tunnel swirled around Corgren and his prisoner until darkness swallowed any color. It lasted several moments,

CHAPTER FOUR

until the darkness whispered the voices of a thousand distant winds. Corgren smiled at the cover of the dragon's wings. His master's wings.

Ath cowered in his blindness and covered his head.

The wings of the spell lifted, and the roar ceased as daylight pierced Corgren's eyes with brightness. He'd been too long in Chokkra. He squinted.

Ath's scream ended as he crouched on the cold ground and trembled.

Corgren laughed. "Are Magdronu's wings so terrible?" They comforted Corgren after his recent suffering. He stepped off the flat rock onto which they'd been deposited by the spell. "Come, we've a meeting to attend." He yanked the chain, and his prisoner shuffled after him.

Down a slope they went, into the camp where Paugren stayed. Corgren scanned the buildings as he approached. Not so much a camp anymore. Several permanent and semi-permanent buildings now stood. One long structure had been built where Paugren once penned imprisoned dwarves. Corgren arched an eyebrow. Curious that, coddling the prisoners in warmth. He strode on, approached the guards, and flashed his master's sign upon the inside of his forearm as he paused. "Which of these is Paugren's quarters now?"

The Rokan soldiers saluted. One guard pointed past several worn tents. "Down at the end, my lord."

Corgren swept past them with his stumbling prisoner in tow. He approached the rough house indicated, built with a raised floor, and mounted the steps to the porch, where he magically locked the chain around a post. His prisoner huddled on the bottom step after nearly falling on it. Corgren opened his mouth, intending to force the blind man onto the ground. He belonged there. But he decided to show him a good turn and let him stay on the step. Corgren turned for the door and paused to glance back at Ath. Perhaps a little coddling might trip him up. He'd slip with his intentions if comfortable. Well, not comfortable, but given a few rewards. Corgren sniffed. "You will stay on the step. You may find a few rewards for your good deed."

A woman opened the door at Corgren's knock. She bowed in recognition of his status as a high-mage of Rok. She motioned toward an office, her face lowered. "This way, my lord mage."

Boards clattered under Corgren's boots as he entered the office. Paugren stood at the window, his hands clasped behind his back. Wearing a thick, red coat embroidered in gold across the back with the sign of Magdronu, his brother matched Corgren in facial appearance, though Paugren wouldn't shave his head, preferring it long and pulled into a straight, dark tail falling between his shoulder blades.

"Pondering some mystery?"

Paugren snorted and half-turned. "Hardly. More weary of this place, this task, and all without proper accommodations. Are you well now?"

Corgren sat in a chair with a sigh. "Well enough to walk. Good thing you were there for that business."

Paugren never turned from the window. "You're welcome, brother. That could have been done better."

Corgren sat straighter and waved his hand. "A lesson taught, nothing else."

"Still, spare thanks for our faithful service." Paugren stepped from the window to the desk.

Corgren cocked his head sideways and squinted. "Going soft on our Master after all these years?" He pulled his sleeve to his elbow and revealed the magical tattoo of Magdronu. "We've gotten much over the centuries with him. Turning away from that?"

"I got you into this, brother. Your pains from that stripped spell are my fault."

"Nonsense!" Better change the subject and figure out where he stood. Corgren waved his arm and indicated the expanse of the room. "This warm little house you've built is better than my dark caverns. Honestly, I don't know how those stone rats live in such places."

"True." Paugren knocked the dark, finished wood of his desk and poured wine in a goblet of silver.

"You even seem to show your prisoners a pleasant time as well."

Paugren paused mid-sip and swallowed. "Hardly, brother. Our master

CHAPTER FOUR

needs blood at his hallowed ground in the mountains. I'd rather they not die here, as every drop is precious to fuel the magic that comes down to us—not to mention our other benefits." He cocked his head with an arched eyebrow and motioned to the other goblet. "Wine?"

Corgren lifted two fingers and waved them side to side. "Best not before the meeting, but I'll likely need it afterward." He frowned at his brother. "Things have not gone as expected, so you better stuff your displeasure of the place down deep."

Paugren looked at his goblet, poised to drink again, then set it aside. He sat on a corner of his desk, arms crossed. "What do you mean?"

Corgren motioned to the cuts on his head. "Chokkra's gate collapsed when my magic met a blade blessed by Eloch. I barely escaped. I think the ranger did as well. He knows our intentions toward him now, so Magdronu isn't pleased. Drop your sudden streak of conscience. Things can get far worse."

Paugren's face paled. "I'm still loyal."

Corgren watched his brother, and several moments passed in silence. *He better be.* "Then why these doubts?"

Paugren stepped back to the window, his boots scuffing the floor. His jaw muscles flexed as he paused in thought. "This meeting won't be easy by far. Unexpected as the incident was, that's on you." He pointed a finger. "Not me. Have a care, brother. I've stuck my hand in the fire for you more than once over the years."

Corgren spread his hands, palms up. "Good enough, just don't let Magdronu notice your..."—he twirled a hand in the air—"questions. I can't afford those." He rubbed his temples and shut his eyes. *No more lessons like the last one.* Corgren swallowed a sudden lump in his throat. "But thanks for your concern." *Best keep the peace with the difficult meeting to come.*

His brother wheeled back toward Corgren. "We'd best be early, then." He motioned for the door.

Corgren stood and cleared his throat as the woman passed in the hall with a blanket. A thought captured his attention. "Have her cover my prisoner with a blanket, would you?"

Paugren chuckled. "Now who's soft? And why have you brought that traitor here?"

Corgren motioned with his hands. "Easy, brother. The man was chained to me in the cave-in and dragged me to safety while I was unconscious. He deserves a little care for his good deed."

"I doubt your sincerity. Here, woman! Give a blanket to the wretch chained outside."

The two mages left the house without acknowledging the chained blind man. They headed for a large canvas tent for their meeting.

Corgren leaned close to his brother, voice pitched low and thumbed over his shoulder in the direction of Paugren's house. "He's up to something. If it were me, I'd have killed my enemy and died with him, at the least. It may be some comforts will make him slip."

"A little intrigue to entertain?"

"Certainly!"

"I must try that with a few of these prisoners and slaves." They arrived at the tent, and Paugren held a tent-flap open.

Corgren ducked inside and found the interior cold but prepared with the ingredients for the spell necessary to commune with their master. He turned to Paugren as he followed and took him by the arm. "Tell me, what's wrong with you? Your mood, the dragon will sense it."

Paugren frowned and sighed. "Nothing to question my sincerity over, Corgren. I'm tired of herding dwarves and wonder if there isn't a better task for me. Let these Beleesh sisters do this."

Corgren chuckled. "Those three? They'd kill half of the camp just from their cruelty. Your way is better for our needs."

Paugren stepped past. "I'm glad you agree with my reasoning. I'm still bored."

"Best not show it to our master."

"Drop it!" Paugren glowered at Corgren. "Or I'll let you bear the whole burden of our spell, since you're the one who failed."

Corgren ground his teeth. He rarely got angry with his brother. But his mood. Magdronu wouldn't be pleased, and Chokkra was bad enough.

CHAPTER FOUR

Lucinda, bloodied and gasping her life away, flashed through his memory. He couldn't lose all they'd worked for because of Paugren. Not now. Not after so long. But he wasn't strong enough to handle this meeting himself. "Fair enough." He pointed at Paugren. "But you just watch it. We've put too much into all this to lose now."

Paugren grasped Corgren's shoulders and leaned close. "I'm just tired of this camp and these dwarves. That's all."

Corgren exhaled and nodded. "Then let's get started."

They approached the table and poured the blood for their rituals into the bowl of coins. Together they murmured their incantation. The stomach-turning green light flickered to life against the white canvas. Magdronu roared through Corgren's mind and the dragon's anger seared his thoughts. Corgren crumpled to his knees.

"I've set plans in place, and they have been thwarted!"

Pressure built in Corgren's head, and he collapsed like Chokkran stone.

~ ~ ~ ~ ~ ~ ~

Ath slouched on the step. Wind, cold but refreshing, swept over him. He shivered anyway. He loathed inaction. Long minutes passed, and he considered using the file. This place was busy, by the sound of it. Best hold back. Although, who'd be watching him? He strained his hearing. Any guard could be watching.

He shivered, blew on his hands, and rubbed them together. Chokkra was warmer. This was some sort of settlement. Some people walked by, and then more. Ath thanked his better judgment about using the file. He turned his head and leaned toward the passersby. It was the only way to tell where he was. Rok, knowing his captors, but...

The clank of metal and heavy tread of boots stepped past him. Soldiers. But they said nothing at all. He could be anywhere.

The door thrust open behind Ath and jolted him upright before it closed. Two pairs of boots clattered on the steps, and he leaned away. Corgren maybe, and someone else. They said nothing that he heard, so he sat and waited.

Someone stepped out of the door. "Here, been ordered t'give ya this." A woman draped a blanket over Ath's shoulders.

A Rokan perhaps, by the accent. Ath wasn't sure. "Thank you."

"Thank the masters. T'weren't my doing." The woman crossed the porch.

"Uh, where are we?" Ath held his breath. *Don't be so obvious about information.* But she paused at the door.

She humphed at him and tapped her foot, and he imagined her standing behind him with hands on her hips. But she was faceless to him. "Rok." She shut the house door behind her.

Ath tugged the rough wool close about him and over his knees. So, it was Rok. His shivering ceased after a few minutes. By 'masters,' she meant Corgren and someone else. But why the blanket? Corgren cared nothing for his comfort. The wizard needed Ath to leverage Athson, but a blanket? It made little sense. The wizard had searched his boot. Likely suspicious. Was Corgren trying to fool him into revealing his plan? He'd use the file with greater care now.

Men strode by Ath. By the clatter and jangle of metal, he judged them to be guards. "...wearied of all the stone rats. Their beards look like horse tails."

Another man laughed as they faded away. "I guess their faces are horse arses then. 'Cept we can pull these tails off."

The first guard laughed.

Definitely Rokans. Ath ground his teeth, the gaps between them pronounced after the recent loss of two at Corgren's hands back in Chokkra. Now, if only he knew where in Rok they were. But even if he could, an escape here was useless without help. He had to choose well, stay ready. He drew the blanket tighter as he hugged himself.

Another set of feet approached, and the conversation drowned out the guards. "...don't know how I'm going to dry all these sheets in this cold. They'll beat me, sure enough."

"Don't fret, Muriel." The second woman's voice rang clear on the cold air.

Ath's head twisted toward the second woman, and he gasped.

"But Dani—"

"Here, now! Watch where you're a'goin." The harsh, nasal snarl of a man

CHAPTER FOUR

interrupted the women.

"Yes, yes." The women's voices sounded strained in Ath's ears.

"Don't dump that wash! I'll give you a beatin'." Slapped skin sounded, and one of the women shrieked. "Shut yer mouth, or you'll get more!"

Feet thumped away, and their voices faded.

"What're you a'doin'?" Breath brushed Ath's face, smelling of onions and ale.

"Uh, just—" What was he doing? Ath pulled his blanket close. When had he stood?

Thick hands shoved Ath onto the steps. He fell and slammed his head. He groaned.

"Next time you raise your fists, I'll beatcha!"

Ath froze. He unclenched his fists. The guard had struck one of those women, and one of them was his wife. He was sure enough, anyway.

The man trudged away.

Ath almost called for Danilla. *No! Don't draw attention.* He sat up and rubbed his head. Warmth formed in his chest. It was her. He was sure it was her voice. He sat down and pulled his new blanket over his shoulders. A sudden smile grew on his face, and he lowered his head lest someone see his grin. She was here. Alive! He must be ready when the time came. And now was as good a time as any to push.

Ath pulled his hands inside the blanket and feigned a shiver. He withdrew his file from its pocket, found the groove in the chain link, and drew the file slowly over and back on the metal. Not too fast, no noise. How long could he work at it? How long did he dare? He slouched and shook. His hand worked the file. He lowered his head to hide his continued grin, and he listened. Now he had a blanket to hide his filing. And his wife still lived. Two little things, and one important detail. That was hope, if nothing. And reason enough to risk working his chain now.

~ ~ ~ ~ ~ ~ ~

Magdronu forced his will through the spell, like his flames over prey. Necessary. Too much independence. Not enough results. These two were minions. Powerful? Yes. Faithful? Mostly. But still minions. Through the speaking spell, he watched their wan faces bear the strain of his presence. *'Guile is necessary for my plans. However, I'm far from weak.'* Magdronu waited for their acknowledgment.

Corgren rolled on the tent floor and groaned.

Paugren steadied himself at the table. *'M-master, you are mighty indeed. But Corgren has just suffered—'*

Magdronu forced Paugren to his knees with the slightest flex of his essence. He flicked through Paugren's mind. What was this boredom with his worthy task? Dissatisfaction with his favor? *'I say what happens, not you, Paugren.'* He flicked the old connection in Paugren's tattooed arm, Magdronu's own mark. *Yes, remember this well.*

Paugren writhed beside his brother.

Magdronu left one brother in agony for the other. He eased his will on Corgren. *'Corgren, we must regain control of Athson and use more leverage. While you ready for our ultimate action in Denaria, you will stand ready for any call I place on you for immediate action. Did he have knowledge of the Bow of Hart?'*

'Master, I think not. He defied me.'

'You needed only to take charge of him and let me slip him from your false noose to manipulate. Instead, you nearly killed him and yourself. Without him, we have nothing to break my enemy's hold.'

Corgren cringed before him.

Magdronu snarled. *'Your powers are mine and not toys of your whim!'*

'Yes, my Master.'

Magdronu eased further. *Now he's got the message. But Paugren needs more lessons.*

'If Athson knows not the location of the bow, then I must guide him to it, even if more leverage is needed. I'll have that sooner or later. Be ready for any plan I activate.' He released Corgren and turned his attention to Paugren. *Unhappy led to untrustworthy. Another task from this lesson.* *'Paugren, since you are so bored with feeding my power and yours, I'll set you another task. Use what resources you have now. Even those sisters. But be wary, this target is far more slippery than you guess. Make as many attempts as necessary for this task, but*

CHAPTER FOUR

see it done correctly if you must do it yourself. She must be removed in the end. Ready for your task?' Magdronu eased his power on Paugren.

Paugren lay still for spare moments and recovered. *'Yes, Great One. I'm ready for the task.'*

'Good. Now...'

CHAPTER FIVE

Limbreth's clutch held firm, but she lacked the strength to wrench free of the Bane's inexorable grip. She whimpered softly as fear as cold as the hand gripping her seized her mind. Her will slowly froze. Would the mindless grip hold? Shame rose with her panic. She loathed herself for them. But her death-grip held faster than anything within her.

The Bane yanked her arm, then tried for her other hand. Limbreth aimed a feeble kick. Wind roared through the doorway with billows of snow.

Then a voice snapped from inside the shelter.

Limbreth clutched the doorway. What were the words?

The Bane paused. The wind only slightly tossed its cowl about as it reached for her locked left arm.

A shout snapped like a whip of light.

The Bane let her go and fled.

In moments, the others arrived at her side. In the moan of the wind, she had not understood the word spoken, but the Bane had certainly been affected by the command. She wanted that word. Her body shivered beyond her control. Limbreth struggled to rise, but her numb limbs flailed out of her control.

Hastra's face loomed into sight along with Gweld and Tordug. Concern etched their faces while they spoke to Limbreth, but their words whispered against the howl in her confused ears. She still grasped the doorway. Her head flopped from side to side. What was wrong.? Her vision slithered toward darkness.

CHAPTER FIVE

Hastra grabbed Limbreth's face and started speaking as she kneeled over her. The Withling's eyes locked onto Limbreth's, and she stilled.

Limbreth heard her own breathing come in ragged gasps. "What's wrong? What's wrong?" But the words sounded like croaked confusion from a wounded animal.

"I think she's better, Withling." Tordug glanced at Hastra. "Shall we bring her inside?"

But the old woman was praying in whatever tongue she used for such dire moments as this.

Beside the dwarf, Gweld pointed to Limbreth's hand at the doorframe. "Not even that creature budged her loose. We cannot until she does so herself."

Feeling edged into Limbreth's other numb limbs, and control eased back in. Her thoughts coalesced into meaning. Her body still quivered, but she sensed her surroundings.

Hastra fell into silence and settled back on her heels.

Limbreth's hand relaxed, and her companions helped her back into the shelter and settled her by the fire.

"What happened?" Hastra pulled Limbreth's blanket over her. The Withling's piercing eyes searched Limbreth for any bodily harm.

Limbreth's teeth chattered for a time and then eased. "I woke and the—the Bane had me." Her voice wavered. "It started dragging me outside, and I could hardly move or make a sound." Tears pooled in her eyes while she spoke. *Coward! Only an old wound saved you!* She stared at her left hand. "It hurts."

"Here, let me." Tordug massaged her arm.

Limbreth sighed and laid her head on her pack.

Hastra touched Limbreth's face. "The Bane is very dangerous. It has a power that pulls your will from you. But how did it get in?"

"It pulled me right past you, Gweld." Limbreth shifted her gaze to the elf. "But you never noticed me."

"What's this?" The Withling whirled toward the elf with some asperity in her voice, and her eyes narrowed into a hard glare.

Gweld backed away, surprise registered in his slack jaw and wide eyes. He spread his hands, palms up. "I was watching but do not remember the Bane entering. Though my eyes never closed, I never saw it, and woke like I was asleep when you spoke, Withling Hastra." The elf ended with his face lowered in embarrassment for his failure.

"Perhaps it was a spell." Tordug paused and looked at the elf in a way that indicated to Limbreth that the dwarf was unsure of the situation and the elf.

"He—he never moved..." Limbreth suppressed a rising sob. *Helpless as a babe.* She hated that too. She bit her lower lip against the wail that wracked her body.

Hastra stroked Limbreth's face. "Are you fevered? We have you safe now, my dear."

Limbreth nodded with closed eyes. But she gasped for air in the midst of her sob. How she wilted so easily. What a coward. She thrust Tordug's hands away from her arm. She was no hero, worthy of such attention. No trinkets changed that, grip or not.

The Withling turned to Tordug and Gweld. "She can't stand watch tonight, I think. We will share the extra watch."

When Limbreth opened her eyes in the following silence, she saw the Withling eyeing Gweld with a frown. The elf shoved his hands in his pockets like a boy caught stealing cookies. The elf retreated to the door and blocked it with the other's packs. He glanced at Hastra, who turned away from him at that moment. His eyes flashed fire, and his face contorted into a murderous leer.

Limbreth blinked. What was that? When she opened her eyes again, Gweld's eyes were fixed on her, but his expression was normal. She rubbed her head. It must have been the firelight. Her mind was tricking her after the Bane. She rubbed her left arm.

"I'm sorry, Limbreth." Gweld drew his long-knife and sat by the packs, his lowered face a mask of dejection.

Don't remember Gweld ever reacting so much. She raised herself under the blanket. "It's not your fault."

CHAPTER FIVE

He saluted elven-style, touching his forehead and then his heart. "You are gracious, but the fault lies still with me."

"I do not know how early we can leave, or even if she can travel in the morning." Hastra turned to face Tordug. "She may not be able, and I must check her before we consider leaving." As she spoke, Hastra pulled out some travel-bread and offered it to Limbreth, who tried to refuse it.

"The storm may keep us from traveling." Tordug's brow creased. "Remember that snow out there?" He motioned toward the door.

"Well enough." The Withling shot her reply over her shoulder as she pushed the food on Limbreth. "We'll worry about the snow as we can, I suppose." She waved the ration at Limbreth. "Take it."

"I don't want to eat more than my share." Her cowardice had drained enough from their group. But in the end, she failed to outlast the insistent Withling. She ate the bread and drank from Hastra's offered share of water. It all tasted like ash.

"We may need to use the fire for a signal to any dwarves who are close." Tordug patted the dwindling pile of wood.

"Smoke is enough to let an enemy know someone is here, but signals may identify us as their prey." Hastra stood and retrieved her own blanket, which had fallen near the shelter door.

"We may have little choice." The dwarf glanced at the roof and the moaning wind beyond it. "There is little enough food and wood. We don't have the proper boots and winter gear for this weather in the mountains."

Hastra nodded with her own frown. "Understood. Perhaps no foe lurks in this storm. I've been in bad spots like this before. Sometimes there are only choices between bad and worse." She rubbed her midsection as if pained and then sat close beside Limbreth.

~ ~ ~ ~ ~ ~ ~

Limbreth bursts from cover and runs in the night amid a silent forest. A hand reaches for her, but she turns away from the grasp. She despairs of fleeing and wheels in circles. She reaches for her swords at her back but falls still and trembling in the dark cold. She stares at nothing for a long time and then sees another hand, and she reaches for it and rises out of water. Hastra chants in her ear, and a glow warms Limbreth. She moves toward the light and finds an arrow flashing whiter than snow. She reaches for it and—

~ ~ ~ ~ ~ ~ ~

Limbreth startled from sleep at a touch on her arm. She pulled away. "No!" Hastra checked her. Her heart thrummed wildly. Not the Bane. Limbreth caught her breath. "Sorry, Withling. I thought—"

Hastra reached for her again. "I should have woken you. I wanted you to sleep, though."

Beyond the shelter door, Gweld and Tordug talked, but she heard little more than the words "snow" and "ice" through the gusts of wind and the creak of the shelter roof. She lay still with the smell of the fire in her nose while Hastra poked her arm.

"Ow!" She winced at the Withling's touch, and Hastra pushed Limbreth's sleeve up, revealing her arm, purpled with a bruise though it was not swollen or cut. Limbreth stared at the discolored skin, flexed her fingers, and grunted in pain.

"Lean into the light some. Let me see better." Hastra adjusted her position and squinted at Limbreth's arm.

Limbreth rolled toward the firelight, and Hastra inspected her forearm further. Limbreth gazed toward the doorway. She yawned and listened for the conversation between Gweld and Tordug. "How long have I slept?" It was surprising how fresh she felt. It couldn't have been long.

"Long enough. It's well past sunrise. Let me see your arm." Hastra tugged at her arm. The Withling murmured under her breath.

"That long? We're not leaving yet, then?" She twisted toward the door. "Ow." She jerked her arm away.

The Withling looked up from her suddenly empty hands, her eyebrows arched.

"You poked me." Limbreth flexed her hand and arm, then rubbed them.

"Look." Hastra pointed at Limbreth's arm.

Limbreth gasped. The bruise was gone. *Thought she was just fussing at me.* "The pain's gone too." She gaped. She had not felt anything until the sharp poke. *I've seen this but not felt it before.*

CHAPTER FIVE

"It was a curse leaving. The pain was not injury at all."

Tordug stuck his head in the door. "Anything wrong?" His eyes danced uncertainly between the two women. "Is the ax-maid able to travel?"

"I think she is now." Hastra stood with a grunt. "That is, if she is not too injured from that poke."

Limbreth glanced at the Withling, who flashed her a wry grin and turned to stow her things in preparation for leaving.

"Good." Tordug crawled into the shelter after his pack, followed by Gweld. "We checked the road. We will have to push along the best we can. The snow is not so deep as I had feared, but we must move and hope for better provisions at the next shelter. We'll go no farther than the next shelter today. We'll take what wood and stores as we can, though. I hope we can signal for help from the next shelter." He pointed at the chimney along the rock face at the back of the shelter. "That was fixed and draws well enough but I can't send any messages through it."

"How far is it?" Limbreth pulled her sleeve down, rolled her blanket, and stowed it in her pack.

"It is less than a full day normally, ax-maid. But in this weather, it will likely be after dark again before we reach it, since we're starting late." He moved to gather wood and food to carry with them. "We must move or be caught in deeper snow, most likely."

They soon left the shelter behind. Limbreth glanced each way along the mountain road as she trudged with care amid her companions. *Glad to move on. Best way to escape that Bane is move away from this isolation.* She slouched. But it could likely do her harm anywhere. She pulled her hood low and wiped a sudden tear from her eye.

The walk lay slick with ice beneath the ankle-deep snow that shifted in the wind. There were frequent slips. Limbreth braced herself with any handholds she found along the mountainside. A fall might lead to a bad injury.

Tordug grumbled about proper footgear. Gweld said little during the entire day, and Hastra spoke less. The wind rose stiff at their backs for several hours while snow drifted in eddies and piled in crevices.

Limbreth plowed ahead with her head down and her jaw set. At least her feet no longer bothered her like before they'd reached the Trolls Heaths. She gripped a crack in the rock. That seemed a year ago now. Her foot shifted on ice. She shortened her stride and tested her next step.

The sun crested invisibly above the clouds, and what brightness there had been soon faded. They slipped and scurried along as best they could. Slopes were the worst. "Might be best to just slide down this."

Tordug shot a grimace at Limbreth. "Good way to break a leg. Almost deadly without the Withling along. That last slope had a lot of fallen rock on it. But if you fall and cannot stop, enjoy the ride and hope for the best."

Dusk was approaching when Limbreth felt the odd chill slipping along her limbs and back. The Bane. She peered back along the road, but the swirl of snow and cloud obscured her vision beyond a dozen paces.

Hastra nudged Limbreth. "I feel it too. I keep wondering why you were grabbed."

"I wish it would go away. I am tired of it skulking around out of sight. I wish I could take a sword to it." Something more than shrinking from it. Slip the noose of her cowardice. She sniffed.

"I think you would be in grave danger if you did, dear." Hastra took Limbreth's arm and pulled her on up the walk. "Let's go before we fall too far behind the others. But a sword is better than nothing, unless it's that grip of yours."

They went on while gingerly stepping over ice.

Hastra righted herself from a near slip. "This thing is here for a reason. But why not the elf at the door? He would have been gone for hours before anyone noticed."

"He is an elf. Maybe the Bane has no power over him—or little enough." Limbreth added the last bit when the Withling shook her head.

"Elves are not immune to the Bane's power." Hastra almost went down again. "Confound this ice. He was affected by the illusion that the Bane cast in the shelter. You were dragged just past him with his eyes open. No, there must be another reason."

"Can't you just chase it away?" Limbreth staggered over a snow-hidden rock as she glanced at the Withling, who grabbed at the young woman to steady her.

"What is given..."

Limbreth grimaced at the words. Nothing before it was given. Best chance was to stick together, then. Snow fluttered in her eyes. The weather was her biggest worry for now. That and shelter, more food. Her stomach rumbled at the last part. *Find that tower and then Ezhandun.*

They soon found a shelter that squatted beneath a drift of snow on its roof. Limbreth stumbled inside with a glance at the spare light that remained in the stormy dusk. Just in time. The glow-moss water had probably frozen in the lantern. She heaved her pack off her shoulders and half-collapsed by it.

Tordug lit a fire and then went outside, coming back with a flurry of snow through the doorway. "Cistern's frozen solid. No surprise there. Plenty of snow we can melt. Got more wood and some further food, but not enough to stay here for days. The dwarves traveling these parts have done a steady job of it. Maybe we can signal someone."

The four travelers ate a hearty meal, and Tordug sang them a song of snow that seemed to Limbreth to keep time with the moaning wind outside. She understood the words. "Teach me the song." Better than chewing her troubles by the fire. She learned the song and more of Tordug's teaching of dwarven protocol.

"More snow tonight." The dwarf sat back when they fell silent and stared into the fire, poking the logs into higher flame. He squinted at the mouth of the chimney. "That one will work better if I need it. That other one was older, needed a rebuild." He chuckled. "Little chance of that these days, unless..." He fell silent and stared at the flames.

Gweld sat with his back to the door when he took his watch, and everyone bedded down. The elf nodded to Limbreth, his face drawn.

Limbreth shut her eyes. *Gweld's determined tonight.* But the Bane would enter if it wanted. Hastra grasped her hand and squeezed. *Better than nothing if needed.*

The night passed without incident and the wind slacked. Morning lay still with snow piled high on the dwarven road. After they checked the conditions, Tordug knelt by the fire and eyed his cape in his hands. "We can't make it far enough to reach another shelter." He shifted his gaze to everyone. "But maybe the wind will clear the snow some today. It's clearing at the moment. I'll try some signals. Get help started this way."

Hastra huddled in her cloak. "I doubt there are any trolls out to see in this weather."

Tordug snorted and a wry grin formed amid his mustache and beard. "Only dwarves like this weather." He built up the fire and started using a thick cloth hanging inside the shelter to send signals with the smoke.

Limbreth watched with curiosity and admiration. "Dwarves are so practical. You take nothing to chance. You have a plan for every instance, it seems."

The dwarf shrugged. "We have learned over many lives how to take prudent action. It is the hard way of the mountains inside and out."

While they sat, the dwarf taught Limbreth more dwarvish speech. After a while, Limbreth rubbed her temples. "It's all so confusing. So many ways dwarves identify themselves by their clans, vocation, and accomplishments. Some braids are so subtle I can barely tell them apart except for the trinkets, and I doubt I know a fraction of those."

Tordug slapped her shoulder with a laugh. "Not that many. Undo your braid and learn with your hands to help your eyes see better."

Limbreth followed Tordug's instructions and learned many new braids. He described where the trinkets went and how they looked. She finally rebraided her hair with her trinkets for warrior, ax-maid, and death-grip—all distinctive designs. She stood and stretched as Gweld and Hastra went out to check the road. "What if I am not only a warrior? What if I am something else too?" Limbreth watched her boots. She bit her lower lip. Should she confide in Tordug? He was like a father at times.

Tordug arched one eyebrow at her question and leaned toward her. "If you wish to declare it, you can be taught the braid as well. What do you have to declare?"

Limbreth glanced toward the door. Hastra knew her identity but said nothing of it. She leaned forward. "My father is Hamgas, King of Grendon.

CHAPTER FIVE

I am the youngest princess."

Tordug stared at her in wide-eyed surprise. Abruptly, the dwarf-lord rose to his feet and bowed to Limbreth in respectful greeting. "It is an honor, Princess Limbreth of Grendon. Why have you not revealed yourself before now?"

Limbreth frowned and switched to formal dwarvish. "That is a difficult matter, Lord Tordug."

The dwarf sat down and motioned for Limbreth to sit with him. After a few moments, he laughed heartily.

"What?"

The dwarf finished chuckling, but his red cheeks bulged with his smile. "You have been most wily, ax-maid. I wondered why you've changed your tune since Marston's Station—even since Chokkra. You have done as you were taught and made prudent alliances when presented. I wondered why you were so vigorous in your pursuit of dwarvish things. I knew it could not be just the honor alone, and now I see it was to learn of the dwarves to gain friendship." He wagged his finger at her. "You are every bit as wise and shrewd as you are courageous, ax-maid. I like that."

Limbreth's face warmed. She suppressed her grin. It didn't wipe the shame from her mind.

The door opened. Gweld's sharp features appeared in the doorway. "What's going on?"

Limbreth cleared her throat. "Nothing. I just said something wrong in dwarvish."

"She just said Makwi was pregnant." Tordug laughed and patted her thigh.

The elf gave a short laugh and called back to Hastra. "Let me help her on the ice."

Limbreth smiled. It was good to see him laugh again. He'd been dour since the Bane. "Later, Tordug?"

"We'll speak of it another time." The dwarf bestowed her with a fatherly pat on the arm. "I'll show you the knot you need, but I haven't got a trinket for an ambassador." He turned to his signals again. "Best send more, just in case."

Limbreth looked around at the inside of the shelter and its contents. "How long can we stay here?"

Tordug pursed his lips in thought. "Not long. Likely we'll need to go tomorrow, regardless of the weather, or we'll run out. We won't leave that much food and wood, just enough for passing travelers in need, maybe a supplement. Too bad we've nothing to spare in our passing for others."

"Can we move to lower roads?"

"It would still be a long march, even in mild weather," said Tordug. "We don't know how bad this storm was in lower valleys."

Limbreth finished her braid. Tordug was worried, by his pinched brow. Meeting their friends or getting to the Tower of Nazh-akun was a big chore. Bane or not.

The afternoon faded into night all too soon. Cold fingers of air crept into the shelter, and it no longer felt warm except near the fire. Even that warmth receded after a while, so that they huddled with blankets over their cloaked shoulders. Concern etched her companions' faces.

Tordug muttered and counted with his fingers about something.

Limbreth patted his hands. "We'll make it." She flashed him her best smile. Would Athson and the others make it, though?

The dwarf paused and looked intently at Limbreth, then the Withling, and shrugged. "No use letting it all bother us. Can't fix the weather to suit us." He shivered and gazed at the interior of the shelter. "Cold can crack stone, though."

They soon fell asleep, and only Hastra roused Limbreth in the night. During her watch, Limbreth sat close to the meager fire. She got warm for a while and then moved off to the door. She listened to the telltale song of the wind. It rose and fell so that the words of Tordug's song returned to her mind. That tune and the words mirrored the storm so well.

The dwarf-lord roused for his watch and approached her. "Go sleep for a few more hours. I'll manage the fire."

By morning, the last of the wood burned on the fire. Tordug brooded by the hearth before he spoke. "We can't stay longer. We'll have to chance it and hope to make another shelter with supplies or meet help. Wear more

CHAPTER FIVE

clothing than you have, and let's get moving."

When they set out, the snow lay so deep on the walk that they high-stepped into crunching snow. Tordug led the way and broke much of the snow open for those behind. They trudged in silence at the grim predicament. The wind soon roused, and with it blowing snow.

Limbreth worked through the cold and snow with her jaw set. The cold left her aquiver. *No energy for this.* The cold sapped it in minutes. Numbness writhed on her limbs. Her feet ached. *Guess that's good.* Makwi knew his boots. Much better for this than her old riding boots. Limbreth plodded forward amid the swirl, her whole body aquiver. How far to the next shelter? Too far. *Just take another step.*

They ate as they could from their supply while on their feet. Limbreth's energy surged but briefly then dropped again. She flexed her stiff hands. *Tordug won't stop. Can't or we die.* What was the time? Had to be afternoon. She paused and watched the waves of snow on the wind. Not from around them. *It's snowing heavily now. Not good.* Her pace slowed to single, slow steps forward.

The snow whipped Limbreth's face so hard that she lost sight of Hastra and Tordug. *Just follow Tordug's trail.* She stumbled on in his wake. She stopped and gazed about in confusion. *There's Hastra. Follow her.* Chill crept into her chest. Not good. *Too tired. Need a rest. No! Keep moving.* But there was something wrong. What? She struggled along the snow-driven road.

Limbreth stopped amid the whirl of wind and snow and swayed. It was late. Getting dark. When did she get warmer? The wind snapped. She shivered and reached for her blanket and cloak. Where were they? Where was her pack? She turned back and shambled up the path, looking for her clothing and pack. Where were her friends? Did they go on without her? Why had they let her lose her things? Did she miss the shelter?

The cold stopped biting her, and Limbreth was glad. She walked on a ways, hoping the shelter was near somewhere. They should've grabbed her. Limbreth staggered to a stop and looked back. There was her pack and some of her extra clothing under it. Where was the rest? Flown on the wind. She shrugged.

Limbreth searched for her blanket. *What are those three lumps by the road?* She went toward them as the wind pushed her. She stood up straight. Her friends, resting, not at the shelter. "Hey." She nudged Tordug. He didn't stir, and she frowned. "Where are my other things?"

The others did not move, so she bent down to them. They were asleep. Limbreth sighed. "Why didn't you tell me it was time to rest?" How irritating. She could have been taking a nap all this time. Blowing snow slammed into her eyes, and she blinked.

Dull lucidity clanged an alarm in Limbreth's mind. She blinked dumbly at the snow. What was the trouble? It was darker now, and they could make a fire, so they would be well enough. She staggered around in the wind for a moment and then sat down heavily. She suddenly wanted to sleep as the wind whistled in her ears.

Limbreth stared at the blowing snow, the frozen dwarf-road, her friends. This was wrong. *Move.* She sighed and leaned back. Too tired. *No!* Her eyes fluttered. *It's dangerous.* She struggled to her knees. *Get up.* The Bane's creeping presence crawled up her spine. Limbreth fumbled for her swords. Her hands didn't work. The cold. It had taken them all. *Get up.* Her body didn't respond. A gasping sob shook Limbreth.

Cold enfolded her deeper, and her heart didn't even respond to her fear with a heavy thud. "Tordug! Hastra! Gweld!" Only the wind heard her.

Hands grasped suddenly at Limbreth in the growing gloom of dusk. She fought them feebly, but they took strong hold of her and dragged her away.

CHAPTER SIX

Many Rokans ran along the walks and surrounded them. Ralda hefted his quarterstaff, but Makwi raised an arm and held him back. "Easy, giant. We may yet talk our way out of this. We can't fight hundreds out here." The giant leaned on his staff as Rokan soldiers arrived, their fur-lined cloaks flapping in the wind.

Athson leaned against the stone and held his hands away from his weapons. His head ached.

The soldiers crowded them with spear-points held ready. Makwi lifted his hands. "Easy, we're just traveling through."

An officer, by his look and adornments on his blue tunic, stepped forward. "Easy, nothing. Who are you? Spies? Where have you come from, that you travel our mountain highways?" The officer's olive-skinned face flushed dark. His accent reminded Athson of Corgren's, though slightly different in its clipped tones.

Makwi's jaw tightened under his beard as he bowed with a wince. "We are but travelers who have gotten lost coming down from the northern passes."

The officer's dark eyes flashed at Athson, and he arched an eyebrow. "What's wrong with him? You look injured, and you have no provisions." His gaze scanned their weapons.

Makwi motioned with his good arm to Athson. "He almost slipped of the edge where the path isn't repaired and hit his head. I injured my shoulder helping him."

"You complain about our care of these roads? Why do you travel with this barbarian giant? He's far from his lands."

Athson stirred. This wasn't going well. He just wanted to rest, to lie down. He opened his mouth, but Makwi spoke.

The dwarf bowed again. "The ways of the mountains are rough by nature, sir, uh, sir. We met this giant away west and have traveled with him—"

"West?" The officer strutted close. "You are not traders. You are either spies or thieves! Bind them! Take their weapons!" He stepped back, drawing his curved sword.

"But we're—" The soldiers jabbed Makwi in the belly with the blunt ends of their spears and clubbed him on the head. The dwarf sank to his knees and covered his head.

Athson pulled his sword. Soldiers milled around him and grabbed at his arms. Athson stumbled into the roadside wall and jammed his sword arm. He lost his grip on the sword. Not again! He snatched at the hilt and missed. Athson peered over the side. The sword clanked and clattered away. The soldiers wrestled him away. They assaulted him with spear-butts. He covered his head and crouched.

Ralda shoved soldiers off Athson and lifted his staff, but they stabbed at his arms. Blood flowed, and the giant gave up against the superior numbers around them.

Athson got to his knees and swayed. His ribs and back raged with pain. Rokans bound his hands behind him.

The giant grimaced as they took his staff and shoved it high between his arms at the elbows and back. Spear-points hovered at his neck. They tied ropes around his upper arms and the staff and then his hands at his waist.

The Rokans snatched Athson's other weapons and tossed them over the wall with Makwi's weapons and Ralda's belt-knife.

They bound Makwi's arm behind his back, and the dwarf grimaced and grunted at the pain from his injured shoulder. "You've no right to attack us here." The officer punched the dwarf in the face.

"You've no right in Rokan lands. These mountains are ours, and we go to the high place for our Lord Dragon."

Ralda and Makwi gaped. Athson groaned. They were prisoners and going

CHAPTER SIX

to see Magdronu? Their only hope was their friends finding them. Perhaps Eloch would lead Hastra to them. He almost laughed. His head must really be injured to start hoping in that old woman.

The officer pointed to the road leading higher. "Get them with the others and start moving."

Soldiers forced dwarves past Athson and his friends. One dwarf with a bruised face and tufts of beard missing paused where Athson had lost his sword. He gazed over the side a moment before the soldiers shoved him along beside Athson. The dwarf cast a sidelong glance at Athson and winked. He stumbled close and whispered amid a grunt. "We talk later."

Athson followed the dwarf, who had taken a recent beating.

The soldiers forced Athson and his companions to their main column, where the officer reported them to a man wearing a headdress of dark velvet and feathers, the latter tossing in the wind. His thick tunic stretched to his knees over thick breeches, and he carried a thin staff. He eyed his three new prisoners, walked up to Makwi, and gazed at his beard and hair. He slapped the dwarf. "You are a filthy stone-rat." He laughed. "No matter. We'll add them to Magdronu's tithe."

The guards forced them away at spear-point as the column wound higher into the mountains along a zigzag climb. They soon came to more prisoners trussed in various ways, but all forced to walk. Athson's eyes narrowed. They were all dwarves. They merged into the line of fellow captives, and Athson stumbled along. Now everything ached, but it felt like his head might roll off his shoulders. The wind whistled in his ears, but he had no way of pulling his hood up. At least he had his cloak. Many of the dwarves didn't, wearing only rags over wounds and dirt. Few looked well-fed. They'd been captives a while.

A dwarf stumbled near Athson. Athson cleared his throat, and the dwarf glanced at him. "Who are you? Where are they taking us?"

The dwarf lowered his head. "Name's Angkwe. You?"

"Athson, from Auguron."

Angkwe arched his brows. "Long way to come for this. They take us to the sacrifice in their high place. We're blood for Magdronu's magic."

Athson swallowed the sudden lump in his throat, but it clung there. Sacrifice? "Surely there's some chance of escape."

The dwarf cocked his head. "Most of these are too weak to do anything now." He checked that no guards lingered near them. "I have friends, but we'll see if they can muster enough strength to help. They aren't many against this company. The Rokans have hundreds here. My friends were below, where your weapons went. They signaled that they'll get more help and follow if they can. Sometimes we can rescue a few before the dragon comes."

The guards shouted for silence among their captives and flourished their weapons.

Athson nodded and lowered his head. There was nothing to do but climb the dwarven highway and wait. He stumbled more than once in the following hours. They spent the night in frigid cold and woke to a thankless dawn amid surly guards who prodded them to their feet when it was time to travel. The guards taunted them and laughed at their struggles on the climb throughout the following days. Snow clouds trailed their route, but only cold and wind assaulted them.

Sometime after noon on their sixth day, a guard tripped Athson with a laugh. Athson struggled to regain his feet after the cruel prank. He shook, seemingly from a fever. His burned hands ached, and his bound wrists chafed. It was hard to catch his breath in these heights. Athson struggled to his knees, regained his footing with effort and shot the Rokan guard a hard glare. That last blow was one more on his growing mental list of abuses. These Rokans were below trolls and Corgren, but they jostled to move up with each unwarranted use of brutality.

"Maybe you will walk faster now." The guard spat, and a sneer spread on his bearded face. He spat again. "Filthy dwarf-friend."

Athson clenched his jaw, even with the blinding pain in his head. He'd remember that face if he got a chance at escape. There were too many guards and little opportunity, so he shambled on up the narrow walk. In these heights, the dwarves had built only narrow paths since there had been little need for trade this way, it seemed. Athson blinked, trying to focus. His

CHAPTER SIX

head still hurt. The Rokans had not helped matters by cuffing him hard on the head several times when they had been captured and bound.

Ralda rumbled behind them. The warning growl was loud even in the wind.

"You be quiet." The guard braced himself with his spear before the giant. But the Rokan's words were tinged with fear of the huge man.

Ralda gave the guardsman a narrow-eyed glare. He cast a glance over the edge of trail and grinned. "Far down." He wiggled his fingers at his waist and chuckled at the Rokan's suddenly pale face. Ralda strained his muscles, and a snap sounded from his staff though the stout wood never broke. His grin broadened. "Not so hard break."

The spear wavered in the guard's trembling hands.

Ralda thrust his jaw up the trail. "You go, maybe no toss over."

The guard backed up the trail. All the guardsmen were afraid of the giant, but they had been able to subdue him with numbers. Guards were spread thin on the long trail. Ralda would overcome several easily if he wanted. Athson squinted. It'd be good to see a few Rokans go over that after their cruelties, elven sensibilities about revenge notwithstanding. Athson cleared his throat and spat over the side. A long way to fall.

Athson's newfound dwarf friend peered through the crowd. "That wasn't wise. That guard might bring others."

Ralda shook his head. "No. He bully. No say I bully him." He shrugged. "But they come, I toss them." He rumbled with laughter, and the staff creaked.

With no guard near them, Athson pressed near Angkwe. "Will someone come?"

Makwi crowded close, as did Ralda.

Angkwe pursed his lips and plodded along the incline with the merciless wind in their faces. "Hard to say. If they got back to the tower, then—"

"Tower?" Makwi stepped closer. "Nazh-akun? We were going there, meeting friends."

Angkwe bobbed his head. "It's not that far, so that could be good. They might send help because of your friends. But unless you've got lots of friends against these hundreds of Rokans, they'll have to wait and hide at that last crossing. Might be a tight time of it."

Makwi eyed Ralda. "Can you break that when the time comes?"

The giant nodded.

Makwi turned back to Angkwe. "Will there be guards?"

Angkwe spat. "Nah. They might leave some lower, but they just give us potion so's we don't holler or try to escape." He glanced at Ralda. "Don't swallow if you can help it, and you might get some of us free."

Short breath sent Athson stumbling. He veered for the rock face. Could they do it? He steadied himself and trudged on with his companions.

Makwi paused at his side, his face tense with his own pain. "You hit your head? No? Good. The mountain sickness still got you. More difficulties, but we'll manage."

The road rose, and Spark padded past Athson, tail curled up. The mountain hound threaded among the guards and dwarven captives. Where was he going? *He's looking for something.* Athson rubbed his sore head and sucked in air. Not enough. His heart thumped faster, and his stomach turned.

The path wound up the sheer ridge in the elbow of the mountain's arm. The upper bulk of the peak obscured Athson's view. They were much closer now. His legs wobbled. Limbreth. Where was she? Coming with the others and the dwarves? Was she well? Would he see her again? Thin hope without help. Ahead, the path climbed into a notch where the western sky opened. Almost there.

Majestic clouds drifted below and above them. But a storm loomed from the northwest. Not a good place for a storm. The guardsman prodded him on again, so he set out with little choice. They'd better get away before the storm, or they'd face the dragon.

Athson's vision went double. He wandered toward the edge. A nearby guard forced him back. He glanced at the olive-skinned man. Instead, he saw a troll. Athson jumped, fell over, and clenched his eyes shut with a shake of his head. Hands hauled him to his feet. He opened his eyes. A guard. *Must be a fit coming on.* He groaned and shuddered at the notion.

CHAPTER SIX

Not now. Maybe Angkwe's friends had retrieved his sword. He'd need it if they escaped.

They were soon walking up-slope on the narrow edge of a gravel ridge that approached the twin peaks of the mountain. Athson's head spun, and he gritted his teeth. *Just keep going.* Ralda would get them free. He shied from the path's edge. It was a long way down, and he wasn't steady. It would be a narrow escape if they made it. *Don't give up. Can't fight like this.*

The climb ended on a stretch of flat stone beneath the higher peak. Athson huffed for air. The guardsmen leered like trolls. *It's the Funnel.* He squeezed his eyes shut. No, worse. Different, but worse.

Even the priests' faces paled. Their leader in the dark feather headdress waved servants forward. "Quickly! Dose them. We must be away ere our master comes!"

Men and women rushed among the captives and forced liquid into their mouths. They forced their mouths shut lest the captives spit it out. They tried Ralda after making him kneel at spear-point, but he laughed at them and snapped at their hands like a dog before they got some in his mouth. They struggled with his face, and he spat much of the potion out. Good for him. But a guard approached the giant from behind and whacked Ralda twice over the head. The giant sank to his knees, gagged out the potion, and rolled onto his side with a groan.

They shifted to Athson. Not good for their escape plans if Ralda was down. Athson clenched his teeth, but they slapped him, and the ogres pounded in his head. His eyes fluttered. More snake-faced hobgoblins leered. "Leave me, troll." They poured the liquid into his mouth, and he gagged. *Bitter.* His stomach flopped in protest. In moments he felt dizzier, but the cold left his body. Athson's thoughts fragmented and came in random succession. The priests chanted while the guardsmen bound them all tightly after forcing them to the ground.

Athson swayed. Trolls sang. He collapsed on his side and stared at the leering hobgoblins. Where were the Rokans? Loose stone poked the Archer's side. It didn't matter, for some reason.

Ralda groaned and stirred, but only a little.

Athson stared into the far distant sky. "The Funnel's so high." No, he wasn't there right now. The other captives groaned occasionally as the sun set and the wind howled. The priests and the guardsmen were gone. They were not going to kill him, then. They left them for dead. Ralda, he was going to do something. Athson rolled over. The giant lay still. That was bad, for some reason.

Lightning flashed. Athson shut his eyes and screamed at the nearness. Wind rushed about the natural table of stone and yanked at his sandy hair and worn clothing. Why did he scream like that? Lightning. The notion of alarm faded in his awareness.

Thunder pounded around him and rolled about in echoes. Athson stirred in his drugged stupor. He opened his eyes. Ralda lay nearby, and beyond the giant sprawled the shapes of dwarves as gloom gathered beneath the storm. *Move.* His muscles never responded to the distant command from his mind.

Thunder boomed again. Another peal answered like massive wings flapping. Athson rolled his head with a groan. A massive black shape settled onto the peak. Yellow eyes glared unblinkingly at them.

~ ~ ~ ~ ~ ~ ~

Limbreth groaned into half-wakefulness. Warm liquid spilled on her lips. She gagged and coughed. Pain shot through her limbs as her body shivered from deep in her core.

"Easy there, gell. Can't warm you too fast. Swallow what you can."

She cracked her eyelids and squinted in the light. After a moment, her eyes adjusted. It wasn't so bright after all. Her eyes blinked and watered. She swallowed a sip of the offered draught as her arms and legs flopped.

A dwarf stooped over her. Rough hands lifted her head gently to the cup again. "Lucky we found you in time."

"Wh-where a-are w-we?" She shivered so hard she barely got the words out, and her voice croaked. If only she could stop trembling. "O-o-others?" Her teeth clattered as she got the last word out.

"We saw the signals and rushed to beat the Rokans to you. We weren't sure about your message, since they aren't the signals we use." His forked beard wagged as he spoke.

Limbreth squinted. His beard was squared, and by the open-hand trinket tied in it, he'd had training as a healer, low fighting commander though he might be. "Y-you l-lead a c-company?"

The dwarf's bushy eyebrows shot up, and he cocked his head. "You know of our ways?"

She managed to pull her braid around with her trinkets of shield and fist gripping bones. She switched to the dwarven tongue. "Greetings, squad leader."

He gasped, and his eyes widened. "How? Who?" He touched her trinkets with his fingertips and then kissed them. "We didn't see these in our hurry. Forgive me, ax-maid." He passed a hand over his eyes and whispered, "Death-grip?"

Limbreth flourished her left arm, but it flopped, and the dwarf eased her down and patted her.

"Who's he, then?" He gave her more to drink.

"T-t-tordug. Ch-Ch-Chokkra."

"He's Tordug? I didn't know he was still alive." His face dropped with a frown under his beard.

Limbreth nodded. Her teeth stopped chattering, and her quivering subsided some. Her eyes rolled. They were inside a shelter. Others spoke in hushed tones, and more snored. "Withling Hastra?"

His mouth opened, and his jaw worked for a few moments. "What are you all doing in the mountains with winter coming hard?"

She shook her head. "Long story."

He pulled a blanket over her. "There, that can go on now." He turned away and spoke dwarvish, but Limbreth didn't follow all of his words. There was something about visitors, Tordug, an ax-maid, death-grip, and Withling. Excited conversation followed, and Limbreth got the gist that not everyone was entirely pleased about something.

"What's wrong?" Limbreth pulled a frown at the dwarf and touched his arm to gain his attention.

He spoke in common tongue, patted her hands, and kissed them. "Nothing, ax-maid. Greetings to you, ax-maid. May your death-grip never falter. This dwarf is Fafwe, whom Elokwe has sent to serve you. We were just deciding what we should do with such auspicious guests as you. We are poor dwarves. Nothing to worry yourself about, in your condition." He waved to the other dwarves in the stone hovel. "Come, greet the ax-maid!"

The dwarves gathered and bent over Limbreth. They each knelt and kissed her hands with murmured greetings almost reverent in tone. Some frowned and others beamed their joy. The stream of names they gave washed over her as her awareness drifted into sleep. Her thoughts faded into oblivion. At least they were safe for the moment.

Limbreth woke much later to more excited conversation in dwarvish. Tordug sat with the squad leader and the rest of the dwarves. The old dwarf's faced glowed red, betraying frustration. Two dwarves rose and left the cramped way-station. *By the light, it's dark, but how late or early?* She noted Gweld standing close to the door in the shadows and motioned him closer as she sat up. She winced at the pain in her limbs, fingers, and toes as the elf approached. She grimaced when she looked at her hands. How swollen and dark!

"Limbreth, you should take care still. You were frostbitten, and Hastra's fallen asleep again. She offered healing prayers for Tordug, but weakness sent her back to her blankets." The elf helped her adjust.

"Thanks." She cocked her head and pointed to his hands. "Did she heal you too? Your hands are well."

He flashed a smile. "We elves are susceptible to cold but not so easily injured by it."

She nodded. "Well, at least one of us is useful at the moment." Voices rose again. "What's going on?"

Gweld looked to Tordug. "It appears we are not so welcome by everyone, though I'm not entirely sure why. It has something to do with Chokkra. Dwarves have strange customs, and they appear to be working out what their obligations to us are. I think they are bothered by Tordug for some reason, but you and Hastra appear to be big enough news to get us more help."

"As Tordug told us. Good thing he's been teaching me when he can."

Gweld shrugged. "Mystery to me, though."

Limbreth listened in on the conversation. There was something about Tordug. They were supposed to welcome a dwarf of such high station without question, from what she remembered. These dwarves held their shoulders so stiffly. *They've yanked their beards so much they should all be beardless by now.*

Finally, they noticed her, and their heads lowered in deference. She relaxed the tense frown on her face. She hadn't meant to show them anger. She chewed at the inside of her cheek and fingered the dwarven rank-badges in her hair.

Fafwe rose and bowed. "Forgive us, honored ax-maid. We did not mean to wake you." He cast a glance at Hastra, who lay sleeping and undisturbed.

She answered with a curt nod but said nothing for a moment. She stroked her jaw. Perhaps it was time to use what Tordug and Makwi had taught her. They honored her so much that maybe…

Limbreth turned to Gweld. "Help me up."

"But your feet—can you stand?" Gweld took her arm with a hesitant touch.

"Just do it." She ground her teeth against the pain as she rose. No more whimpering about sore feet. A dwarf stood if possible to ask aid. "This ax-maid is honored by Fafwe's care. You have found us in our need and we—I ask for more of your assistance. I'm sorry I don't know all the words yet in your tongue." Her bow was a bit wobbly, but it got their attention.

Fafwe bowed again and started toward her. "You are most kind to notice this humble dwarf, ax-maid. There's no need to trouble yourself."

Limbreth held up her swollen hand as Gweld steadied her. "Tordug is my honored companion and teacher." The dwarves murmured, and Fafwe's eyes widened as he restrained a gasp. "He knows best how to tell you our needs as we labor against enemies most dark on our desperate quest. I know your resources may be meager, but I ask for your continued forbearance in aid."

Tordug grinned at her, tension easing from his face. The other dwarves muttered and nodded in obvious approval. Fafwe bowed again. "It shall be so, honored ax-maid." He ended with a flourish of salute.

Limbreth returned the salute, and the dwarves nodded again. She sat with Gweld's help and a thinly restrained wince.

Gweld pulled a blanket over her and held a cup of hot drink to her lips. "That got their attention. Well done."

She took a sip and dabbed her lips as the warmth spread in her chest. She flicked her eyes at the elf and back to Tordug, then grinned. She leaned close to Gweld. "It was simple. They were so caught in the past with Tordug, they forgot they hosted a Withling and an ax-maid. I just needed to ask for help and mention Tordug's honor as a companion to end whatever they were debating with him."

The elf held the cup to her lips again. "Well, whatever you just did, you got us what we need for as long as we need it. Now, if you could end that storm… I've scouted several times while you three were out, and I don't know when it will end."

She sniffed. If only she could chase the Bane away so easily. But this effort was the least she could do for Tordug after all his mentoring. It was a start. Her father would be proud. She was certain of that. Limbreth stroked her braid and fingered the trinkets there. She'd won a measure of renown, and she intended to use it well—for her, Athson, and her other companions.

Before they set out for the Tower of Nazh-akun, Hastra blessed Limbreth and healed her injured extremities. With first-light still an hour away, they trudged into the snow, a few dwarves assisting Hastra, who still bore the effects of collapsing in the snowstorm. Drifts of snow lay thick upon the road, but the party of dwarves cleared much of it in their passing, and by midday the snow dwindled away.

Tordug tugged his beard. "It seems we weren't far from making it out of the storm."

Fafwe spat. "Storm went east rather than south. Road's better ahead. We'll make the tower tomorrow."

True to Fafwe's prediction, they arrived at Nazh-akun the following day before the sun crested overhead. The square tower rose high by

CHAPTER SIX

a broad hollow of the mountain where roads connected from several directions—higher, lower, and on the same level Limbreth and the others had traveled. They passed guards at a low wall around the tower and walked into a narrow courtyard. Several thick, wooden doors allowed access inside, and upon entering, Limbreth and her companions found the interior lit with lamps and a fire on a wide hearth. The broad tower of square construction housed rows of bunks and sacks of supplies while stairs climbed into thick rafters, presumably toward a door to the top. Limbreth walked near the hearth, curious to see that it vented smoke to the rear down a narrow hole. Other dwarves spoke quietly to the side at a table, their faces drawn with some earnest consideration. Some of their rescuers greeted the other dwarves.

Limbreth switched to dwarvish as Fafwe warmed himself at the hearth. "How does this hearth vent?"

Fafwe pointed to holes in the front. "There are vents constructed to catch a draft from outside the tower at various points. It creates a draw that flows under the fire grate and keeps the current of air flowing back." He pointed up. "Keeps the view up top clear."

The conversation from the table drew Limbreth's attention. A frowning dwarf spoke. "They got Angkwe first. We're too few to challenge such a large party of Rokans. Suppose we could go rescue them. Got just enough time, now you've returned with more, Chertug." He nodded to Fafwe's group. "And that these others have come helps too."

An elder dwarf hooked his thumbs in his belt. His gray-and-brown beard was tied in several different knots for leader, trader, and warrior. "How many dwarves are there, Hirstwe? They going to the dragon's sacrifice."

Hirstwe wiggled his fingers as though he was counting fast. "Got to be several hundred Rokans. They had their priests, and they're on the road up to that summit." He spat and wiped his bearded mouth. "They caught some others just after Angkwe. Big man, even from where we saw him, another dwarf who had an injured arm, and a smaller man than the first with a bandage on his head. The Rokans threw their weapons over the wall, and we collected them afterward." He motioned toward the wall by another door.

Limbreth's gaze followed the motion. Her eyes flared wide. "That's Athson's sword!" She pushed into the middle of the conversation beside Tordug. "Those were our friends. We've got to go after them!"

~ ~ ~ ~ ~ ~ ~

Magdronu-as-Gweld watched and listened to the pointless drama before him. The stories from the various groups got sorted. He turned and examined Athson's sword as he listened to the dwarves grumble about Tordug's presence, then find their respect for Limbreth and Hastra. Then they realized it was Makwi who was in trouble, and that got them motivated. Weak Tordug. He should have commanded a rescue effort. Gweld smirked at the sword. Like it would help anyone but Athson now. He'd see to that—somehow. Magdronu-as-Gweld stood and wheeled back to the crowd.

"But one of us needs to go." Limbreth pleaded that she go even if they didn't trust Tordug for the mission.

Chertug raised his hands toward Limbreth. "Ax-maid you may be, but Duliwe will have my head if I don't present you to him."

Tordug tugged his beard and stepped close to Limbreth. "There's a time to win honor and a time to bow to protocol."

Limbreth rounded on Tordug. "If we don't save Athson, there's little use in the protocols or our mission."

Tordug opened his mouth.

Just the chance he needed. Magdronu-as-Gweld stepped among the three of them. "Limbreth, I'll go with them. I'm sure these dwarves know their business in the mountains, and I can easily keep up with them."

"And you are?" Chertug eyed Magdronu-as-Gweld with a pinched brow.

Tordug interjected before Magdronu-as-Gweld could answer. "This is our companion. The worthy ranger of Auguron, Gweld. He's an archer and scout of great renown."

"Arrows aren't much use in this wind."

Magdronu-as-Gweld patted his elven long-knife. "I'm adept with a blade as well, if it comes to it."

CHAPTER SIX

Chertug paused and glanced among them. "Good enough, if that satisfies you, ax-maid." He motioned Magdronu-as-Gweld to follow him. "Stay close and follow orders. You don't know our ways, but I suppose a ranger can hold his own among warriors and scouts, eh?"

Magdronu-as-Gweld followed the dwarves to the tower door. A rumble grew in his chest. He'd devour these companions in a matter of hours. *Easy now. Don't show your hand to the others yet.* He subdued the rising fire within him. *Not so eager, a little patience.* He pretended to check his bow and gear as he went. He'd bring back just Athson for Limbreth to dote over. Then for his other plans for them all.

"Gweld." Limbreth approached. Weary circles from their frozen ordeal still painted her eyelids.

Magdronu-as-Gweld turned to Limbreth. Her anxiety delighted him. He leaned on his bow and played his part as Gweld. "Yes?" He glanced from her to Tordug and Hastra where they sat. Anxiety adorned their features and radiated from them. If only he could stay and taste their fear more. He gloried in their darkest emotions most. But his dutiful part, and sacrifices, called to him.

"Bring him back."

"You know we will. We have surprise on our side. And Eloch." He smiled more at his false use of his enemy's name than in reassurance.

"Limbreth, don't hold them up." Hastra stirred on her pallet.

The Grendonese woman grimaced at the old Withling. "I won't."

The old woman's weakness grew with the passing of each day. How long would Eloch keep her on this impossible task? And the tension between Hastra and Limbreth? So unexpected and delectable to his senses. Though not as deep as Athson's cursed emotions. He waved to Hastra. "We've plenty of time, Withling."

"Best not linger." Hastra offered her farewell without hesitation.

Magdronu-as-Gweld restrained a smirk. He played the part too well. Not even she guessed. And wouldn't until it was too late. With an elven salute, he turned away and slipped out the door before he laughed at the notion. The dwarves offered stout gestures of their warrior welcome. They'd be his scorched sacrifice in mere hours. Magdronu-as-Gweld followed them into the mountain-scouring winds but longed to glide on the air instead of crawling behind these doomed dwarves.

The hours of walking passed without pause by the dwarves. Gweld feigned slight weariness for their benefit. But they covered the distance to their destination with ever-increasing stealth as they drew closer. They approached each intersection with growing care.

Gweld smirked when they weren't looking. Death stalked their heels. They didn't even suspect it. They soon halted at an intersection. "Chertug, how far to the final climb? Can we beat the night?"

The dwarf, his beard knotted several different ways with several trinkets that glittered in the sinking sunlight over the mountaintops, hushed Gweld as they sent scouts along a rising stair to a soaring climb higher up the mountainside. He waved Gweld to him. "We're here, but the climb to the top will take a while. We need to take care lest we are caught by lingering Rokans."

"Why is that?" Gweld knew all the answers, yet he played his part.

"Rokans sometimes leave a guard, lest the sacrifice be disturbed. They hallowed those heights to their false god years ago. We used it for our meetings of import and our important festivals. It's not sacred, but it was important. We should make a fast climb."

"What about a guard here, since you're concerned?"

"Not a bad idea."

"Why not me? I'm only just recovered. I get around the heights well, but not like you dwarves."

"Even better, but we'll leave you a few others to help."

"Not necessary. You'll need every man you have to get people down. If there's trouble, I'll use arrows and retreat up so that you'll be warned coming down."

Chertug stroked his beard. "You're right." His scouts returned and reported in dwarvish. The officer turned back to Gweld. "Looks like we're clear, so we'll spare you as rear-guard. Don't stand and fight more than a few. Just warn us of any trouble."

CHAPTER SIX

Magdronu-as-Gweld smiled and saluted them as an elven ranger. "Good luck. You have no worry with me at watch." Heat swelled within him. A perfect disguise to surprise these extra sacrifices. Should any escape, he'd maintain his disguise. He saluted them as both a ranger and a dwarf, the latter learned from observation.

Chertug grinned and waved to his squad. "Move out, or we'll be too late." He glanced at the ragged mountaintops with a rueful shake of his head. He saluted back dwarf-style. "We've not a moment to spare."

Magdronu-as-Gweld watched them until they passed around a shoulder. "The timing will be perfect." Now to wait. As Gweld, he watched for anyone that turned back. Darkness stretched over the eastern side of the Drelkhaz Mountains and deepened into a starlit sky further east. From the north, a storm rumbled over the heights. Time to move. He could wait no longer. *Must change.* He staggered toward the retaining wall and climbed atop it.

The wind rushed into Magdronu-as-Gweld's face. He leaned and leapt into the abyss of night. With his innate magic, the elven disguise twisted away, and Magdronu's true form whirled into the air. His wings snapped and, as a dragon, he rose on the faltering thermal winds. Back to his nature. His accursed nature. Even this would be thrown off soon enough.

As Magdronu, he glided below southward peaks until well out of sight. Leagues rushed past within minutes. He rose on currents over the jagged peaks covered in snow and gained the western side of the mountains. The sun sank red in the west. He roared flame and swept north toward his hallowed grounds for his sacrifices.

At the approach, Magdronu slowed, wings flapping toward a triumphant landing at a peak overlooking his trussed and drugged victims. He landed upon one of the twin peaks overlooking the sacrificial ground. Lightning snapped around the mountain, but Magdronu crouched, heedless of the storm assaulting the heights, and cast a hungry gaze over the mass of his offering. His eyes narrowed at an incongruity among the forms. Athson! There he lay! Leave him to escape. He'd bend his knee after this frenzy.

Magdronu shifted shape. Magdronu-as-Gweld observed Athson's condition, but Athson saw his elven form. He shifted back to Magdronu. Let him think that through in his addled state.

Now for these others and those coming for the rescue. Rocks rolled underfoot as he approached, and the storm raged lightning and thunder around him. How appropriate! Magdronu prowled closer to his victims.

~ ~ ~ ~ ~ ~ ~

Athson stared, entranced by the eyes on the peak above the him and the others.

Spark surged into view. The mountain hound barked and growled but didn't charge.

"Hey, Spark!" Athson smiled. "Where you been?" His dulled mind clanged a distant bell of danger. What? Oh yes, the dragon.

Lightning flashed, and he saw the great, scaly hulk crouched upon the peak. Claws the length of a man grasped securely at the stone summit. The barbed tail lashed in flashes of lightning.

Athson's eyes welled with tears. He'd never find his father. Never see Gweld or Limbreth again. Lightning flared. Gweld sat on the mountainside, solemn, watching like a bird of prey. He licked his lips.

"Gweld! They made it!" Athson called to the others and flopped his eyes back to the mountain peak. The dragon crouched there. He groaned. What was he thinking? It must be whatever they'd given him! Or a fit...

Stone crumbled under the dragon's feet when it moved down the slope with its bat-like wings splayed for balance and its tail flicked side to side. The monster stalked toward Athson and his companions. Bound and drugged. Helpless! A shout boiled from Athson's chest.

The wind died. The Lightning gouged the mountain. The creature's great maw yawned open and displayed fangs as long as Athson. It stepped onto the table of stone. Athson's drugged vision fixed on Magdronu. Spark advanced on the dragon.

Lightning seared the mountaintop again. A figure stood beside Spark, between Athson and the dragon.

Crack.

It was a man, but not too tall. He stood with his feet apart and ready, a staff in his hand. The wide brim of his hat flopped in the wind. The trader?

CHAPTER SIX

How was he here? Athson squeezed his eyes shut. This must be a fit. He opened his eyes to the same sight.

The monster roared. Fire bloomed and spread toward the unflinching figure. Blazes lit what fuel lay around to burn. Athson glimpsed remains lying about— charred and broken bones of past victims.

Flash.

The great maw snapped at the man. He stood firm and swung his staff. The wooden stick, no more than a twig to the dragon, struck its nose. It flinched away and roared in pain.

In the firelight, the trader stamped his foot at the dragon like it was a vicious dog. The dragon slunk away.

"Go!" The single word reverberated like thunder and shook the mountaintop.

The dragon roared defiantly and wagged its head. Fire spewed again, and lightning pounded at the trader's feet. He didn't move.

This time the man clapped his hands. Athson cried out at the thunderous boom, but his cry was lost in the noise of the dragon's snarls of rage.

The dragon burst into the air. It winged into the dark morass of the sky. Lightning silhouetted Magdronu in several punctuated flickers.

Athson stared, his jaw slack. His gaze drifted back to the figure now silhouetted by Magdronu's residual flames. The trader turned to face him. Who was he? Athson squinted. The wide-brimmed hat on his head folded in the wind gusts.

Athson blinked.

Dark figures carrying torches charged out of the night into the firelight. His heart sank at the sight and he groaned hoarsely. His eyes fluttered. "Trolls!" He rolled onto his back and awaited a fatal blow.

CHAPTER SEVEN

Athson floated in darkness. Hands grabbed him and carried him away. Hushed voices mingled with whistling surrounded him. Then darkness shrouded him, and he lost awareness of his surroundings.

Gruff voices dragged Athson from his stupor much later. Spark lounged nearby and panted. He must be safe if the mountain hound was relaxed, unaffected by anything.

Makwi's voice drew Athson's attention. "Well met, Chertug. How came you to find us?"

Athson lay on his back as an older dwarf wrapped his head in a bandage. Ralda squatted nearby, watching, his head also bandaged. "Where are we?" Athson started to his feet, but the dwarf gently forestalled him. His head spun just from that movement. His eyelids drooped. *Need sleep anyway.*

The dwarf over him continued binding his head. "We're off the mountain and stopped on our way to the Tower of Nazh-akun. Just rest. You shouldn't have been on your feet with this lump on your head."

Athson peered around him. It looked like the end of a crevice. Here the wind barely rustled, but the cold remained like a blanket. Patches of white rolled beneath blue sky overhead. Good. At least there was no snow.

Chertug stroked his tan and white beard, then bowed. "Honored one, we are pleased to have found you. Some of my squad witnessed your capture and recovered your weapons. They returned to the tower and reported. We were unsure of attempting a rescue with small numbers and had to wait a

CHAPTER SEVEN

day or so to set out regardless. But others arrived who knew you and your friends. Withling Hastra directed us to attempt the rescue, as all but the elf were not ready to travel after nearly freezing on the road." The dwarf spat to the side and wiped his mouth.

Athson sat up and fell back with a groan. "Hastra? Were there others? Where's Gweld? What of Limbreth?"

The dwarf tending Athson frowned. "Easy there, young one. Let me bind your wounds, or the Withling will never let me hear the end of it."

Chertug bowed to Athson. "Yes, Hastra. The others I know little of now, but Limbreth is well enough. They needed rest, but Gweld came with us and guarded our retreat lest Rokans sneak back to check for any escapees. He's down by the road on guard now." He motioned along the shadow of the cleft.

"Good." Athson let the dwarf tend his head. He could sleep now if they'd all be quiet.

"I'm sure enough they are well, ranger." Makwi turned back to Chertug. "You arrived just in time?"

Athson stirred, and the dwarf with the bandages steadied him again. "I saw the dragon. Someone fought with the dragon, and then trolls came. Who defeated the dragon? You fought off the trolls?"

Chertug wagged his head. "Nay, we saw the dragon and thought we had come too late. But something chased him away, so we rushed in to look for survivors." He scratched his bearded cheek and cut his eyes to Makwi. "There were naught of trolls, just us. We saw no one fight the dragon. We don't know why the dragon left, though."

Makwi tugged his beard. "We don't know either. They drugged us before leaving us to be cooked." He waved his hand toward Athson. "This one needs medicine or his Eloch-blessed sword, or he sees things. But we were all drugged and Ralda was stunned by the Rokans. Otherwise..." Makwi shrugged, grimaced, and rubbed his injured shoulder.

"Elokwe knows, then." Chertug lowered is head a moment in reverent silence, as did the others around them. "But Champion Makwi, are you well enough to travel? We must hurry or risk being found by more Rokans, and we are few."

Makwi stretched his injured shoulder and grunted. "I'm well enough to travel and some help in a fight."

"Good, then we're heading for the tower as soon as we can."

Athson sighed and lay still after the conversation ended. Good news but he saw what he saw. His brow furrowed. But no trolls? Must've been his head and that potion. He stuck out his tongue at the memory of the bitter taste. He shifted his gaze to the other dwarf over him. "Have any water? That potion left a foul taste." The dwarf sat him up and gave him several sips. Athson laid on his back. His head spun even with his eyes closed. Sleep, he wanted that now. "Thanks, must sleep."

"That's better, I still need to wash your burns." The dwarf finished wrapping Athson's head and pulled out more water. "This is from snow-melt and good for these things. I have some salve for the pain."

Chertug turned to the others and began asking after those who were brought from labor camps. He spoke dwarvish, so Athson followed little and turned his attention to the dwarf tending him. Ralda sat slouched forward, his head in his hands.

Athson almost drifted away into sleep as the dwarf worked on his burned hands. "Your beard—you have a healer's knot."

The dwarf glanced at Makwi. "Is this one a dwarf-friend, to know these things?"

Makwi shrugged. "He's traveled with me for weeks, so something useful has worn off on him."

The white-bearded dwarf turned back to Athson and chuckled as he continued his work. "I'm Leifwe and a healer."

"I'm sorry, I'm Athson of Auguron. What happened to those trolls?" Too tired, he slurred like he was drunk.

Makwi worked his shoulder. "He's an elf who's not an elf. If you could spare some time from his elf-prattling, could you look at this shoulder?"

Leifwe shook his head. "There's too many to look after with this un-elf, dwarf-friend, and this champion's blathering. Chertug, see that those others are fed and tell me of any serious needs." He motioned to his bag.

CHAPTER SEVEN

"Otherwise, give them a salve for what ails them."

Makwi grunted at the healer.

Chertug nodded. "Yes, we do need to move quickly from this shelter soon." The dwarven leader motioned to his men to start tending the others who bore scrapes, wore little for the cold, and looked little fed. "Bring some of the firewood they can use it as cudgels in a pinch, since we don't have enough weapons."

Makwi stirred. "I'll take a piece until I get my weapons back. You have them at the tower?"

Chertug nodded. "Aye, honored champion. We left all that was collected from a lower road. We traveled quickly and light, so we didn't bring them. His sword too."

Chertug soon completed organizing his company and, after reports from scouts watching routes, they set out. They gave Athson a draught for his pain, and he faded toward sleep in earnest as the dwarves readied for their departure. They lifted Athson on a stretcher. His awareness faded as the dwarves jostled him at a jog. He stirred once as his bearers spoke.

"This ranger's heavier than he looks." The lead dwarf grunted after his words.

"No time to turn weakling, Orstug," The dwarf at Athson's feet huffed in effort for a few moments as his braided and knotted beard wagged with his gait. "We'll all get cooked on the mountaintop if we don't get clear of the Rokans."

"Doubt this is all worth it."

"Oh, it will be. We'll gain more fighters if we win free."

Athson lost track of the conversation, his last sight being the afternoon sky as his eyes closed.

~ ~ ~ ~ ~ ~ ~

Hastra stirred from sleep, and her residual snore dwindled into wakefulness as hands shook her awake. She wet her dry lips with her tongue. "What is it?" She brushed her hair from her face as she blinked at the low light and pulled her blouse closed over her old wound. *So soon?* She'd only slept moments. Hastra rubbed her eyes.

Limbreth tugged at Hastra's hands. "They've come! Athson, he's unconscious! And Makwi's hurt too. So's Ralda. Hurry, Withling Hastra."

The Grendonese woman pulled Hastra to a sitting position. The noise of people entering the tower brought her to awareness. Hastra scanned the knot of dwarves who assisted injured dwarves into the tower. There were so many. Time to work.

"Athson, where is he?" Hastra swung her legs to the stone floor and avoided bumping her head on the upper bunk. Best not injure herself in haste. Her strength slipped almost daily as it was. No telling how long she had left for Eloch's call. She swallowed. She'd died before, at Withling's Watch, but she didn't relish it at the end of her long mission with the bow prophecy. But there was every hope beyond that eventuality.

Limbreth took Hastra's hand and pulled her along. "This way, on the other side." Limbreth wiped her eyes and sniffed.

The last bit of sleep relaxed its grip on Hastra as she shuffled among groaning dwarves.

"See, there she is, I told you we were blessed with a Withling."

The shaking hand of a dwarf extended from a bed. "Bless me, Withling. I can't believe it's a real, live Withling."

Hastra took the extended hand. "Bless you. I must go attend others, but I'll return to you." She released the weak grasp as Limbreth pulled her away. If this kept up, she'd waste precious time getting to Athson.

"Yes, Withling, I'll wait." The battered dwarf lay back. "Just to see her is enough."

"Come quickly!" Limbreth pulled harder.

Hastra pulled away from her, her annoyance with the younger woman almost slipping from her lips. "I'm coming, dear, but I don't want to trip over anyone." How many had returned with the rescue party? Fifteen? Twenty? She'd be weary all over again once she finished with this many. "What's the time?" This tower let precious little light in, even during the day, so lanterns and torches blazed at all hours.

"It's late." Limbreth sighed and straightened her braid. "Or early. I don't know. I've been watching for them for hours."

CHAPTER SEVEN

"You should have slept, my dear."

"I couldn't, so I waited with the watchmen. Please hurry, he's so pale!"

Pale? No wonder unction to look after Athson was so strong among all these wounded men. "Patience." Hastra cleared her throat at the sound of irritation in her tone. "Let an old woman step through this crowd without tripping."

Limbreth waved her arms. "Make way for Withling Hastra."

Hastra sighed as voices moaned for her. She passed men who bore singes, scrapes, cuts and bruises. They needed more than her. "I can't attend all these men at once. Feed those who can eat and make the others comfortable enough to sleep while they wait."

As Hastra passed the dwarven healer, he stood and bobbed his head. "I'll organize the help and see to their feeding."

Hastra opened her mouth and paused. She almost, almost let loose a harsh response that Athson was the priority, but she caught her words. "Very well." What she didn't say was more important than what she said. She quickened her pace. Now for the ranger. Her—Athson's, she corrected herself—errand and health were most important.

Dwarves laid Athson upon a bunk and parted at Hastra's approach with Limbreth. Hastra withheld her gasp. Pale understated the ranger's condition. As she muttered her Withling's prayer for guidance, Hastra touched Athson's face, arms, and legs. Clammy skin was bad, as was his head. She nodded to herself as guidance from Eloch distilled in her thoughts amid her prayer tongue. The head first, definitely.

Limbreth stirred and grabbed Hastra's arm. "Please hurry."

Hastra paused and found tears in the young woman's eyes. Funny how her attitude changed with need. Hastra almost mentioned Limbreth's distance since Chokkra but bit her tongue. Eloch didn't want it said. She'd asked Limbreth to guard Athson with her life, but she'd not anticipated the young woman would grow such deep feelings for him.

Hastra patted Limbreth's hand and moved it away. "My dear, don't interrupt." She returned to her prayers and examination. Burned hands—there was a tale behind that, and—

Limbreth rose to watch, then moved and stood close behind Hastra.

Hastra turned her head and found Limbreth stooped over, her face close to Hastra's shoulder. "Limbreth, if you can't contain yourself and stop interrupting me, I'll have you removed—ax-maid or not."

The dwarves nearby muttered, and a few who hadn't noticed the trinkets in Limbreth's hair rumbled remarks with wide eyes. Limbreth stepped back with a glare as she bit her lower lip and a tear glistened on one cheek.

Hastra rubbed her old scar where nothing beat in her chest. If only Limbreth knew what Eloch could do—indefinitely. She resumed her prayer and touched Athson's head.

He writhed under her hands and spoke too low for Hastra to hear. She leaned close, continuing her prayer, and heard his croaking whisper.

"Father, why'd you go hunting? Why did you leave us?" Athson grimaced and twisted his head. "Mother, why did he go hunting so far, to Howart's Cave?"

Hastra drew back with a gasp.

Limbreth stepped close and pushed at her shoulder. "Withling, why the delay?"

Hastra shrugged Limbreth's hand away. *Darkness of night dimmed the room around her. She walked a wood beneath the winking stars, stalking as if after prey, with a bow in hand. Hastra touched her face and felt a beard.*

Eloch revealed a vision.

The stench of fetid water rose from down-slope as a massive shadow reared overhead. Hastra strode around the natural edifice, touching the stone with her hand, walking slightly sideways so as to keep balance on the loose dirt and rocks underfoot. Working her way to the lower side of the rock formation, she found a narrow cave. It yawned wider and sucked her into its darkened depths.

Light grew stronger as she flew toward it. The back of a gray-haired man hove into view as she stepped out of the pulling motion of the vision. He turned with a gentle smile, no surprise displayed in his gaunt face. She handed him the bow...

Hastra gasped as the room reformed in her vision with its flickering lights and groaning of wounded and suffering.

"Withling Hastra, are you ill?" Limbreth knelt close, gazing at Hastra, her

CHAPTER SEVEN

brow pinched with concern.

Hastra closed her gaping mouth and nodded. If her heart still beat in her chest, it would be flopping and up in her throat. "It was a vision. I've seen where it is."

Limbreth covered her mouth with a hand and spoke through her fingers, "You mean the Bow of Hart."

"Shush, don't mention it here." But Hastra nodded.

Limbreth's eyes flicked wide, and her jaw dropped. "Where?" Her question was barely audible.

"Not now. Let me finish with Athson before his injuries finish him." Hastra turned back to Athson and continued her prayer. The boy knew and didn't know all along.

Athson's eyelids fluttered open as Hastra shifted her hands from his head to his hands. Limbreth kneeled beside him and wiped her eyes.

Hastra held Athson's hands when he tried to touch his brow, and his face displayed a mild wince. "Be still, and the pain will pass." She bowed her head and muttered until the singes faded, then she stood.

No rest for her yet. She scanned the bunks and found Makwi sitting on one further down the row, his face drawn with pain. She patted a strand of hair into place and moved to the next bunk. Best take them one at a time and talk to Makwi when she got to him.

As Hastra moved to the next bunk, Limbreth grasped her hand. She turned to the Grendonese woman.

"Thank you, Withling." Limbreth's face spread into a smile. She released Hastra and laid her head on Athson's chest, and he stroked her face.

Hastra shrugged and sat beside a bruised dwarf on the next bed. Those two were almost maddening. Limbreth's face beamed—actually beamed for the first time in days, if not weeks. A smile spread on Hastra's face. Limbreth's smile meant much when it came to working with Athson, almost as much as knowing the whereabouts of the Bow of Hart. Hastra touched the dwarf on the bed and began her prayers.

By the time she got to Makwi, his head was nodding into sleep. At her touch, he stirred. "Would you rather sleep or do this now?" she asked.

Makwi ground his teeth as she moved his arm. "Now's best. It's frozen in pain."

Hastra began her prayer, touching his shoulder in several ways. The familiar surge of warmth spread along her arm as healing power went into the dwarf. His tensed posture and expression relaxed over the moments until it was done, and Hastra paused. "How did this happen?" She tilted her head in Athson's direction as she assisted the weary dwarf onto the bunk. "And his head?"

"Corgren trapped us at the gate. He knew we were in Chokkra all along. He had Ath and wanted to trade for the bow." Makwi's eyes fluttered toward sleep.

Hastra's eyebrows climbed at this news. "You found Ath? Where is he?"

Makwi shook his head on the pillow. "Couldn't save him. Busted my shoulder trying to force the chains at the gate. Corgren had them cursed. Athson wouldn't have none of Corgren. I have to hand it to Athson, he saved me and Ralda. The wizard threw fire at the two of us, and Athson leaped in front of us with that blessed sword of his. Knocked everyone off their feet, and the entry started collapsing." Makwi waved his hand toward Ralda, who lay asleep by the fire with his head and arms bandaged. "The giant saved us then. He used the sword to break the chains and carried us away as the mountain caved in. Your words proved true. Just us and no more had time to get out—and just the right bunch to do the work."

Hastra rubbed her cheek. News indeed! "What of Corgren? What of Ath?"

The dwarf shook his head again. "Don't know if they made it. But keep an eye on Athson."

"Why?"

"He's already tried to go find his father when his head was injured. I imagine he'll be out the door soon enough."

"Limbreth will keep him close. Besides, there's no way to know if Ath's alive or even if we need to worry about Corgren anymore." She stood to go.

"I don't think she'll keep him, and she might just go with him. My thanks, Withling, for the shoulder and all."

CHAPTER SEVEN

Hastra inclined her head dwarf-style to honor him. "An honor to serve Eloch and you, champion. However, I know where the bow is, and Ath is likely buried. I think Athson can be persuaded to go for the bow."

Makwi's eyes closed in his weariness. "Maybe, but I think not. He's keen to find his father, as would I be in his place." The dwarf settled into the rhythmic breathing of sleep.

Hastra wobbled to the next bed, weary herself. She paused and watched Limbreth and Athson. There must be a way to ensure the ranger went after the bow. Surely, he'd see the sense of it, maybe do it for his father's memory now that he knew his fate for sure? Well, almost. She sat on the edge of the bed by the next dwarf and took a breath. *What is needed is given.* She laid her hand on the dwarf, and he stirred from sleep.

"Withling."

"How can I help you, um…" She gazed at the dwarf's beard and its squared knots like a wall. "Master stonecutter?"

He grinned at her knowledge of dwarves. "Well, there's my elbow been aching this last year, and it got worse when those dirty Rokans…" Hastra healed the elderly dwarf and soon arrived at Ralda's side and knelt to bless and heal him. He woke during the prayer and she kissed the weary giant on the head.

Hastra glanced over her shoulder at Athson again as the dwarf continued. There must be a way to keep him on the path for the bow.

~ ~ ~ ~ ~ ~ ~

Athson stirred from his dreams of fire and pain and stared at the darkened rafters above. Soft groans, snoring, and whispers touched his ears amid the dim light of a few torches. He frowned and squinted.

Corgren had wanted the Bow of Hart and threw fire at Makwi and Ralda. Athson had leapt between the spell and his friends with his sword. His sword. Where—? He touched his hip and found the weapon. He sighed. Still there. He needed it against the fits, and he remembered losing it, though not clearly. Twice maybe?

His eyes snapped wide. His father had been there, a blind shell on the end of a chain held by Corgren. But it had been his father. The hall collapsed and someone—Ralda—carried him to safety. But what of his father? Athson rolled to a seat on the edge of a bunk and saw Limbreth asleep with her head on the edge of the bed. He reached for her. Spark lay beside her.

"Athson."

The whisper turned his head along the row of bunks.

Hastra beckoned. "Leave her to sleep. Come, I have food for you."

Athson followed the Withling past snoring dwarves and frowned at the familiar faces. Weren't those dreams? Where was he? He slipped past the sleeping dwarves with Spark trailing and found Hastra waiting.

"Come, there's food by the fire." She led the way into a wide hall of trestle tables built low for dwarves, and sat next to the fire that warmed a chill off him.

"Where did you come from?" He took a swallow of water and a bite of bread while he watched Hastra.

"You arrived hours ago. But I suppose you don't remember it all." Hastra touched his head.

He flinched away. "What are you doing?"

"Easy, I'm just checking your head. Makwi said you hit the stone floor hard back in Chokkra, and you haven't been yourself." She checked his eyes, looking at them intently in the firelight.

"Where are we? What's happened?" She released him and Athson sliced meat from a haunch and ate. "Goat?"

"Mountain goat. The dwarves have been hunting." Hastra nibbled at bread and swallowed. "Ralda carried you and Makwi from Chokkra."

"That I remember, then some traveling. I was looking for someone." *Father.*

"Yes, you were injured and left Ralda and Makwi looking for Ath. Makwi said you were about to fall from one of the high walks when they found you and pulled you back. That's when the three of you first spotted the Rokans."

"Rokans? The ones we were after?" He touched his head. There had been a lump. His hands, he gazed at them. No longer burnt. He cocked his head at Hastra. "I remember the injuries. You healed me?"

"Yes, but not before the Rokans captured you. Go ahead and eat more. I don't know it all, but Makwi told me plenty. When he and Ralda found you after you wandered away, there were Rokans far below on another path. Makwi didn't know if you three had been spotted, but he pushed on to avoid them. But the three of you were captured by a large troop of soldiers and priests of Magdronu. They took you up to a mountaintop and left you with some other dwarven captives as a sacrifice to the Dragon." She brushed crumbs from her clothes.

"Why?" It made no sense, but the vague memory of walking in the night and almost falling returned. So that wasn't a dream. He paused a moment and stared at the fire. But there were also dreams, maybe a fit or two as well. He turned back to the food. All that had happened flowed into images he needed to sort between real and false.

Spark lay by the fire. "What do you think?" Spark wagged his tail.

"I think they just caught you and decided to get rid of you. Makwi said they thought you were spies. The sacrifices feed Magdronu's magic. I'd heard it was going on, but I didn't know it was this many." She waved her hand toward the doorway and the bunks of sleeping dwarves.

"And how did we get away?" He covered his question to Spark by going back to his food.

"You dropped your sword over the side of a road."

Athson stopped eating and stared at Hastra. So, he'd likely had a fit. He shifted his gaze to Spark. The mountain hound barked and snarled in his memory, a silhouette against Magdronu and fire. "What—?" He cut off his question to Spark.

"It fell near some of these dwarven scouts. We got word and sent a rescue party for you."

"We escaped the Dragon."

"Yes, curious that. The others swore you said the Dragon was afraid of something and wouldn't land to feed."

"It was Spark, I think."

Hastra sat up straighter. "He was there? Of course, I should have realized he was. Is he here now?"

Athson motioned to the hearth.

"Well done." She stretched out her hand the hearth. "The rescue party brought everyone here."

He frowned. The trader was there too. "Hastra, is there another Withling with a floppy hat?"

"Uh, there are only three left and that doesn't sound like Howart. Why?"

"It's just that I keep seeing this old trader in a floppy hat. He was there and helped chase off the Dragon."

Hastra sat up straight. She'd seen him long ago at Withling's Watch. "That might have been Eloch."

"Really?"

Hastra nodded. "He healed my hip once at Withling's Watch before, before…" She flashed him a smile and ignored the memories of the slaughter and blood. "Anyway, you seem to be blessed." She frowned and squinted toward her pack. "But that can't be right. It's not Eloch's way. But then who would it be?"

"I wouldn't know."

"But someone was there and acted with what was given." Hastra rubbed her chin. "It's a puzzle now that I think back and I've just assumed and never thought it through." She shrugged. "What can I say, old memories…"

Athson gazed around at the rafters and tables. "You stayed here? Where are we, anyway?"

"Now you get at our tale." Hastra rubbed her breastbone with a slight frown that passed quickly. "We left Chokkra hoping to meet you at one of the old dwarven shelters along the way but never found you. We were higher than you apparently, so we got caught in snow after the Bane tried to take Limbreth one night. The dwarves—they're stationed here out of Ezhandun to spy on the Rokans—rescued us from the snow. We would have died if it weren't for them looking for us after Tordug sent up fire signals from our last stop. Gweld went on your rescue, being the only one of us hale enough to travel immediately."

Athson looked around. "Where is he anyway?"

"I don't know. Out watching, hunting, or scouting, I suppose. I haven't seen him since everyone returned. I've been busy with you and the others."

CHAPTER SEVEN

She motioned toward Athson's head and the rows of slumbering dwarves as she spoke.

A few moments of silence passed, and then they spoke at the same time.

"I need to find my father."

"I know where the bow is."

Athson stared at the Withling, who returned his gaze with a measuring squint. They were going to disagree again. He clenched his jaw and slouched slightly. He'd argue only if necessary. He could leave when he wanted.

Athson swallowed. "What can you tell me about my family history?" He needed to know more about his enemies and why they wanted him so badly. "My father is more important than I realized."

Hastra shoved a stray strand of gray hair behind her ear and smoothed wrinkles from her skirt. "Athson, based on what Makwi told me, your father likely died. Maybe even Corgren as well, and that's one less enemy to worry about." She leaned forward, placed a hand on his, and squeezed. "The bow is more important now, the only thing. Surely your father would want you to keep it from Magdronu now. I'm sorry that he was alive all along and now he's gone again."

Athson watched the Withling's wrinkled hand for a moment and then pulled his away. He shook his head and ground his teeth. "He's alive. I know it. I need to find him. I've lived well while he's been a prisoner. He's more important than the bow."

"Athson, you're grieved all over again, I understand. But you must see that there's little chance he survived."

"Tell me why. What are they after? Why is my family—me, now—what they are after?"

"They want the bow to—"

Athson shook his head. "No, there's more to it than that. Please, tell me what you know."

Hastra cleared her throat, opened her mouth, appeared to think better of what she was going to say, then spoke. "The bow is in a place we both overlooked. When you were injured, you mumbled that your father went to Howart's Cave to hunt that fateful day. That's where it is, and—"

"Where? Who?" Athson remembered the name.

"Howart. He's a Withling and lives at a cave not many days from your old home. Your father must've taken the bow there for safekeeping." She shrugged. "Howart may not even be alive. Athson, getting the bow is the best way to draw out Corgren and your father if they're alive."

"That's all well and good, but I need to find my father. Tell me more about what is going on so I know what I'm really up against." Athson stared at Hastra, who blinked and waited.

She sighed. "Very well, perhaps it will help you understand. But will you hear me out regarding the Bow of Hart? We've come too far and suffered too much not to try and retrieve it."

Athson squinted at the Withling. A bargain? What game was she playing with him now? He rubbed his chin whiskers. "I'll think about it. But tell me the truth about my father if you know something from Eloch."

The Withling cocked her head as if listening again. She nodded and sighed. "Back around three hundred years ago, Hart dominated southern Rok. As you know, there are a number of ruling houses in Hart. One of them is your family."

Athson stood and paced a few moments, then wheeled toward Hastra. "You're sure of this? My parents never mentioned this to me."

The Withling nodded. "Your family had gone into hiding for several generations, along with the Bow of Hart."

"And what else is there?"

Hastra opened her mouth, but at that moment, an outside door opened, and several dwarf guardsmen entered. They reported to Chertug, who gave them orders. One left, and the others spread out, waking the sleepers. As Athson turned back to Hastra, the dwarven captain came to her.

Chertug saluted. "Withling Hastra, my scouts report there is a Rokan troop approaching. We must leave quickly. We'll divide our numbers into three groups to escape along the roads and to the forest in the valleys. There's not much time, maybe minutes."

Dwarven officers began organizing their men and their wards. Roused dwarves scrambled for their belongings or to grab what weapons and

CHAPTER SEVEN

supplies there were.

Athson ground his teeth. "Are you sure we must run? We have numbers too."

Chertug shook his head. "They have numbers and likely mages. We are too few to protect so many ill-nourished." He shrugged. "Besides, we aren't a defense force, just one for scouting, and this place is not that well prepared for a fight."

At that moment, a rumble shook the tower, and dust fell from the rafters. Athson rushed for his bow and Limbreth. His family, the bow, and the search for his father would have to wait.

~ ~ ~ ~ ~ ~ ~

Tordug snatched his ax as he started from sleep when Fafwe nudged him. He relaxed at the sight of the dwarf. "What is it?"

Fafwe frowned and glanced down the row of beds where others woke more dwarves. "Rokans are coming in numbers. We're leaving. You're with me." He glanced down the row at Limbreth, who stood searching for Athson. "You and your ax-maiden. We'll split into groups and take different roads so we all have a chance to escape them."

One of Chertug's other squad leaders shouted, "Grab everything you can now! Supplies first!" He turned to a slow dwarf who'd been rescued. "Don't grumble! The Withling has helped you all, you've eaten, so now act like free dwarves."

Tordug rolled from his bed and turned to Fafwe. "How many?" He stroked his beard. Fafwe didn't want him along, but he couldn't lower his status by leaving him. Squad members rushed past to assemble their wards, and Tordug snatched up his pack.

"Several hundred." Fafwe shrugged. "Too many for us, and this tower is no longer properly fortified and supplied. Could be as many as five hundred, and we think there are mages with them." The dwarf walked toward Limbreth and snagged her sleeve. "You're with me and him." He pointed to Tordug.

"Mages?" Tordug stepped closer. "Why would they send mages?" But he sighed at a thought. It was Athson and the bow, or nothing.

"Just get ready. We leave in few minutes. There's not much time." Fafwe stepped away to gather his squad and other rescued dwarves.

"I want to go with Athson." Limbreth drew her cloak about her shoulders and strapped on her swords.

"I'll need you with me. I need you trained more, should I need your help at Ezhandun."

"Why can't he come with us?" Limbreth shouldered her pack as Athson walked up for his things. She touched his shoulder. "We're to go in different groups."

Athson paused, his gaze shifting between Limbreth and Tordug. "What's this?"

"Haven't they told you who you're with? We split up for different roads so they have to split their forces. This way one group has a chance to get through."

Athson grabbed his bow and pack. "Why don't we stand and fight?"

Limbreth nodded and rounded on Tordug. "Yes, why?"

Tordug grabbed Limbreth's arm. "There are far too many for that. There are—"

At that moment, heavy thuds sounded at the far door. Dwarves scurried like ants for the other door. Athson ran toward the pounding, drawing his sword. Limbreth started after him, but Tordug held her back.

Limbreth glared at him. "Let me go! I must help! I'll go with him."

Tordug's words erupted with a snarl. "No, we go now or risk being trapped. The others must get him out now. They'll surround us."

The far door burst asunder, and pieces rained among the dwarven armsmen arrayed to act as a rear-guard to allow the rest to escape.

Limbreth pulled away as Athson, Gweld, and Ralda pushed toward the door and lent their strength for the defense. Rokans poked spears through the destroyed doorway, and dwarves forced them away.

"Out, this way." Tordug turned toward Fafwe, who motioned for them to hurry, his face red and beard bristling beneath a deeply furrowed brow. The dwarven officer slipped out the door with his squad. Shouts echoed along the mountainside outside.

CHAPTER SEVEN

Tordug pulled at Limbreth's arm again. "Come, ax-maid, they're leaving without us!" He couldn't hesitate now, not again. He couldn't fail again. Shouts sounded around him, and he slouched.

"Tordug!" He raised his head and found Makwi, who motioned to him. The champion was going for the door.

"Go with Hastra!"

Too late. Makwi turned to defend the door. But then he turned and nodded his recognition before hacking at the Rokans pushing through.

Makwi knew what was needed. He'd do it. Now to get Limbreth moving. She'd slipped away without his attention, and Tordug went after her. He reached for her arm.

Fire burst through the doorway. Dwarves fell back. Limbreth fell, and Tordug crashed to his knees. His ears rang. The wizard was here! He grabbed Limbreth as she rose. "Are you hurt?" He wasn't sure about his knees.

"I'm fine."

"It's time to go. That may be Corgren!"

"What about Athson?"

"The others must bring him. Fafwe is gone, and we're with him. He knows the best ways for us."

Instead, Limbreth turned as if to rush to Athson's aid. She paused, and her eyes grew wide. She wheeled and brushed past Tordug, her face pale. "Yes, we must go!"

They leaped out the door and raced down stone steps after Fafwe's squad. Tordug could just see them in the available light, winding down the stairs for a lower road. He swore at the slick footing in the night, but Limbreth never hesitated. What had gotten into her? His boot slipped on ice, and Tordug righted himself. Best pay attention to his own feet instead of hers, or they'd make the trip quicker than necessary.

They gained a lower road and heard Fafwe's squad marching away. Rokans called above the tower in the night, their torchlight flickering on the steps above them. Limbreth charged after the dwarves. Tordug heaved his pack on his shoulders and followed. The lass was fast as a deer.

A few minutes passed, and they caught up to the squad and slowed their pace at the rear. Limbreth huffed, but she looked pale even in the limited light. Tordug wasn't sure of her actions, so he just caught his breath instead of questioning her.

Fafwe ordered a scout to trail them farther back.

"Good, but not enough by far." Limbreth stroked her braid and clenched a fist as she huffed a cloud of breath in the cold night. The wind rose and whipped her hood around her face, and Tordug lost her expression for a few moments.

He glanced over his shoulder at the scout fading into the shadows behind them. "He'll call a warning if we're followed. We're not stopping for a long time, anyway."

Limbreth rounded on Tordug and bit her lower lip in hesitation. "I shouldn't have left. But I had to."

The squad members shushed her and kept moving.

Tordug took her by the arm and moved her along. "Let's keep up and be quiet, lest we attract attention. The darkness will hide our retreat."

She pulled away from his grasp and grabbed his shoulder. "It won't matter."

"Why?"

"The Bane was back there. It's still after me. There's neither Athson with the sword nor Hastra to help me."

Tordug's jaw worked a moment, though he found no words. Emptiness rose in his belly, colder than the wind. They were trapped on this mountainside. He stumbled on with Limbreth, her posture rigid as an icicle. Failure haunted him no matter what choices he made. Beside him, Limbreth sniffed and her shoulders shook in silent sobs. Tordug yanked his beard hard and ground his teeth. He'd fight the Bane if it came to it. He glanced over his shoulder again but saw only the night and heard the fading sounds of fighting. He hated running—and losing.

CHAPTER EIGHT

Athson pressed through the milling dwarves standing at the door. *Thud! Boom!* The Rokans beat on the barred door, which shuddered with each blow.

Crash! The door burst asunder.

Athson threw his arm up to protect his eyes and staggered. Dwarves at the door fell wounded, jagged pieces of wood impaling them. His ears rang, but Athson held his sword on guard.

Rokans leapt through the door, slashing and stabbing at the fallen dwarves. Ralda swung his staff and knocked several of the Rokans to the ground. The giant leapt among them and forced the arms-men back.

Stunned dwarves scrambled to their feet in the respite. Their leader shouted to his men to stand firm, his face bloodied by several cuts from door fragments.

Athson winced and glanced at this arm. He also bled from several wounds.

"Fire!" Ralda leapt out of the doorway.

Flame slashed through the door, and dwarves fell screaming and beating at their clothing.

Gweld shouted something lost amid the noise. Athson leapt over dwarves. *Flat, hold the blade flat.* The voice, last time he'd ignored it. This time Athson held his blessed sword flat, raised at his face.

Fire spat through the door again and struck the sword. It faltered against the blade, though it forced Athson back a step with the force. A cowled figure, shorter than him, stood in the doorway. The Bane? No, too short.

He shouted and attacked it with a stab.

The figure dodged and screamed a word. It twisted in ragged shadow and was gone. But Rokans jabbed at Athson with spears.

Ralda answered with pokes of his staff in their faces. "Another!" The giant dodged away with a grimace.

Athson glimpsed the face of a pretty woman as she raised her hands. He held up the sword flat forward again. Fire spewed through the doorway. Athson leaned into it, his jaw clenched. Again, the sword consumed the magic flames. When it dissipated, Athson grinned at the woman, leapt at her, and stabbed with his sword.

The mage dodged back, her face a mask of anger and fear. "Fall back, this isn't the one we seek!"

Rokans fled, firing arrows. The mage spoke a word with a smirk and a dark glitter in her eyes. She twisted into shadow and was gone. Another nearby did the same.

Wounded dwarves groaned inside the tower. A hand grabbed Athson at the shoulder as he lunged after the Rokans. He wheeled back to the tower and found both Gweld and Ralda grasping him.

"We need to gather the wounded and retreat!" Gweld sheathed his long knife and motioned to the others.

Ralda wiped sweat from his brow and motioned with his hands. "We go, no keep tower." The giant held his singed arm, and the end of his staff bore a blackened sear from the magic fire.

Athson inhaled, nodded. "Right." He whirled and helped a dwarf to his feet. "Here! Any dwarf salves for burns?"

"Quickly, tend to everyone, and then we leave." One of the dwarven officers directed his men and approached. "I'm Ingwe. You three are with me. We split into the remaining groups assigned."

"I'll hold the door and find my group later." Makwi stepped forward, his ax ready. "It will delay the pursuit."

Athson glanced at the bustle of dwarves ducking out another door. He took a deep breath and exhaled slowly. The Withling was with them, and she paused, her eyes fastened on him. Their conversation wasn't finished.

CHAPTER EIGHT

Hastra left with the other group of dwarves. Perhaps she was avoiding telling him what he wanted to know. He swore under his breath. He'd find out at Ezhandun and decide what to do later. Ath was important, but Athson needed support and help to find his father. He wasn't giving up just yet. He clenched and unclenched his jaw several times after Hastra slipped out that door with the other squad.

Makwi slapped his shoulder. "Don't worry, ranger, I'll find them and take care of the Withling. Tordug wants it so."

"Speaking of him, where is he?" Athson searched the tower with his gaze as dwarves hustled for their belongings. "And where's Limbreth?"

The dwarf champion hefted his ax and checked the door where Ralda still stood guard with a few dwarves. "She's gone with Tordug and Fafwe. You three will go with this last squad." He pointed to Athson as well as Gweld and Ralda.

Athson clenched his jaw. He wanted to talk to Limbreth. He shifted his gaze to Gweld, who checked his bow. At least Gweld was along to confide in.

"Come, we leave now while we can. Those Rokans will return soon and bring that mage-fire on us." Ingwe motioned to his squad, then paused to nod to Athson. "That was well done with your sword, ranger. It must have some virtue to stop the dragon's magic. You are welcome among us."

Athson nodded. "Thanks. I'll get my pack." He crossed to the bunks and found his things. After a quick check for the inheritance, he hoisted his pack.

As Athson shouldered his pack, Gweld approached. "You look like you've lost something."

"It's just that I missed Limbreth. We hardly spoke before all this happened." Athson hefted his bow. "And I needed to finish talking to—"

"Time to go!" Ingwe waved his men out a tower door into the night.

"It's fine, Ralda. Do what you must." Makwi clasped hands with the giant, who turned away from the dwarf champion and crossed to them.

Ralda paused at the door. "Go you, Athson." His fingers wiggled briefly, and then he ducked out the door after Ingwe's squad.

"Sure, Ralda." Athson sighed and motioned for Gweld to go first. "We'll talk about it later."

Spark flashed past Athson with a slight growl after Gweld exited. Athson followed. Odd that Spark seemed upset. His personal apparition rarely offered much hesitation or warning. He shrugged and exited himself. *Must be Rokans near.* The cold wind embraced him, and ahead it ruffled Spark's coat. But he wasn't real. Spark's hackles were up. Athson had best watch for some surprise, like those mages. He hunched against the wind and hustled after Gweld, Ralda, and the dwarves as they descended to a far lower dwarven road. He arched a brow at the soft glow of Spark in the night. What really bothered the dog? Athson nocked an arrow. Whatever was out there, he'd be ready.

~ ~ ~ ~ ~ ~ ~

Limbreth rolled from under her blanket with a groan and a grimace. She worked her shoulder against an ache and then paused with a hiss. Her gaze shifted around their shelter, searching the shadows. She trembled at the chill along her spine.

"You're cold by the fire, ax-maid?" The dwarf standing guard motioned toward the wood. "We have little but can put more on."

She shook her head and answered in dwarvish. "No, it's not that."

"That creature that follows you, then?" He pointed at Limbreth's arm. "Your death-grip aches for the fight, then?"

"There's no fighting the Bane." Tordug sat up and gave Limbreth a reassuring pat on the shoulder. "There's only running from it."

The guard grimaced at Tordug and said nothing in return. But he grinned cheerfully at Limbreth. "You'll beat this enemy, ax-maid." He chewed on some dwarven jerky.

Limbreth's face quivered. The fool knew nothing. Crazy dwarf! The Bane froze the soul, and ten ax-maidens with the death-grip meant nothing against its power. She bit her tongue, but her lips quivered with the effort to hold her rant to herself as she inhaled a ragged breath and then exhaled through gritted teeth. "It's near."

The guard chuckled. "Your gift calls to defeat it."

CHAPTER EIGHT

"If it comes, you won't even know it's here." Limbreth rolled back into her blanket and faced away from the dwarf before he could answer. She watched the fire as a single tear rolled along her cheek. Her heart pounded. They needed to run, she needed to run.

Limbreth drifted into sleep but squirmed awake more than once. The Bane whispered out of the shadows in her dreams. With her aching shoulder, she rose none too rested later with the others and ate her ration of jerky.

Tordug sat apart from them all. They—she—needed Athson and his blessed sword. He had to have escaped. He must have. She shouldn't have run. She tore the jerky with a savage bite and a grunt. Hastra had told her to protect him, and she'd only failed him.

The dwarf next to her elbowed her. "You keep eating our food, and you'll grow a beard soon. He stroked his own dark beard as the others laughed.

Limbreth laughed with them. Nothing was funny about her predicament. She held her braid in front of her mouth. "And just as bow-legged and just as worthy of a hairy kiss, eh?" There, she'd mustered some jibes for them. Tordug nodded when she glanced his way.

The dwarves laughed, but Fafwe silenced them. "Quiet. We'll draw Rokans like flies to a carcass."

One squad-man muttered under his breath. "There's no one in this lonely pass."

Fafwe stood and gathered his belongings. "Time we moved on."

The squad rose and readied their weapons and packs. Grumbles and groans passed among them. One of them snuffed the fire. Limbreth stood and stretched as she worked on the jerky some more. She squatted by her pack and fiddled with it beside Tordug.

The disgraced ruler of Chokkra leaned close. "Your dwarvish is getting good," he whispered in the common tongue with the mildest of smiles.

Limbreth continued working with her pack and replied in the common tongue, "You're all crazy."

He patted her hand. "You'll get all the nuance soon enough. We'll talk later on the trail."

"I doubt I'll ever get it." She hated herself for the negative admission. Must be the Bane. "They shouldn't treat you this way—ever." Limbreth frowned at the dwarven squad as they rose and gathered their gear. She'd never understand this kind of honor system. Limbreth stroked her braid and the trinkets woven into it that bespoke her status, which she barely understood. Crazy dwarves. She'd thought Tordug and Makwi weren't sane, but this crowd took the champion's title.

Tordug stood with his pack and ax. He bestowed a smile on her and offered her his hand, the meaning of her diplomatic status ignored by the others just because they largely ignored their former king.

Limbreth took his hand and shouldered her pack as she rose. She checked her swords for readiness. Little good they'd do her against the Bane. She grimaced at the thought.

The dwarf who had offered her the jibe elbowed her in passing. "We'll get you a proper ax in Ezhandun if you're uncomfortable with those toys." Some of the others snickered.

Limbreth smirked and clenched her left hand around her braid just at his face-level. "Didn't need one to get this."

He slapped her on her pack and ducked out of the shelter door ahead of the others. He signaled the all-clear after a few moments, and they left.

Their line spread out along the dwarven marching road until they veered onto a long stair. Wind buffeted their every step, and clouds rolled overhead in a variable sky. The stair ended at length, much to Limbreth's relief, but the road still descended and rarely led higher.

All morning, Limbreth watched the shadows as she walked. She often found that she held her breath even though the telltale chill never slithered along her backbone. She exhaled once again and brushed a strand hair from her face. The blasted Bane. Had they lost it? Was it after one of the others? Athson, most likely. She hoped not. And she had run from her duty. If not Athson, then who? Why her at all? To get to Athson. Her stomach knotted at the thought.

"We need to talk." A hand touched her arm.

Limbreth jumped and gasped. "What are you doing?"

"Easy." Tordug cast his gaze at the other dwarves. "You're jumpy." He

CHAPTER EIGHT

spoke the common tongue. "Still feeling the Bane?"

They continued walking. "No, just thinking about it. I didn't hear you approach."

"I spoke your name twice."

"Oh." She sighed. The Bane had frayed her nerves. "What, uh, what do you want?"

Tordug leaned close. "We may need to talk our way into what we need if we arrive first. I'll need your help as an ax-maid."

She lowered her head toward the dwarf. "Why me? I don't know enough. I can barely speak and keep from ranting, let alone follow a complex protocol of honor."

"Makwi and Hastra should be together. But what if they're delayed or worse?" Tordug paused for effect. "You'll bring enough honor for me to get what we need."

"Look, I know you wanted me along to be seen, but it was all up to Makwi and Hastra. I can't do this." Not with the Bane lurking in the shadows. Her stomach flopped and her heart skittered at the thought of the Bane touching her again, dragging her away. She shook her head. "I can't."

Tordug stopped her on the road and glared firmly at her. "That's not like you, and certainly makes me rethink those baubles there. Do you still have a backbone?"

Limbreth swallowed. Fear gripped her backbone. She cleared her throat, and her eyebrows knit together. There was Athson to consider. If she couldn't stand by him, then she could do this. She nodded. "I'll try."

"Good." Tordug turned her along the path. "Let's start now." Without giving her a chance to answer, the dwarf launched into a set of instructions and terms about handling a meeting and what requests she needed to make as well as how to phrase them.

Limbreth soon found herself stumbling over the ritualized honor responses and what gestures meant what. She bungled one sequence for a third time and swore under her breath.

Tordug cocked a questioning eyebrow her way and cleared his throat. "Again."

A groan escaped her throat. Tordug just didn't understand. She couldn't think with the Bane at her heels and Athson possibly in danger. She wet her lips. *Grab hold of yourself, girl.* She took a few deep breaths, like when calming herself before a practice duel, and started again. This time she got it.

Tordug nodded in approval and slapped her on the shoulder. "Let's end now." He looked around for no seeming reason. "It's getting on, and the others will bunch up before we stop. It'll likely be dark soon. Practice some of the other things I've taught you on the squad. It'll help."

Her mouth twitched. "They treat you so poorly. It isn't right."

Tordug's bushy brows knit together. "It is fitting among dwarves. I know it's strange for you, but this who we are." He pointed to himself, a squad-man, and then to her. "But you'll change that, won't you?"

Limbreth walked several steps before she nodded. "Let's hope so." Maybe she'd do something about it around the fire.

Their scout ahead waved his arms as he came back around a bend where the dwarven road wound around a shoulder of the mountain. The squad halted. The dwarf trotted toward them and saluted Fafwe once he arrived.

Limbreth pressed closer with Tordug. Her hand twitched. It was likely trouble ahead. Maybe just debris blocked the road. They'd passed that a few times. She glanced toward Tordug. He fingered his ax haft. She leaned closer to hear the report as the wind sang in her ears.

"Rokans are marching this way, maybe twice our numbers."

Fafwe stroked his beard and cast a glance at Tordug, who offered nothing but a stony expression for his advice.

Limbreth frowned. The command was Fafwe's, but a little consultation from an older commander wouldn't hurt. Crazy dwarven pride. She held her tongue but not her frown.

The scout gripped his ax tighter. "They have the numbers. Perhaps we can go back and find a defensive position."

Fafwe shook his head. "No, Eakwe hasn't returned from that direction. Ezhandun is forward, and there may be Rokans following in greater numbers. Do we have time to form up at that bend and surprise them?"

CHAPTER EIGHT

"Yes, but we must hurry."

Fafwe waved his arm. "Ahead, then. We hide against the mountainside and spring on them as they come around. We'll force them over the edge if we can and maybe take the advantage of timing and position quickly. What are their weapons?"

The squad marched double-time, and the scout went beside Fafwe. "They have a mix of short spears and swords."

Limbreth followed the pace, her breath puffing in her face. The rear scout hadn't reported? She chanced a glance backward but saw no sign of anyone coming. Strange. Maybe there was trouble behind them too. She hoped it wasn't the Bane. She pushed her braid out of the way and kept moving.

Fafwe halted them at the sharp bend in the road. He motioned for them all to lean in line against the mountainside. His whispered command passed along the line of dwarves. "Stay silent until it's time. We spring at them with shouts and force as many over the side as possible. Mark the spearmen first before they can turn on us."

Limbreth passed the commands along and drew her swords. Time for a little ax-maiden work. Her heart raced, and her face flushed. She breathed slowly, deeply. She stared at the low wall along the road, where open sky bespoke the drop beyond.

They soon heard the sound of men marching. Hands gripped tighter on ax hafts around Limbreth. Fafwe raised his hand to signal their attack. The first two lines of Rokans rounded the curve. Fafwe's hand dropped.

The dwarves shouted and charged between the Rokans and the mountainside. Limbreth screamed and ran behind Tordug. Fafwe veered into the Rokans and lowered his shoulder as they reacted with their weapons. The others forced more soldiers over the wall. Rokans fell with screams of despair on their lips.

Limbreth shouldered into a Rokan spearman who stepped forward and lowered his spear too slowly. He fell, and she stabbed him in the neck above his mail. He fumbled his spear as his life gurgled away.

Limbreth wheeled and almost tripped on the fallen spear. A Rokan stabbed at her belly. She dodged sideways and parried but fell over the fallen Rokan and slammed her shoulder into the wall. The swordsman raised his sword. A sneer danced on his face behind the cheek-guards of his helmet.

Limbreth lifted a sword to parry and roll.

An ax crashed into the Rokan swordsman's leg. He screamed, and blood spewed from his wound. He went to a knee but held his sword and twisted toward his attacker.

Limbreth slashed at his throat. The Rokan fell back and clutched his blood-pulsing throat in his last moments. She scrambled to her feet and back into the melee.

Around her, dwarves shouted and men cursed. Limbreth sliced, parried, and stabbed amid the churning fighters. She fought near the wall, too near for her liking with all the bodies and weapons at her feet to trip her.

A sudden chill ran along her spine. Something gripped her, and she wheeled away and turned. The Bane stood reaching for her. Her limbs trembled. Limbreth stabbed slowly. The Bane slithered aside. She remembered Athson's faltering attack back in Auguron. It was no joke now.

The Bane reached for her. Limbreth cowered. She hated herself in that moment. She dropped the sword in her left hand, grabbed the Bane, and her arm locked with the chill. Her knees wobbled, and her heart thudded in her throat.

She stabbed weakly with the other sword, then collapsed to her knees. Her locked hand and arm felt frozen. Pain from her arm brought a rush of tears from her eyes. But the death-grip held the Bane at bay.

Around her, Rokans and Chokkrans surged in a slow, fierce dance. A wail escaped her lips. "No! Tordug!" She forced a weak cut at the Bane with her right arm.

The Bane slapped the sword from her grip. The blade clattered into the wall and fell on the road. The looming creature grabbed her arm and pulled Limbreth away from the battle.

She resisted with feeble kicks, but her struggles weakened. Only her death-grip worked. Limbreth's eyes fluttered as she heard the soft hiss of

CHAPTER EIGHT

the Bane amid the clash of fighting. Her vision narrowed into darkness rimmed with fading sunlight. "No! Help!" But her voice sounded like a squeak in the wind and the din of battle.

The Bane pulled her inexorably away as her resistance waned.

CHAPTER NINE

Darkness surrounded Magdronu-as-Gweld and those with him who crept along the dwarven road. Ralda bumbled like an ox while the dwarves, furtive as they attempted to be, thumped along the stone road. Magdronu-as-Gweld smiled, but he held the heat lurking in his belly. They only thought danger followed them. But he made sure there wasn't—for now. Beside him, Athson muttered under his breath about Limbreth, Hastra, and Spark. Magdronu-as-Gweld quirked an eyebrow. Best not to glance at that creature.

Magdronu-as-Gweld squinted as he listened to Athson. He needed to transform into his true form, but he had time before Eloch's curse drained his magic.

Athson patted Spark. "Good dog." His murmurs turned to another subject. "Hastra wants me to go there, but I won't go. I need to find father."

Spark's tail didn't wag.

Magdronu-as-Gweld tilted his head and leaned slightly closer. That fool guardian spirit parading as a dog didn't trick him for a moment. But Athson hadn't figured out his "friend" yet. No wag meant *no* or disagreement. Spark wanted Athson to go somewhere? Magdronu-as-Gweld held his gaze steadily ahead and cleared his throat. No sense tipping Athson off that he could actually see Spark. "What are you muttering about?"

Ralda grunted ahead of them. The giant's hands flicked in the darkness, like anyone could see or even cared what else he meant. "Nothing, just prayer, thanks."

CHAPTER NINE

Magdronu-as-Gweld frowned. Nitwit, like all his kind. He swallowed his sharp retort as usual. "Uh, I mean Athson. He's going on like half of Rok isn't after us."

Athson drew closer as they trudged the dwarven road. "It's what Hastra said back at the tower. She knows where the bow is, or thinks she does."

Pleasant news to his ears. Magdronu-as-Gweld allowed himself the flicker of a grin. This darkness hid his expressions as well as his magic hid his true form. "When did this happen?" Best get the whole tale and see where this led.

"Well, I spoke while I was unconscious and Hastra was healing me. She said I talked about where my father went on his hunting trip."

"Where was that?" Better and better. Magdronu-as-Gweld refrained from the deep purr of pleasure of his dragon's form.

"He went to Howart's Cave just before the village was sacked. Hastra heard this from me and claims she went into a vision and saw that the bow is at this place."

So, it's at that other Withling's hidden home. He had never found it because Eloch protected it. Magdronu-as-Gweld rubbed his chin. "Who's Howart, and where's the cave?"

Athson patted Spark again and adjusted his bow over his shoulder. "Hastra says he's a Withling like her. I've heard of the place, but I never knew who Howart was. I don't think I should follow her anymore. That bow is likely lost for good, and I need to find Ath. She claims he may not even be alive, but if he is, the best thing is to get the bow to draw Corgren out—and my father."

"Interesting. But where does she want you to go now?"

"It's supposed to be in the marshes south of Depenburgh. I've never been there, but we used to call it the Nightmare Marsh when we were kids. People said it was haunted." Magdronu-as-Gweld sensed Athson's shrug. "Just tales to scare us kids."

Magdronu-as-Gweld feigned a sigh. "I'll never understand why your people do that. Doesn't seem funny."

"Yeah, I suppose. But anyway, I think it's time you and I parted with

Hastra and went after Ath. We won't capture that Domikyas now. Right, Spark?"

Magdronu-as-Gweld stifled his laughter. If only Athson knew the truth of it all. Magic controlled his family no matter how they sought escape from his control. *Oaths are oaths.* He cleared his throat. "You sure you don't want some Soul's Ease? That dog's not real."

"Hastra says it is."

"Hmm. So now you do want to follow her instructions?" Magic controlled his desires more deeply than Athson would ever guess. Magdronu-as-Gweld adjusted his grip on his bow. Waiting was proving better with each moment.

"No, I just think it's better to find my father than wasting more time on this bow." Athson huffed a little as they climbed some broad, shallow steps.

"But Hastra's likely correct. Your father is likely dead from that cave-in." He patted Athson's shoulder to encourage him. "I'm sad to say it, since you just found out he still lived. But Hastra may well be right: find the Bow of Hart, and if Corgren and Ath are alive, then Corgren will come, seeking his trade. Then you'll have your chance to save your father." *Bait.* People always went for the emotional bait. But this was easy, with the magic hold on Athson's family.

"Well…"

Magdronu-as-Gweld almost laughed at Athson's predictable hesitation between choices. Heat flared in his belly. He needed to get away and fly in his form soon. He needed to set his bait further and contact Corgren. Removing Hastra from the equation was definitely best. "Well, we best hold our tongues, lest we draw Rokans on us. We can talk later."

Spark growled and held his tail low and still.

"Easy, Spark." Athson patted his dog a final time.

Pity that the boy didn't understand his guardian at all, or he'd understand his danger.

Later, when they entered a dwarf shelter by the road, Magdronu-as-Gweld volunteered to scout along their back-trail. He'd meditate on this news, send his orders, and fly as a dragon, if ever so briefly. He trotted back along the dwarven road. Best not to dawdle. He needed as much distance and

CHAPTER NINE

time away from Athson, Ralda, and the dwarf squad as possible. Magdronu-as-Gweld let the night swallow him and he hummed as he went. He'd lay his traps well this time. Paugren and the Beleesh sisters needed to do their part one way or another. Paugren needed a few magical items just in case Hastra proved as slippery as always. He found a desolate spot against a rock-face behind a pine thicket and sent his summons, *'Paugren.'* Instructions for a potion and a disguise should get results if nothing else. His pleased rumble of laughter startled a sleeping bird from a tree.

~ ~ ~ ~ ~ ~ ~

Corgren strode past the ranger's wretched father. He paused and watched the babbling fool as he played with the chains that locked him to the tunnel wall. The slave had saved him, and he still didn't understand why. Ath was halfway to crazy, but his motive must rise from something. He wanted to live. Corgren pushed through his doorway and shut himself within its confines. Best to watch him closely. Corgren sat and sniffed. Still, the blind man had saved him from sure death. *Reward him with a quick death when the time comes.* Corgren chuckled at the thought. Anything else was weakness.

Papers lay strewn on his desk, carried from Rok by trolls and slaves. Corgren read through his latest reports. Plans were advancing for his part. He just needed his objective, though he harbored little doubt of his master's intent. The dwarves in the north bore little consequence in the larger plans—except as slaves. Rok stood poised to strike wherever necessary, likely west. And his trolls, well, that was a simple matter.

The stone in the ring on Corgren's finger flashed, a welcome return to function now that he was back in Chokkra. Magdronu summoned him. Corgren grabbed a bowl and a knife. Ecstatic dread flooded his mind, and his nostrils flared. First the blood, and then the majesty of the Dragon.

He went back to the slave and clutched his arm. "Your contribution to the cause is needed."

The blind man ground his teeth but said nothing.

Corgren cut just a finger and dribbled the slave's blood into the ceremonial bowl. The gem flashed blood-red. Corgren wrapped the wound. One day Ath would break and make a sound, and he could take a finger for payment.

Corgren stood and watched the slave's clenched fist shaking with pain. But then there was the debt owed. Perhaps the quick death instead.

Magdronu waited, so Corgren wheeled back to his quarters, placed the coins of Hart in the blood, and spoke the spell. The marvel of power rose in his mind. Few understood the Dragon and his motives, so foreign to their way of thinking, the normalcy of what must come with his master's rise above Eloch, the usurper of this age.

The visage of the Dragon rose with the light above the bowl, the horned head shimmered amid heat. Instead of a rumble of threat, the Dragon's purr of pleasure greeted Corgren, though the pain still throbbed and he suppressed a gasp. "Master, I answer your call."

"My faithful Corgren, most useful of all, since we met up on the river." Merciless fangs gleamed in the light. "I have a mission for you. You have the ranger's father?"

"I do. It is his blood I used for the spell." Corgren's lips quivered with the effort. Was all forgiven?

"That is well, since I now require him and you this very hour."

"What of my preparations?" Corgren gripped the desk as his face quivered. A mission. A chance to prove himself.

"That attack must wait, as you well know. I have information that will lead us to the bow. But I need you so I can lure Athson to it. Paugren will remove the Withling so she can no longer hinder my plans. Without her, I'll encourage Athson to go for the bow in hopes of finding his father. But he must see that you both are alive so I can entice him properly." The Dragon's purr rose. "I'll need Athson to get the Bow of Hart from Howart's Cave where Eloch undoubtedly protects it from us."

Corgren ducked his head. "As you wish, Great One. Where shall we go?"

"Here are the instructions." Pain and images flashed across Corgren's thoughts in a whirl of colors. *Steady, endure.* These were necessary to live in the coming age of his master's glory. When it all faded, the spell snapped away, and Corgren almost fell over.

Corgren gasped and waited for his heart to slow and his head to stop spinning. At length, he snapped at his troll attendants, who came running.

CHAPTER NINE

"Bring the man. Gather six fists of your brethren. We raid!"

When Corgren stepped out of his room, the traitorous wretch stood among the trolls. Ath shifted his stance and almost fell over as he adjusted his boot. Corgren stepped close to him. "We've a job to do, you and I."

~ ~ ~ ~ ~ ~ ~

Ath paused and listened to the silence around him. He waited for any sign of furtive movement. Even the slightest whisper of his tool might cover the approach of a troll. Discovery wasn't an option now. He fingered the groove in the chain link. It remained narrow. Good. It was his world, that thin notch, his only hope. Ever since he'd found the rough metal sliver after the cave-in, Ath had guarded it, working only when he was certain he was alone. His ears gave him that much sense of his surroundings.

Right now, Corgren muttered in his quarters, and Ath risked a few spare moments of work on the chain. His patient work would pay off. He smirked. He'd wait for just the right time to act. Just when Athson needed help. Ath waited and worked the file in the groove once, twice, maybe three times. Paused. Listened. His thoughts screamed into the silence. "Patience." His muttered word carried like a shout in his ears. He covered his mouth.

Careful, Ath, old boy. Once he'd nearly been discovered and dropped the little file at the sound of approaching footsteps. He'd searched the floor in haste where it had pinged. At the last moment, he had found it and placed his worn boot over it and slouched. The trolls had laughed and spat on him in passing.

Ath exhaled. *Held your breath at that memory? Well, pay attention, or there'll be no reason for patience.* He wiped his grimy face at the memory of troll spittle.

A rumble throbbed from Corgren's quarters. The wizard watched him closely, and he didn't know why. This was Magdronu, he remembered that much, and slouched at the loathsome presence emanating from the nearby door. Words echoed in the halls of Chokkra. "You go to attack Athson. Take that captive too." Words faded into the noise of the Dragon's presence.

Ath gasped and covered his mouth. Athson! Too soon! He wasn't ready, not yet! He started filing at the link with sudden fury, grinding his teeth.

Within a short stretch of time, orders in trollish snapped from Corgren's room.

Boots clomped hear him. Ath palmed his file, fiddled with his chain links, and muttered nonsense. The trolls wouldn't understand, but he imagined it helped the image of an addled prisoner.

A troll yanked him to his feet.

Ath dropped the file. It bounced off his leg as he stood. His heart beat into his throat. The sliver of metal slid along his shin and settled with the edge against his leg. He imagined it balanced on the edge of his boot cuff, braced against him. He held his breath and dared not move. Cold sweat broke out on his forehead as the trolls muttered. What could he do? Something! Anything!

"Well, well." Corgren's voice sounded clearer as he stepped into the hall.

The trolls about Ath shifted.

How many where there? It didn't matter. Ath shifted his stance, leaned over, and knocked the file into his boot as he feigned adjusting it. He stomped once, twice on it. Everything was silent around him. He clenched his toes, certain the trolls were about to pull his boot off—or worse.

Corgren's breath brushed his face. "We've job to do, you and me. We're off with these trolls, and I'll explain when we get there. Oh, and it's cold where we're going, so try not to freeze."

Cold? Ath almost laughed. *They missed it, old boy!* What did he care how cold it was? He still had the file, his only weapon against the wizard in the whole time of his captivity in darkness.

The harsh words of Corgren's spell assaulted Ath's ears. He cringed, glad he'd never seen what they did to that old woman back in the Troll Heaths. Then Ath slouched. But he wasn't ready, regardless. The file may as well have been bread, for all the use it was now. Noise swirled amid the cold. He just was not ready to help Athson. Ath's teeth chattered.

CHAPTER TEN

Tordug charged with the others amid the eruptions of shouts on the road. He lowered his shoulder into one Rokan and pushed with his legs. He grunted with the effort. The soldier flailed his arms as he fell over the side with a scream.

A spear thrust at Tordug as he turned. He parried it with his ax haft and stabbed with the spike of the ax-head into his attacker's throat. Blood gushed, and the Rokan fell, grasping for his throat with gurgled cries.

Limbreth disappeared into the milling combatants.

Tordug pulled the spike free and engaged another Rokan soldier. *So may all the slayers of innocents end.* He hacked at a swordsman, who leapt back. The fight wove in a dance of gore and screams while the dwarves sang, their voices low.

Another Rokan thrust a spear at Tordug out of the knotted melee. He dodged and whacked the weapon lower with his own haft. He lunged with a short stroke at his foe's knee and crushed the joint.

The Rokan fell with a scream but pulled the spear back under Tordug's legs. Tordug caught his balance and stepped over the spear-haft and then chopped at his attacker's belly. He turned from the bowel-stench of the dying man at the flash of something dark. Dwarven war-song faded on his lips.

The Bane was dragging Limbreth away. At a glance, he took in his pupil's feeble resistance. His hopes of honor regained slid away with the fell creature. Limbreth's head lolled like that of a child's ragdoll.

"No!" Tordug charged the Bane. He chopped at the grasping arm, and his ax bounced away. But the Bane released Limbreth. Tordug lunged and pushed the Bane. His shoulders struck the black-clad figure. Tordug grasped at it and found the robe more shadow than cloth. But it did have substance. He yelled and forced the Bane away. It slid over loose stone as Tordug shouted wordlessly. The Bane struck the retaining wall. Tordug howled his effort. How heavy it was! Then over the creature flopped into the open air.

The Bane fell with a hiss instead of a scream, its robe fluttering in the wind. Tordug glimpsed the shade billowing like a cloud darker than crow's feathers. Then he slid back along the wall, his knees suddenly weak. He flopped and gasped. His vision narrowed as a Rokan stepped close and drew back for a killing strike. Tordug fumbled with his ax with weak hands. The Bane's cursed touch had killed him. Tordug squinted at the expected blow and stared his death in the eye.

A hand grabbed his attacker's sword arm. The Rokan struggled to free his arm with a grunt. Tordug mumbled the dwarf-song and raised his ax. His face twitched with effort as he stabbed with the spike. The Rokan dodged back and, unable to free himself from the grasp, pulled a dagger with his other hand. The Rokan's grimace flashed under the faceguard of his helmet as he kicked Tordug's ax away and reared his arm for the killing slash.

~ ~ ~ ~ ~ ~ ~

Even after their descent into the high woodlands of the mountains, Athson kept an arrow nocked. He, Gweld, Ralda, Spark, and the dwarves stalked the trail as darkness crept closer from the east. Athson paused and listened. No birds sang. No squirrels rustled in the underbrush. He shifted his gaze.

Spark stood half-hidden beneath an evergreen, hackles up and head lowered.

Gweld turned to Athson. "Hear something?"

"That's just it, I hear nothing in the forest."

"It just evening coming on. Let's go before the others take all the good spots to sleep." Gweld motioned along the trail with his head and turned back toward the others.

CHAPTER TEN

Athson's eyes narrowed. Should he say it? Spark stalked on, hackles still up. "Spark's got his hackles up."

Gweld wheeled. "*Your* hackles are up. You've been that way since we left the tower."

Athson started walking again and passed Gweld. "You've got an arrow to string too. Besides, why shouldn't we be on edge?"

"I don't have my arrow quarter-drawn."

Athson turned his head and watched to either side. "Something's stalking us, and Spark knows it. It's just too quiet."

Gweld sighed. "You and that imaginary dog of yours. It's just evening, and we've lost the Rokans. They drove us away, and that's that."

"Then why put your arrow to quiver?"

"Athson, don't be so—"

Athson wheeled around and faced Gweld. "Be what? Careful? You taught me the very skills I use now. Am I so wrong?"

Gweld patted his shoulder. "Easy, Athson. I'm not saying there isn't need for caution, but I'm not basing my decisions on Spark." The elf paused and gazed steadily at Athson. "You sure you don't need Soul's Ease?"

Athson tapped his sword hilt. "Quite sure. And I'm not so sure Spark isn't real."

Gweld groaned and continued past Athson. "Really? I think you need some medicine."

Athson followed his old friend. "Really. Spark's the one constant of all my experiences since the Funnel. He's even warned me away from trouble any number of times."

"That's just you and the ranger skills you've learned, not an imaginary dog." Gweld crept along, suddenly crouching, and then trotted after dwarves. "But you may not be wrong. C'mon."

Athson trotted after his friend. "However, I did see you up on the mountaintop when the dwarves rescued us."

Gweld halted and cocked his head with a furrow on his brow. "You what?"

Athson pulled up beside the elf. "We kinda thought maybe you, Limbreth, Hastra, and Tordug might come with some dwarves, since they knew we'd been captured." Athson shrugged. "My head hurt so bad, and they gave us that potion. Must've had me confused, and I thought you were up there with us. Another reason not to use more Soul's Ease, maybe."

Gweld set out again, this time walking. "Well, I was there, just down below standing guard."

Athson followed. "Yeah, but it was a tough spot. Thought I was having a fit. I may have, but with that lump on my head, it's hard to tell."

They eased among the trees in the failing daylight until their squad leader called a halt behind a screen of trees growing against a ridge of rock that rose back into the Drelkhaz Mountains. They set a cold camp and ate from their rations of what the dwarves called *pukh-muk,* a version of dried, ground meat mixed with nuts and honey.

Athson gnawed on his hardened rations, his bow at hand. He preferred this boiled into a mush, but they traveled without fire for now. He frowned and listened as wind whispered in the trees. Too bad he slept with dwarves. They snored, even if softly.

Murmured words passed among the dwarves. A guard stood watch at either end of their camp. Spark lay on the northern end of camp, watching the trail, though he often turned his gaze back toward Athson and stared at Gweld for a moment before watching the trail again.

Athson finished his meal and leaned back against the cold rock face. Spark's hackles were down. He'd best sleep while he could. The stillness seeped into his mind. Funny how Spark acted oddly since Chokkra. Come to think of it, the mountain hound often stood between him and Gweld. Strange. Athson opened his eyes and looked at the elf.

Gweld wiped his hands as he finished eating and noticed Athson's attention. "What?"

"Nothing."

"You sure about the medicine?"

Athson leaned his head back and shut his eyes. "I'm sure." But he wasn't sure of Spark and Gweld. They were both faithful to him. He exhaled slowly. Maybe Gweld was right about Spark. Just his imagination. But then his imagination was uncannily right when his senses were mute—or rather,

CHAPTER TEN

when his skills revealed nothing.

Shouts woke Athson. He started from sleep and grabbed his bow as he stood. He reached for an arrow as dwarves rushed past.

On the north side of the camp, their watchman lay on the ground and wrestled with a shadow. The snarl revealed the attacker as a troll. Weapons clanged in the crisp air.

Athson snatched his sword free instead of an arrow. *Too dark for that.* He charged into the fray as more trolls attacked out of the night. Gweld shouted, but Athson didn't understand him. He parried a sword thrust at the last moment and jumped back.

Light burst around them. Fire blossomed in one of the trees. Dwarves dodged from the flames.

"Mage!" Athson thrust forward to attack the magic-wielder. He parried and countered several attacks as he sought who had cast that fire.

Athson paused, and his face flushed with heat. Corgren stood along the trail, his hand lit with flame.

Athson shouted and charged the wizard. Fire spewed at him. He lifted the blade, the flat forward. A hard lesson learned. He grimaced, turned his head, and closed his eyes. The wizard fire met the blade and threw Athson back a few steps. He slammed into a troll, which grunted in reaction, then squealed as a dwarf chopped him down. As his vision cleared from the flash, Athson leapt at the wizard.

Corgren sneered a moment, wheeled, and ran back up the trail.

Athson chased the wizard. "Where's my father?" He'd catch the wizard and beat the answer out of him.

"Athson, stop."

Athson ignored Gweld's shout and charged on. Sounds of fighting faded around Athson as he gained on the wizard. Corgren cut uphill over some rocks, and Athson scrambled over a massive rock after him. "You're mine, wizard!" He lunged through the squat firs and extended his bow to clear limbs from his face. He jumped from a rock into a depression and stopped. Firelight flickered around him.

Ath sat on a rock next to Corgren and a hobgoblin.

~ ~ ~ ~ ~ ~ ~

Hastra escaped the Tower of Nazh-akun with Chertug and his squad of dwarves, a mix of scouts, warriors and former Rokan captives. They gained a high road and scurried into the night.

Several hours passed and Hastra stirred from her silent travel with the dwarves. Makwi hadn't come. Chertug didn't seem concerned. But she'd seen the glimpse of a familiar face among the Rokans, a Beleesh sister. It had been years since she'd seen any of the three turncoats, former Withlings, who now served the Dragon as especially effective mages. She rubbed the old scar at her heart and an unction rose in her. *'Offer them forgiveness.'* Hastra halted and dwarves pushed past her. Now? She should turn around?

The rest of the dwarves went on by Hastra. She sighed and slouched. She'd have to go back and make the offer. But why now? She shook her head, shrugged and set out toward her enemy in the dark of night. *A Withling served no matter the consequences.* She knew that better than any. What was needed was given–even forgiveness for a prowling enemy.

Not long after she turned around, Hastra passed a few crevices. A shadow stirred from one and a hand clamped over her mouth. Hastra grabbed at the hand over her mouth and inhaled to scream.

"Shhh! It's me, Makwi. Rokans are close." The dwarf released his grip.

"Where have you been?" Hastra lowered her voice regardless of the roaring winds at these heights. Why did they take such a high route?

"Why are you headed back to them?" Makwi grabbed her arm and guided her back toward the dwarf squad.

Hastra pulled away. "I've had—I was looking—" She sighed. "I can't say just now." She regretted the words, but she shouldn't tell Makwi yet.

Makwi cast a sidelong glance at her. "You should know better."

"I know." She rubbed her face where the dwarf had held her. "Those three mages? I may know who they are."

"Hmm, friends among that lot?"

"Hardly, I should think. But they were once Withlings."

Makwi fumbled with his ax. "Withlings? Back there?"

"Yes, sisters once in my order but corrupted by Corgren and his brother."

CHAPTER TEN

Makwi walked faster. "And you were going back to, what, catch up on old times?"

"No, nothing of the sort. It's just that they may need me."

The dwarf almost halted. "Need you? More like they'll slip a sword between your ribs and have done with you, Withling."

Hastra rubbed where the old wound lay beneath her heart. She shook her head. Not as simple as that. "No, they can't just now, though they'd love to try, I'm sure. They just need to know…" She trailed off into silence. She'd said too much, maybe.

"Know what?" Makwi groaned, his voice pitched low. "You mean they're welcome back? That they can change again?"

Hastra cleared her throat in answer.

"They've likely killed so many people and done so much wrong since those days. I don't see that they're much interested, Withling." Makwi grabbed her hand and pulled her along the dwarven road with the wind swirling. "Let's get out of here while we can."

"Can't say as I like it much either, Makwi, but Eloch's will is best followed. I know that much." She wouldn't be alive without Eloch's purpose. Corgren's knife flashed in her memory. *He plunged the dagger into her heart. The pain seared her mind a moment. Then she floated away.* Hastra rubbed the death-wound through her thick clothing.

Makwi marched forward and dragged Hastra in his wake. "Isn't our mission more important?"

She followed with halting steps. It was a distasteful message to her, that much she admitted. And what of Athson? He needed her to guide him, lest he falter in his own wayward intentions. But there it was. The unction to invite the Beleesh sisters back to Eloch and the Withlings. Her mouth went dry and tasted bitter. But Eloch wanted it done. She pulled away from Makwi. "If it's Eloch's will, then what is needed is given."

Makwi waved his arm in the direction he wanted to go—the direction Hastra wanted too. "We're falling behind, and they won't wait on us."

"I must try." And what of Athson if she was caught? She needed to tell him more. The desire to lie to him to get the foolish youngster headed for the bow rose in her mind. *Yes, just tell him of a vision or something to get him moving.* Everyone knew Withlings couldn't lie. They said only what was necessary but didn't lie. She brushed hair from her face. If she openly manipulated Athson, then she wasn't a Withling. She'd have failed altogether. But how to do both?

"Why not leave them a message?"

Hope flared within her thoughts, and she grabbed Makwi's hand. "Yes, a message. Do you have something to write on?"

"You have that book of yours in your pack."

Hastra twisted her hands at the dwarf. "No, I can't use it just to send missives."

"Well, then, we capture one of their scouts and tell it to him."

Hastra raised her chin and tapped her lips with her fingertips. It would have to work. "Yes, I suppose it's fine. But mind you, he must be out."

Makwi chuckled. "Why, Withling, what is needed is given. Let's hide over here."

They ducked into a seam of rock and waited in the darkness beneath the stars. It wasn't long before they heard someone moving near their crevice. A shadow slipped past them, sword drawn and the bearer alert, pausing to listen often.

Makwi leaned close to Hastra's ear. "I'll check for others, and then we'll leave him the message."

She breathed back, "I'll wait here."

The dwarf crept out of the crevice and checked back along the road. He waited and then motioned Hastra out of the hole. They set out after the Rokan scout.

He whirled and held his sword on-guard at their approach.

Makwi held his hands up, away from his weapons.

The Rokan edged closer. "Do you surrender, stone-rat?"

"Never!" Makwi started forward, but Hastra held him back.

Hastra stepped forward, her hands clasped before her. Words sprang to her mind. "Your weapons are of no use right now."

The Rokan gasped and grimaced, unable to move. "Magic! You've cursed

CHAPTER TEN

me!"

"Hardly such, since I serve Eloch."

"What do you want with me if not to kill me?"

"You're led by three mages. Sisters by the name of Beleesh, I believe?" Hastra stepped closer.

"Yes." The soldier gasped. "You've cast a spell on me! I didn't want to say that."

Hastra smiled. "What is needed is given. But I have a message for them, and you will carry it." She glanced at Makwi and held her hand out to him. "Stay back, I will deliver it." She stepped near the scout.

The Rokan ground his teeth. "Sorcery! I won't listen."

Hastra sighed. "Nothing of the sort. Really, it's a bit insulting, since that comes from Magdronu." The scout's face tremored as she leaned close with a whisper. "You're to tell them, 'There is but one master of all, and he is Eloch. They are welcome to repent their betrayal and return to him.'"

The Rokan's jaw worked wordlessly as he blinked.

Hastra smiled and waved Makwi on after her as she started away. "You'll stay here until they come along, and then you'll deliver that message."

They hustled along the dwarven road amid the wind and starlight for a long time.

At last, Makwi spoke, "What did you tell him?"

She turned her head and offered the dwarf a stern gaze. "That is for the sisters, not you. Now come along, or we'll never catch those dwarves."

Makwi swore and moved on at a trot. "Tight-lipped Withlings!"

She smiled at his complaints, but more at the relief of delivering that message. What was needed was given to her and to the Beleesh sisters.

~~~~~~~

Limbreth gasped as Tordug slid onto his backside with a grunt. Her eyes fluttered. A shadow fell across her, and she flinched. The Bane? No! She squinted and found a Rokan soldier about to strike Tordug. She reached for him and clasped his arm. Her own grasp locked, as well as her arm, and she groaned in pain.

The Rokan dodged Tordug's weak attack, whipped out a dagger, and drew back to stab the dwarf. Limbreth yanked the soldier off balance. He pulled back but failed to loosen her death-grip. She groped with her other hand and touched a sword hilt. She grasped the sword and stabbed blindly toward the attacker.

He screamed and fell, thrashing as he went. Limbreth released the sword but not the Rokan's arm, and he dragged her around in his death-throes. The noise of fighting touched her ears as she struggled against her own grip on the dying man.

"Tordug! Help!" Strength returned with her senses, and she stomped on the Rokan's arm but failed to pull her grip loose. She kicked with her other leg.

Tordug quivered and stirred feebly. "Here, let me."

The dwarf worked at her unyielding fingers. His hand was as cold as ice. Her spine felt that way. Limbreth ground her teeth with the effort of freeing her grip.

The remaining fights clattered to an end around them. Limbreth lifted her head, half-thinking they'd be surrounded by Rokans. She sighed. Only dwarves survived. But the Bane! Where was it? Fear lent her renewed strength.

Some of the dwarves swore in their own tongue at the sight her unrelenting grip. Fafwe knelt and struggled with her hand. She stared the dwarven officer in the eye. "I can't, I can't…" She couldn't face the Bane again.

Fafwe touched her shoulder with an expression of wide-eyed awe and spoke in dwarvish, "Easy. Relax, ax-maid."

Tordug recovered some of his strength and helped pull her free. The two dwarves helped her to her feet as she rubbed her arm.

Fafwe stammered, "I never—I thought you made it up. But it's real."

Tordug cleared his throat. "Of course it is!"

Surviving dwarves stood close and watched Limbreth. Somehow, she worked feeling and motion back into her arm and hand. *Oh, but that hurts.* She turned to look over the wall as much to hide her tears of pain as to search for the Bane. "I see Rokans down there but not the Bane." She turned back, mostly to Tordug. "It's not dead." She slumped. Limbreth's hope of

CHAPTER TEN

escape from the creature faded like a puddle on a hot day.

"You fought this Bane." Fafwe motioned to Limbreth and Tordug. "You captured it and cast it over. It was a mighty deed."

Limbreth cleared her throat. "That you note a humble deed touches this ax-maid." She shifted her eyes to Tordug, who winked in approval that she'd gotten in a timely, traditional response. She pressed her lips together tightly. Humble indeed! Desperate to escape, not mighty. "But it cannot be defeated. We must leave ere it returns."

Fafwe nodded and grinned, his gaze shifting between Limbreth and Tordug. "You've had a good tutor." The officer turned to his men. "Alright, enough staring at the pretty ax-maid. Let's get these bodies over the side and tend the wounded we have."

The dead Rokans were heaved over the wall while the wounded were tended. Most bore only minor wounds. Limbreth regained her swords, cleaned, and sheathed them with help. She lent what assistance her pained arm allowed. Two dwarves lay dead, and they were wrapped in their cloaks and carried to a collapsed shelter, where the others constructed hasty cairns for them and spoke prayers for their dead. Limbreth learned the words in case she ever needed them.

The troop soon departed in earnest with a scout sent ahead. But the squad traveled slower with the wounded. Limbreth walked with her head down until they found a shelter well after dark. She lay staring at the fire while the wounded groaned in fitful sleep. *This isn't what I expected.* She wiped a tear and hoped Athson fared better than her. She'd fought poorly, hesitantly even, before the Bane attacked. Her faced flushed with heat. First the Banshee, now this. *I'm no help like this. Not at all.*

Limbreth woke from fitful sleep later, her dreams interrupted by the Bane looming out of the darkness. Her teeth chattered as she woke but only from the dream. She rolled onto her back and stared at the low beams half-hidden in the fading firelight. *I'm useless this way, princess or not. I can't help Tordug or the others like this.*

She frowned. But that was it. She was a princess, used to learning etiquette and the ways of diplomacy. She hated those duties, but she had skill that

Tordug and the others needed. She smiled. She did have that experience, and she'd use it to learn from Tordug and help get them what they needed if necessary. If only she could evade the Bane. But she'd try—for Athson.

CHAPTER ELEVEN

Athson's chest heaved, and he gasped. "Father."

Ath shifted at his voice. "Is that you, Athson? Run! Don't let him—"

Corgren slapped Ath. "Silence!"

Athson hefted his sword. "Do that again, and I'll kill you."

The wizard displayed a cruel grin. "One step, ranger, and he'll die." He motioned with his hand, and the hobgoblin held a dagger at Ath's throat.

Athson's breath returned, but his stomach boiled and his mind seethed. "I'll kill you both with arrows." His low growl carried across the bowl-shaped depression in the rock.

"You're good but not that good." The wizard drew a wolf-head dagger. "We'll kill him either way."

Athson tightened and loosened his grip on his weapons. He could do it. Maybe. Where was Gweld when he needed him? "What do you want? You brought me here to talk."

Corgren's laugh rolled with mockery. "You see, wretch? He's smarter than you. Maybe he'll get right what you and you traitorous ancestors didn't." He motioned to Athson with his free hand. "You know what I want. Get it, and he lives."

Traitors? This was news. Athson's vision narrowed with his frown. "What do you mean?"

"You know what I mean." He leaned toward Athson's father. "Maybe he's not so smart."

Ath opened his mouth, but the hobgoblin yanked his head back and pressed the blade closer. The blind man shut his mouth.

Athson stared. His father was a shell of the man in his memory. Scarred eye sockets. His face smudged with dirt and covered with a patchy beard. His body gaunt, drained of vitality.

Athson ground his teeth. "I should kill you regardless, wizard, right now. The world would be rid of a monster like you!" He cared nothing for elvish views on revenge in that moment. But he needed something more. "What do you mean 'traitors'?"

"My master and I can give and take away. Want a taste of what you can have?" Corgren cupped has hand over one of Ath's eye sockets and uttered a spell. Green mage-fire flared beneath the wizard's fingers. Ath sat up stiff with a cry, and his face trembled.

Athson took a step forward. "Stop it, or I'll—"

The troll pressed the knifepoint at Ath's throat. Blood dripped from his neck.

Athson halted.

Corgren grimaced with effort until the flare of his magic faded. The wizard slowly removed his hand to reveal a healthy eye in place of a ruined socket.

Ath's good eye blinked, and he gasped. "I can see!" He gaped for a moment at Athson and then grinned, revealing chipped and yellowed teeth. "You've grown into a fine—"

Corgren pulled Ath's head back. "Enough talk!" The wizard smiled at Athson. "A down-payment for the bow." He raised a single finger. "But remember it doesn't have to be permanent." His grin faded into a sneer. "I can make him suffer."

Athson gaped at his father's eye. A miracle from this evil bastard? His eyes narrowed. "What game do you play? Once you have the bow, you'll kill us!" His face flushed hot, and his fists trembled around his weapons.

Corgren's sneer grew, and his gaze flicked ever so slightly before he blinked.

"Answer me!" Athson took a step forward despite the hobgoblin's threat

CHAPTER ELEVEN

to his father.

Voices shouted behind Athson, back on the trail.

Corgren's gaze shifted over Athson's shoulder and back to him. "My time is short. Your family is rotten like a dying tree. Get the bow and bring it to me at the Funnel. Maybe you'll get a reward. We shall meet again. You know the place."

An arrow sliced out of the darkness. The feathers brushed Athson's cheek in passing. It flew past Corgren and missed him by less than an arrow's vane.

Corgren's sneer flashed. "Nice try!" He raised his hand, spoke several harsh words Athson didn't understand, and snapped his fingers. The wizard, Athson's father, and the troll swirled in tattered shadow and sudden wind, then vanished.

Light faded in the depression. Athson paced. Traitors? He should have killed the wizard. His father was dead regardless. His father's ragged image remained etched in his mind. But he needed to save him if possible, to take him to a better life with the elves.

Voices echoed over the rock Athson had traversed and footsteps sounded among the fir trees. Spark slipped into the shadows and growled. Athson had never realized the mountain hound stood beside him. Tree limbs rustled, and he held his sword on guard. Could Spark have helped? Maybe.

Gweld emerged from the scrubby pine trees on the rock.

Athson sheathed his sword. "A little late. I had Corgren here, but there was a hobgoblin holding a knife to my father's throat. How'd you miss?" Athson chewed at his cheek in thought. Corgren had moved his eyes when he threatened to kill Ath anyway. Did he see Spark? Athson glanced at the dog. An interesting thought. Maybe next time he'd see if Spark would do something.

"What? Here?" Gweld jumped into the bowl. "Your father is alive? I had a bad angle with you in the way, or I could have killed the wizard. I didn't see much else. If I'd have known your father was there I would have taken more care."

Athson grimaced. And his father had an eye back! *Doubt that lasts or that he gets the other one.* Athson nodded as he moved toward the elf. "Yes, both he and Corgren are alive. I should have killed him. Why didn't you follow?"

Gweld motioned to the forms of dwarves among the trees. "We had our hands a little full of those trolls. But they ran away not long after you chased Corgren. If you'd waited, I could have helped."

Athson brushed past the elf and ground his teeth. Wait? Never! Next time he saw Corgren, that wizard was dead! "This little trek of Hastra's ends. I'm going to find my father."

Gweld laid a hand on his shoulder. "You can't."

Athson wheeled, almost striking an arm of his own bow against Gweld's. "I have to, or they'll kill him."

"You need the bow, and Hastra can get you there. Along with the rest of us."

Athson stepped back and looked around. *This is from that dream after Chokkra. He jumped in here and said the same thing.* Dream and reality merged. Should he listen? "I can rescue him without the bow. It's probably rotted away in this Howart's Cave." Athson waved his hand in angry dismissal, more at the fact that he had dreamed this than anything else. He wanted to kick something.

Gweld shook his head. "You won't find him without the bow. Hastra's correct. The bow will draw them."

Athson looked away in thought. The word *traitors* echoed from his tense conversation with the wizard. He needed more information, and Hastra likely had it. He sighed and ran a hand through his hair. "Alright, I'll stay, at least as far as these dwarves go. I'll listen to her. But I'll make my own decision then. Will you go with me, whatever I decide?"

Gweld hesitated. "Athson, I'm your friend. We'll do what's necessary."

Ingwe pushed through the firs. "What's all this? Some elf poetry needed for a few trolls in the night? Let's get moving before more turn up, shove an apple in our mouths, and truss us up for Magdronu's meal."

Ralda strode out of the trees and offered his hand.

Athson climbed out of the rock bowl with the giant's help, and Gweld soon followed. Athson doubted there are more trolls near. Corgren just

CHAPTER ELEVEN

wanted to taunt him into getting the bow. He hesitated. "I wonder how Corgren found us."

Gweld shrugged. "Likely a report from those Rokans or their mages. Someone probably spotted our escape."

Ingwe motioned his squad away. "Likely we've been spotted by the Dragon." He motioned to Athson. "Had his eye on this one since he escaped the sacrifice."

Athson followed the dwarves through the trees. "If he's watching, it's because they want the bow." He glanced skyward through the tree limbs. No dark shape passed overhead, as in his vision back at Eagle's Aerie. He followed Gweld, Ralda, and dwarves onto the path. Athson's memories trailed him like ghosts, like that Bane.

But Spark walked with his hackles raised.

~~~~~~~

Magic swirled them from the illusion of lights in the bowl of stone into the stony dark of Chokkra. Corgren chuckled and pushed past Ath. "You played your part well, traitor." He motioned to the hobgoblin and added in troll tongue, "Bring him. Have the horns blown for the captains to assemble."

Ath hobbled, the clink of his chains marking each halting step.

"Your son will do what's required of him now. He'll bring the bow to us for your sake." Corgren laughed over his shoulder. "He dances like a puppet on a string in a child's farce at a fair. He's Magdronu's toy now."

An odd silence followed Corgren. "What no defiant reply for me? Stunned to see your son so close?

Ath didn't answer, just followed on the chain.

Corgren wheeled and grabbed Ath by the throat. "Consider this payment for your help after the cave-in. Defy me, and I'll take it back!" Corgren secured the chain in the passage with a few words of magic and he entered his chambers. He needed the troll captains to set his plans in motion. Pity he'd left even a few of his other trolls behind him. Numbers were needed soon. But if they survived they'd return. Corgren snorted. Most likely they'd get themselves killed.

Ath's chains clinked as he moved outside.

A piteous fool there. Soft too. Corgren stroked the beard he now grew. It was a near thing, that Ath had saved him from the cave-in, chain or not. *You wouldn't have saved such an implacable enemy as yourself.* Corgren narrowed his eyes. Ath had a reason. Was it noble forgiveness? He doubted that. The man's family line lay under a curse. No, the wretch had a plan—or thought he did. Corgren arched a curious eyebrow and peaked out his door as trolls approached from farther along the passage. Ath counted the links in his chain and muttered aimless names. He displayed a half-cracked mind. He bore watching. Corgren determined to keep the one-eyed man close, and all the more now, with that single eye. That way he'd give Ath a quick end for saving his life. When the time came.

Trolls swaggered past the chained man and spat on him. But when they entered Corgren's chambers, they slouched in deference. Corgren wanted to purr like his master. Proper respect. When they'd all entered, Corgren shut his door and spoke troll tongue.

"Prepare all the companies. We begin the march through the Neath—likely in a matter of weeks."

He smiled as the trolls laughed. Magdronu had passed the subtlest of signals in how he missed with the arrow. They were to invade Auguron Forest when the arrow arrived and they possessed the bow. And they'd burn the city like that village ten years ago.

~ ~ ~ ~ ~ ~ ~ ~

Corgren came later and released Ath's chain. "Take him to a cell and guard him well."

Hobgoblins dragged Ath down the passage and made several turns before they hurled Ath into an old storage room and ran his chain through an old iron ring set into the wall. The door slammed, and the lock *clicked*.

His mind whirled. After years of darkness, real light in his mind. Just one eye, but something. Images flashed like treasure. Athson. It was really him! Trees in the night. Firelight. Even the dark confines where Corgren took him stood out like gold. He wept his sudden joy and adjusted the rag around his head over his missing eye.

Ath's breath caught. He could work faster now. Just listen and watch.

CHAPTER ELEVEN

Then work. They'd even put him in this room alone. Trolls snarled beyond the door, but he was alone here. Of course, with his sight, they couldn't just let him sit anywhere. He was no longer helpless. In the dim light from under the door, Ath gazed at his hands. Sight! He laughed in silence.

He gathered his chain and found the grooved link. Not near enough progress. He'd change that. Ath worked the rough metal from the sole of his left boot. Time to work. He would be ready when the time presented itself. Wherever it might be. His boy was alive and needed his help. He choked back a sob in his chest and rubbed the file three times before he paused and listened.

Ath worked the little file in earnest. Athson would have his help. He'd be ready when the time came. Ath sawed the file in the groove again, again, again. The chain clinked with his movement. Trolls approached outside his cell. He listened, slid the metal tool into a pocket, and waited for them to go. They were spying on him now. He rattled his chains. *Create regular sound of movement.* The shadow under the door stepped away. Ath retrieved his file. *Work faster.* Now he could. He couldn't believe Corgren's gift. Almost insane, but he had his chance.

CHAPTER TWELVE

More days passed as Fafwe led them from high rolling roads to high forest paths, where winter cold crept lower from the north. Tordug quietly tutored Limbreth in dwarven protocol. Since the Bane, she'd been far more apt. He shuddered at the memory of the Bane. He leaned close and talked out of the side of his mouth, "You felt that thing lately?" He hadn't asked in several days.

"Yes." Limbreth frowned.

Tordug clucked under his breath. "Like a stray dog."

Limbreth sniffed. "I'm sure not feeding it."

He chuckled. "Might could train it if we did." *Take the bait while the others are listening.*

She rolled her eyes and then squinted at him. "Maybe some bacon. Anyone with a scrap? I'm fresh out."

The other dwarves were nearby, and one piped up. "Ate all mine, but I'll make you a leash for your stray from my belt." The others laughed.

Limbreth hooted a moment with the dwarves, then added, "No thanks! I wouldn't want you dropping your pants and slowing us down while you waddle like a duck." She acted the scene out for them, and they laughed all the harder.

Fafwe scowled at his squad. "Cut it."

Tordug smiled. Fafwe had actually included her in that scowl. He exchanged winks with Limbreth. But she likely needed to hold her own with Duliwe—a different skill. By his reckoning, they were close. He inhaled.

CHAPTER TWELVE

She'd be ready. He frowned at his boots. She had to be, if the others weren't there yet.

Fafwe's squad ventured west into a maze of game trails. By midday, a low escarpment rose above the trees. The squad led them through stands of crowded fir until they entered a narrow where scrubby cedar grew along natural walls of stone. Here, they followed a series of switchback turns while the defile widened, climbing until they crested the bluff and found a meadow valley sprawling longer than it was wide beneath steep, wooded ridges.

Limbreth shaded her eyes against the afternoon sun. Tordug paused. Ezhandun. It had been many years since he'd hunted bear from here. He glanced back. He'd seen guards concealed up the path and back in the lower forest. Not enough men to defend this, just enough to slow a concerted force long enough to empty the valley. He sucked at his teeth and took in the village. Low, brown lumps of buildings festooned the valley below the tree line farther up the valley. Dwarves walked among those humps, some even leading a pony. He scanned the valley meadow. Other dwarves herded cattle and scattered fodder from hay bales amid patches of snow. Thin herd and few people. Tough times. He set out after the squad.

Fafwe stopped and waited for Tordug to reach him. "We'll take you to rest and inform Duliwe we have visitors."

Limbreth fell into step beside the squad leader. "Aren't there guards?"

Fafwe grinned and cast a sidelong glance at Tordug. "You passed them climbing up the narrow. And we have already passed scouts."

Tordug hid his frown behind a swipe across his mouth. Fafwe hadn't told them anything about being watched on their approach to this valley. Duliwe probably knew there were "guests" already. He spared a quick glance at Limbreth and shrugged. He'd tell her when the time came.

Limbreth pointed at the brown humps. "What are those?"

Fafwe chuckled. "Ah, you've not seen how dwarves live outside a hold. Those are houses and barns and such. This is an old settlement that once traded its wares in Chokkra." He switched to dwarvish. "Take them to the tall barn to wait. Best not march them into Duliwe without a proper report of these—uh—guests."

Tordug hid his smirk. He forgot that more than Tordug listened. He'd almost called them something else but then realized he had an ax-maid with him. *So he doesn't trust us still. This might be far tougher than I expected.* He shook his head but otherwise ignored Limbreth for the moment. *The Bane lurks somewhere near and these dwarves are as prickly as a thorn.*

As Fafwe strode away for the main settlement, the squad led them toward a larger outbuilding. The soldiers were silent in their duty, though they maintained their aloofness with Tordug and their politeness with Limbreth. *Like they just picked us up in the forest.* At a barn, they opened the doors and lit a lamp.

Limbreth ducked through the low door and stood straight beneath low rafters. Tordug followed into the mingled scents of dung and hay. An insult. Subtle, but an insult nonetheless. It was colder in here. Probably very warm when filled with animals.

Tordug swung his pack from his shoulders and sat beside her. "It won't be long." He sat on a hay bale. "Duliwe knows we're here. This is an insult. We're meant to smell up his hall." He crossed his arms. "If we didn't need them, we'd just leave."

Limbreth crossed her arms. "So this is a real dwarven welcome. Tougher than expected, eh?"

Tordug scratched at his bearded cheek. "They're careful this near Rok. It may be an old settlement, but it is hidden. They took pains to hide the roads here years ago. Still, they're not sure of you, or they'd welcome us with better surroundings."

Limbreth removed her pack. "Speaking of which. They never warned us of guards. Did you see anything of scouts?"

"Yes, but I thought you had too. No?" He chuckled. "Athson needs to teach you better tracking skills."

"Humph." Limbreth sat down. "Maybe we could wait for the others?"

"Duliwe won't wait. They'll present us as soon as he's able to see us. But they'll definitely offer you aid, even if it's not enough. Just use the correct words. But I think we'll have to stand up to him first." He shrugged and

CHAPTER TWELVE

offered a thin grin. "Us dwarves and our ways, you know."

Limbreth stood again, and began pacing and kicking straw. She eyed him like a strange cat, then sighed. "Well, the sooner the better, I suppose." She stood straighter and squared her shoulders.

She sat beside Tordug, and he patted her leg. "You're a princess, so act like one. You'll do well, gell. Let me start. He'll be angry first, and then you step in with what I taught you."

"I don't see—"

"It's our way. Just let the meeting take its natural course, and you'll win the day. After all, you have the sunny disposition of a dwarf by now." He grinned

She chuckled. "Sunny? Not with that Bane on my heels." She relaxed her stony expression into a crooked smile.

They settled in and waited. Limbreth lay flat on a hay bale. Tordug leaned back and shut his eyes.

Fafwe entered with a grunt and a gust of frigid wind at his back. Limbreth rolled off the bale. Tordug sat up and twitched an eyebrow at her. She must have fallen asleep. He sniffed. Probably did himself. He stretched like he'd just gotten out of bed and beamed as fresh a dwarven grin at the officer as he could muster.

The squad leader beckoned. "Duliwe will see you now, Tordug. Bring her if you must."

Limbreth sighed and blinked.

Tordug followed Fafwe. So, he thought her useless in this? And they were ahead of the others. Fafwe offered a respectful bow to Limbreth but squinted. "Ax-maid."

She brushed hay from her cloak. Outside, it was dusk. How long had they slept? The squad stretched outside. It must have been hours. They hauled their packs onto their shoulders and set out with Fafwe across the snowy meadow.

Tordug cleared his throat. Duliwe must've been busy, or he'd intended to throw them off somehow. His stomach rumbled. He inhaled fresh air. Or Duliwe wanted them smelling like that barn. Tordug bet on the latter.

Early stars glittered overhead, but Tordug had little time to consider their beauty, even as one flickered out of the eastern sky. The brisk night brought him to full wakefulness. Tordug leaned close to Limbreth. "Stand close to the door when we enter. I'll speak with him first. You step in later. You'll see when, if you remember the rules of honor and defending it for another. Just like at that shelter."

She nodded. "Not quite what to expect, after all you've taught me."

Tordug shot her a quick glance. "Keeping us into the night in a barn isn't what I'd expect. He doesn't want our presence widely known—yet."

Tordug's nostrils flared. Duliwe had played this well enough to hope he could send them away with a few days' food. Not hopeful at all. Tordug rubbed his palm across his thigh and swallowed a sudden lump in his throat.

They arrived all too soon at the squat door of a low-roofed building, larger than any of the other dwellings. Tordug remembered it. He'd stayed there years ago on hunting trips. He shook his head. A different time.

Fafwe opened the door and motioned them through it. "Duliwe's Hall."

Tordug strode in, and Limbreth ducked in behind him. Warmth from a cheerful fire in a central hearth brushed his cheeks. They discarded their packs by the door. Fafwe closed the door, and Limbreth slid into the shadows along the wall while Tordug stepped into the brighter glow of the fire and a few lamps. A dwarf hunched over parchments scattered on a table, his back to them. Gray strands fell on his shoulders from a crescent of hair below a gleaming bald crown.

Tordug cleared his throat and began in dwarvish. "I'd have expected a warmer greeting, even considering—"

"This is not the past, when riches flowed to every settlement." The dwarf stirred his hand over the parchments. "We're at constant war with Rokans here."

"Still, a better welcome than a barn and a nap in the cold for hours is due your—"

"You come after long years of silence in your dishonor and think you deserve a full welcome of fealty?" Duliwe pounded his fist on the table, and a candle swayed in its stand. He turned, his lips pulled into a frown, and

CHAPTER TWELVE

glared at Tordug. He stood a moment, and Tordug measured him. Several scars crossed his exposed cheeks above a beard woven in warrior's braids and festooned with trinkets of leadership. "Very well." He ducked in the barest bow of fealty possible.

Behind Tordug, Limbreth stifled her gasp. Duliwe's eyes never shifted to her. *Good, he discounts her.*

"What do you want here, bringing the memory of defeat into our meager struggles?" Duliwe stood with his hands on his hips, his feet spread apart.

Tordug assumed a similar stance, unyielding. "I've come at need from Chokkra."

Duliwe snorted. "Gone to check your sums of losses or to bury the dead?" He waited for no answer but waved his hand at Tordug and turned to lift a dented, silver goblet. "It's no matter to me what you did there. Better that you had died than come here and bring Rokans or trolls on us!"

Tordug's cheek twitched. Duliwe drank without offering anything to his liege. A slight insult, but only slight considering Tordug's lost status. "I've traveled in the company of a Withling on an errand for her. Our journey brought us here, thanks to the fortuitous help of your men in the mountains. We are in need of supplies to continue on the errand given by Elokwe." Tordug motioned the sign of reverence at his forehead.

Duliwe answered with the wisp of an answering motion. "Those laggards should have left you to die in the cold. Or to the Rokans for their sacrifices." He stepped closer. "You've been away, while we deal with the hard things, those losses."

Tordug squinted. No backing down. "I heard rumor of that over in the west. Didn't know it was so bad. My man helped bring some of the people in from that."

The other dwarf motioned to Limbreth in the shadows. "That's not a man."

"Her? She don't cow to Rokans either. She backs troll-bands down with nothing but a horse and a spare friend or two."

Duliwe sniffed and took a long drink with arched brows. "Tell me a better tale, Tordug."

"Really?" Limbreth spoke in dwarvish with a low growl and challenge in her tone. She stepped into the light.

Tordug almost smiled. Almost. *Remember, you stand in for Makwi as my champion.*

She stepped past Tordug. "You'd let an ax-maid of the death-grip freeze on a mountainside? The Lord of Chokkra too?" She motioned, palm-up, to Tordug.

Tordug paid her high honor with a flourished bow. He gazed at Duliwe and grinned.

~ ~ ~ ~ ~ ~ ~

Duliwe laughed and motioned the cup and a glance to Tordug. "You'd let this foreign gell without standing raise your honor for you?"

Limbreth snatched the cup from his hand with a slosh of wine that fell across the right side of her white leathers. She whirled, took one knee, and offered the goblet to Tordug, who took it. Before Duliwe could stir from his surprise, she rose and whirled again, drawing a sword with her left hand and holding the point to the sullen dwarf's neck. With her other hand, she drew her braid around from her back.

Duliwe's eyes widened as Limbreth's trinkets flashed in the firelight. His jaw worked, but he choked on his words.

Sheathing her sword, Limbreth ground her teeth and offered her honor to Duliwe with an ax-maid's bow and the death-grip salute—left-handed. She followed that with a champion's flourish and then stood with her arms crossed and legs apart beneath the low rafters—like royalty. "I am Limbreth, Princess of Grendon, Maid of the Ax." She lifted her left fist. "I grip death." A sudden thought caught in her mind. "I am the Silver Lady of Auguron and both Patroness and Protector of the Wayfarer on the Road. I stand with my honor, in place of Makwi-angk-tho, for Tordug, Lord of Chokkra. Honor him as you would me! Hear him!"

Duliwe stepped back and reached for the table without looking. His cheek quivered beneath the edge of his beard. He shifted his squinted gaze to Tordug. "How could you let outsiders copy our fashion and tradition without due honor? You can't just march someone in here with these

CHAPTER TWELVE

claims!"

Tordug crossed his arms. "Makwi and I pried the sword from her hand. Makwi has done so again since that time. She is worthy of the honor. Ask your officer, he's done the same. The whole squad saw her death-grip."

"What of the verse? Let's hear that!" Duliwe crossed his arms.

Tordug's voiced lowered to a growl. "Makwi still composes her honor-verse. You shall hear it when he comes—if it's ready."

Duliwe's face flushed. "Where is Makwi?"

Limbreth heard surrender in his voice.

Tordug launched into a summary of their travels without revealing all of the details about the Bow of Hart. His every statement snapped with underlying demand. He took a breath and then ended. "We have come here on the mercy of Elokwe in need to continue our journey at his will."

Limbreth suppressed a smile. Tordug's hesitation had left him. She stared at Duliwe, who hesitated. "Well? Shall we recount the story of all our scars, Duliwe? Here, I'll start!" She motioned to the repair in the left arm of her leather armor. "A troll arrow went straight through in an ambush." She held her fist forward and grinned. "But I beat them back with this arm. It is an ugly scar for one so young and pretty as I!"

Duliwe hesitated, then burst into laughter. "It seems Tordug rises in the honor and trust of his companions!" He shook his head as he poured more goblets of wine. "Few can say they have traveled with a High Champion, an ax-maid with the death-grip, and a Withling!" He handed a cup to Limbreth and raised a finger. "But these other two need to come and vouch for these tales! Until then..." He went to a knee with a grunt. "What is it you need, Lord of Chokkra? Half the village will complain, and the other half will want to throw a feast at this sight."

Limbreth sipped her cup of wine and exhaled in feigned satisfaction, covering her relief. She'd done it!

~ ~ ~ ~ ~ ~ ~

Clouds opened over the mountains, their darkened hulks backlit with bands of orange, red, and purple while snow showers drifted east into the gathering night. Athson trailed most of the dwarves, as well as Gweld and

Ralda, while they climbed a rising, narrow gorge along a switchback path. Ice festooned the rocks, so Athson stepped with care.

Spark escorted him, as he often did since Chokkra. The mountain hound almost got underfoot except he wasn't there—at least in a tangible way. Spark bounded to the next elbow-turn in the path and waited for Athson, as patient as ever.

Athson followed over the rocky terrain with weary steps, his internal debates nagging his steps. Should he even bother with this stop at Ezhandun and Hastra? He did need information about his family, if nothing else. And Hastra had that, if anyone did. Rock shifted under his boot, and he braced himself against a boulder for his next step. And there was seeing Limbreth. If only she were safe and wanted to help him, he might just go it all alone with her and Gweld.

At the turn in the path, Spark bounded ahead before he waited again. If only Athson knew with certainty that the mountain hound really existed. He yawned at the long day of travel which the dwarves assured neared its end. Some days he almost agreed with Gweld about his imagination. But then he remembered the dog biting surprised trolls that night at Marston's Station. And then Corgren had ignored Spark almost on purpose in those tense moments several days earlier. *Don't think about Corgren—or your father.* He ground his teeth and trudged toward the next turn on the winding path amid the gathering evening shadows.

They emerged at length atop a bluff with the last fingers of sunlight stroking hay fields and stands of pine decorated with snow. Athson paused a moment and viewed the area. White humps of various sizes rose in the distance. Buildings of a settlement. They'd arrived at Ezhandun at last. But had the others? He followed the dwarves and his friends along a path in the snow.

They soon arrived at a low, long building and entered a door. The scent of hay and animals greeted Athson. A barn? "What are we doing here?"

Ingwe motioned them inside. "We bring people here until we're sure of them. Rest a while, and we'll report that you're with us and settle your arrangements."

CHAPTER TWELVE

Athson glanced at Ralda, who shrugged and sat against some hay bales rather than stand hunched under the low roof.

Gweld frowned and crossed his arms. "We fight with you, and this is how we're treated?"

Athson stood near Gweld while Spark sat unnoticed near Ralda. "Yes, we fought trolls with you just days ago. We helped defend the tower while everyone escaped. Isn't that good enough?"

The dwarf's gaze shifted to his men and back to Athson and Gweld. "We're careful here. Our commander makes decisions about who we accept. At least we let you keep your weapons because of the aid you gave us."

Athson's eyebrows rose. Their arms were an issue? "Well enough, then. Will you send word of our friends if they've arrived?"

The dwarf saluted them with fingers to his lips and a wave of his arm. "I'll send word." He told six of his command to stay with them as hosts and left with the others.

Athson exchanged a glance with Gweld, and they sat next to Ralda. He eyed the dwarves by the door. They seemed casual, speaking dwarvish tongue, but they were guards, no matter what word was used. He turned his head slightly and listened. Judging by the voices outside, the rest of the squad stood watch as well. He leaned close to Gweld and whispered, "What do they think we're going to do, throw off disguises and attack?"

Gweld sighed. "It rankles me too, but it's their way, not ours. Best we let them work out their details—"

The buzz of Ralda's snoring interrupted their conversation. The giant's head nodded and he rubbed his eyes where he sat against the stacked bales of hay. He propped his head against his hands.

Athson yawned and glanced at Gweld. "That was fast."

Gweld shrugged, and an exasperated expression flashed across his features. The elf shifted after several minutes passed, got up, and stalked over to the doors. He looked at Athson. "I'll watch." He gripped his elven long knife, but the dwarves on guard never reacted.

Athson yawned again and waved his agreement to the elf. He found a spot for his own head, and his eyes drooped, the smell of hay in his nostrils. Something warm nestled against him, and his sleep-fluttering eyes registered Spark close. *He's never that close. Maybe he's cold.*

Raised voices drew Athson awake with a start. Beside him, Ralda's snoring paused and then continued. He motioned ranger-style to Gweld. 'How long?'

The elf returned the motion. 'Few minutes.'

Athson frowned. It had felt like hours. The sound of a familiar voice drew his furrowed brow into an arch. Was that Limbreth?

"I don't care who said what, my friends are in there, and I'm here to see them."

Athson stood, his legs stiff, and nudged the snores out of Ralda.

"What?" The giant reached for his staff.

"We've got visitors." Athson moved toward the door.

A fist thumped on the barn door. "Open up, or I'll start using these thick heads out here to batter it down." The dwarves outside chuckled at the threat.

The guards inside hesitated.

Gweld sighed. "Look, we're not prisoners, are we?"

The dwarves shrugged and glanced at each other.

Athson cleared his throat. "Just let her in. You know her."

Two of the guards drew the bar and pulled the door open.

Limbreth, wearing a white fur cloak, swept inside like she owned the barn. The cold breath of early evening air on her heels cleared the sleep from Athson's head as much as the sight of her. Behind him, Ralda muttered and stood. Limbreth's gaze took in the dimly lit barn with a grimace that widened to a sudden smile like a sunny day when she recognized Athson. She covered three quick strides in a heartbeat and staggered him with a hug and an earnest kiss. His head spun anew but not from injury. Limbreth drew back from the embrace and punched at him with a grin. "That's what you get for going to fight when you should have left with me and Tordug."

Athson chuckled. "What? And miss all the fun at that tower door?"

She laughed and turned to the dwarves nearby. "He'll grow a dwarven beard before long!"

CHAPTER TWELVE

The guards laughed, and one replied, "He's made a start at least. But he needs a few knots and braids yet."

As she turned back, Athson fingered the edge of her snow-white cloak. "Where did this come from?"

"A gift of warmth from Duliwe, who leads these dwarves." Limbreth pulled the fur close about her and stroked it.

Athson's breath caught for a moment at the sight of her. "It suits you well." He imagined her sprawled on it, her skin aglow in firelight. His cheeks warmed, and he gazed at his boots. That kiss had warmed his chill.

When he lifted his gaze, Limbreth displayed a sly smile with one eyebrow raised, hands on hips. "Suits me, eh?"

He swallowed. Had she read his thoughts? His cheeks flushed so much, he expected them to light and heat the barn. But she seemed to welcome the thought. He scratched the back of his neck. "More than suits you, I guess. It looks good on you."

One of the guardsmen muttered, "Bold, isn't he?" The others snickered.

Athson cleared his throat, and now Limbreth's cheeks flushed in the lamplight. *Easy.* He needed to focus on what was important. But weren't they important? The sudden memory of his father's ruined, haggard face wiped away his smile. Lucky for him, making that choice to defend the door. He'd have never seen his father otherwise. Maybe. He lowered his voice. "We've news."

Limbreth's smile melted, but the embers of her ardor lingered a moment on her cheeks. "As do I, but yours seems the weightier by your expression." She lifted her hand toward his face but drew it back, aware of their dwarven audience.

He motioned her toward Ralda. The guardsmen closed the door as the two of them stepped into the depths of the barn. Gweld joined them. Spark bared his fangs but remained silent.

Athson grasped Limbreth's gloved hand. "I've found my father."

"You have? Where? Is he here?" She glanced around.

Athson shook his head. "No, I've only seen him. Briefly. But he's alive. And so's Corgren." He and Gweld related their story to Limbreth, whose face grew stern. Athson ended as he ground his teeth. "I'll find him if I can—and that wizard." He'd see Corgren dead for his crimes, along with that Domikyas, if he ever caught him.

"Where are they now?"

Athson shrugged. "Don't know, but I need to hunt Corgren down and find my father. But there's more." He needed space to gauge her support. He touched Gweld's arm. "Excuse us a few minutes." Gweld and Ralda stepped back as Athson led Limbreth into a darkened corner.

One of the dwarves called out with a laugh, "Shall we clear the barn for you, ax-maid?"

Limbreth waved her arm dismissively. "Oh, go dice with a bear!"

The dwarves chuckled but turned to talk among themselves.

Spark followed and lay nearby, as if he guarded them. Good old Spark.

Back by a stall, Limbreth lowered her voice and stood close. "What else is there?"

Athson's face twitched as a lump rose in his throat and he fought down a sob. All the loss of his years rose in a wave. He wrapped his arms around her in a sudden, tight embrace. He sniffed and ignored the dwarves muttering and chuckling. She held him in return, seeming to sense his jumble of emotions. At last, he drew back. "I must find him. I don't know how. Will you help me?" The emotion in his voice surprised him.

Limbreth watched him, her concern displayed in her eyes. "Athson, I'll stand with you. You know that. But how can we find them?"

"Hastra, is she here yet? She spoke of a way back at the tower. She wants me to get the bow so they'll come to me. Gweld thinks I should go along with her plan."

Limbreth wet her lips in thought and shook her head. "No, Hastra and Makwi aren't here yet, and there's some concern about that. She mentioned she knew where the bow was, but I know nothing of the details."

"She heard me speak of a place, Howart's Cave, where my father went hunting. Depenburgh was sacked while he was away. She thinks my father hid it there. If that's true, why doesn't Corgren get it himself?"

"I don't know. Maybe Eloch holds them back, since there's a prophecy

CHAPTER TWELVE

involved. But both Hastra and Gweld seem well reasoned in this." Her hands brushed along the soft fur of her cloak, and she cast him a speculative glance. "You're the hunter, but perhaps the best way to catch the bear is to use bait."

His stomach tightened. "Meaning me." It might well be the best way to find them. Athson sighed. "I think so too, but I just don't trust Hastra's judgment. I'd rather just go after Corgren." He gripped his sword hilt tightly and clenched his jaw for a moment.

Limbreth lowered her gaze and murmured, "I—I don't like that she wouldn't let us go with you back in Chokkra." She lifted her head and fixed him with a steady gaze. "Gweld and I should have been able to help you."

Athson nodded. "I wish you both had been there. But it was a narrow thing to escape as it was. I fear she may have been right, much as I hate to admit it. Still, I fear she's used me—us"—he waved his arms to include the others in the barn—"for her own ends. Whatever that is. I want to start at daylight, get supplies, and head out with or without her."

Limbreth shook her head. "It's not so simple." She brushed his thin cloak. "We need clothes for the journey suitable to traveling the mountains in addition to supplies and rest. I've been able to secure temporary help as an ax-maid of the death-grip." She lifted her chin with smile of pride as she stroked the trinket woven dwarf-style into her braid. "But at the moment, it only goes so far, since Tordug's honor is still low among these insane dwarves. We need Hastra and Makwi both to really get what we need."

"I don't understand. Shouldn't your word and influence be enough?"

"Yes, it is, but they need confirmation from Hastra and Makwi. Makwi most."

"Well, I guess that makes some sense, but still..."

Limbreth stepped closer and glanced at the dwarves at the door. "You don't understand. Makwi's a dwarven champion, and they'll respect that as well as the word of a Withling that I'm who Tordug claims. Makwi has high honor. Tordug tries to distance his own from Makwi."

"I know the dwarves blame Tordug for Chokkra, but why distance his honor like that?"

"Makwi is heir to Chokkra too. He's Tordug's son."

"Really?" He hadn't seen that coming. Athson rubbed his chin. But it all made sense—obvious sense, now that he thought about it. Why else would an honored dwarf serve a dishonored one?

Limbreth nodded in answer to Athson's question. "Tordug's honor is damaged so much that they won't listen to him except because of me—and Makwi and Hastra, when they arrive. I think I agree that getting the Bow of Hart means rescuing your father, Athson, but we'll have to wait this out."

Athson sighed and paced a few steps in thought before he faced Limbreth. "It seems I'm constrained. But then, I need to talk to Hastra. We didn't finish at the tower, and I still need more information from her about my family."

"Such as?"

"Such as why my family is considered traitorous by Rokans."

~ ~ ~ ~ ~ ~ ~

The wind dropped, and snow brushed their faces as Hastra followed Makwi along the darkened dwarf road. They discovered a guard along the way, who directed them to a half-dilapidated shelter squatting in the crook of a rock formation. They slept out of the wind for several hours, though a crumbling wall and the gaping hole in the roof afforded them little warmth.

Hastra shut her eyes to the cold. She'd slept in worse places over the years. What was needed was given. Even that message, though she understood little of her sudden unction to bring these lost Withlings back in the fold. She snorted. Wolves among sheep. Just like at Withling's Watch. She tremored. She found the thought more chilling than the cold. Her thoughts blurred into sleep.

The dwarven squad stirred and woke Hastra hours later. She yawned and stretched as she ate some dwarven travel meat. She arched her brow at first taste. Sweetened? Usually it tasted more salty.

Makwi entered the shelter and shook snow from his cloak. He tugged his beard. "The scout says Rokans are coming, fast-marching. Better go and eat on the road."

Hastra stood and grabbed her pack, as did the rest of the dwarven squad.

CHAPTER TWELVE

"They're coming in this weather? I'd hoped..." Her voice trailed into her thoughts. She'd hoped they'd listen to the message and at least turn back.

Makwi hefted his pack and hesitated at the door, his thumbs hooked in his belt as the other dwarves marched out. "That message must've just made 'em mad."

Hastra paused a moment. "'It was Eloch's wish, though we may little understand it now.'" She pushed past the dwarven champion and trudged onto the road.

Shouts carried on the wind. Hastra peered over her shoulder. It was still too dark to see. She glanced east over ranks of valleys and squat ridges where a sliver of pale light glimmered with the promise of a new day. She shook her head. A long day of walking and dodging Rokans lay ahead. She bumped into a dwarf. "Excuse me. I wasn't watching." She wasn't herself, not since Grendon. Certainly not since leaving Auguron. She felt it in her energy for even her service with healing and such. How long would Eloch's blessing last? To the very end of this mission with the bow? She pulled her hood over her head and trudged after the others. What would be needed would be given in proper measure.

"Hurry, Withling! They must've marched all night." The dwarf pulled her along.

Makwi slithered into a crag and winked. "I'll take care of their scouts. Hurry on."

A lump formed in Hastra's throat, but she managed a nod. *He's brave and trying to live down his father.* "Don't linger long. I'll need you." *We all rely on you more than we should.* She turned and hobbled after the squad. No sense in hovering. Makwi could take care of himself. She tucked wisps of flailing hair in her hood, shifted her pack, and shuffled through the windswept snow.

It wasn't long before Makwi jogged past Hastra with a motion for her to follow him. He found Chertug and stopped him. "Got the scout. But he laughed as he died and said we're trapped regardless." The champion turned his attention to Hastra. "He also carried that other scout's head. Said it was the sisters' reply. I left my own message for the Rokans, though."

The other dwarf stroked his beard a moment in thought. "You say trapped? How? We're far from intersecting roads."

Hastra pushed closer. "Those mages can likely use magic to travel. It costs them, but the Dragon seems to be replenishing the powers bestowed on them with all these sacrifices."

Chertug crossed his arms and stared at his feet. "They could have soldiers ahead and behind."

Makwi nodded. "They aren't too far behind at the moment. But if we flee without looking ahead, we may find ourselves surprised. Truthfully, I don't think that scout meant to tell me, but he wasn't thinking clearly when he died." He turned his head and spat.

Snow swirled between them on a sudden gust. Hastra cocked her head. "What was needed was given, though I dislike killing these Rokans." She shrugged. "Sometimes our choices lead to bad ends."

Chertug motioned his men into a march. "Let's discuss this as we go. Get a scout ahead." One dwarf surged into the lead. Chertug drew his ax from the loop on his belt. "So do we find a defensible position and fight, or do we surprise the foe ahead or behind, so as to lessen the numbers we face?"

Makwi hefted his own ax. "We've only twenty-five in our number. I've not found out how many trail us, but I think they mean to stop us with a smaller force ahead and crush us from the rear. They seem to be holding back for now. I say we ambush the ambushers and clear our escape. We've not got the numbers to stand and fight."

Chertug coughed. "I don't think these Rokans are experienced with fighting on these roads, nor at these heights. But we've no shields among us to march in ranks and push them back. We'll have to stay on the mountain side of the road when the attack comes." He turned to his men. "Stay to the right and expect an attack ahead. May be a Rokan mage with them. That one's for the Withling."

Hastra sighed, her breath ghosting in the cold air. For her? What could she do against spells? She mumbled her prayers and calmed her nerves. She ended with a muttered, "What is needed is given." The dwarves around her spoke the same words in answer. Maybe they understood she was just a

CHAPTER TWELVE

mystic and no fighter.

Their scout signaled the way clear beyond a shoulder of the mountain. They rounded the sharp, blind turn and followed the road into a deep horseshoe bend between two spreading arms of rock that rose and fell in a sheer cliff.

Makwi called to Chertug, "Best we hurry or be exposed as we cross to the far side." He pointed to the sharp turn across the distance from them farther south.

Hastra wished for a bridge. The pace picked up, and she hurried with them, lest their pursuit spot them before they exited the turn. At times, Hastra found she held her breath. Were the Rokans close? Their scouts hustled ahead and through the deep turn. She glanced skyward as the wind blew snow in her face.

"Here and up there." She turned her gaze to Makwi. He pointed out crags.

"What?" She passed one of the cracks in the rock, wide enough for one or two of them to squeeze into but deep enough for several people.

"We can take cover in them if necessary." Makwi moved ahead, looking for more hiding places.

Then Hastra understood, as their scouts trotted for the far turn out of this horseshoe. The scouts wound around several slight curves in the road. Makwi understood their predicament. They were exposed here from either point, especially to arrows. Thunder rumbled along the cliffs about them. Hastra bit her lip and watched the scouts lope toward the approaching point. They were so close. They were going to make it. Her stomach clenched.

The scouts closed to within a hundred paces of the point. A figure stepped around the point, the wind tugging at its dark cloak. The two scouts hesitated. Fire leapt from the stranger's hand.

Hastra gasped and clutched at her old wound, a sudden lump in her throat.

The mage-fire rolled through the snow and wind. The scouts flattened themselves against the rising rock. The fire passed them and smote the edge of a slight outcrop of rock, but part of it kept churning toward them.

Hastra stared. One of the dwarves struggled with his flaming cloak. His beard caught in the flames as he staggered back into the middle of the road.

Another ball of flame rolled toward him. It engulfed him, and he fell over the wall, trailing smoke and fire.

"Back against the rock! Hold your cloaks still in the wind!" Everyone shrank against the rock on their right. The first attack *whooshed* past them and struck farther down the horseshoe bend. Hastra risked a glance. The second spell struck the mountainside farther away. *Boom.* The flames whirled away on the wind.

The mage walked down the dwarven road with a casual stroll. The second scout shouted and charged from hiding. The mage halted, wisps of long hair whipping from under the hood that hid the face.

Hastra squinted. She'd wager it was one of the Beleesh sisters. Betrayers! *There was mercy for them if they'd accepted.* The unction from Eloch stood Hastra straight. She'd offered mercy, but Eloch withdrew it now.

Flame, smaller and more direct, sprouted from the mage's gloved hand at the attacking dwarf. The scout fell into a rolling drop under the smaller attack. Rokans rounded the point behind. The scout came to his feet and took a second, smaller ball of mage-flame in the chest, throwing him back engulfed in tongues of fire. He struck the mountainside and tumbled along it before crashing onto the road. His burning hands beat feebly at the consuming conflagration.

Bam!

The roadway shook, and Hastra fell to her knees. Flame rolled among them. Dwarves howled and beat at sudden flames. She searched for the source of the other attack.

Chertug yanked off his smoldering cloak. "Into the crags!" He pointed the opposite direction. "Rokans!"

Hastra's spinning head cleared enough that her eyes found the Rokans and two mages casting fire as they rounded the northern point. She scrambled for a crack in the rock. Dwarves dove for cover behind the retaining wall. Hastra's mind registered only a few singes from the last attack. But more flames fell among them. Dwarves screamed and whirled amid flame. Hastra covered her face with her arms to ward off the heat.

They were trapped!

CHAPTER THIRTEEN

Hastra recoiled from an incoming blast of fire that slammed into the mountain. Shards of rock and ice showered her and the dwarves with her. She struggled to her feet, her ears ringing. Dwarves screamed, rolling in fire, and a few fell over the retaining wall. Others squatted at the wall. She spotted a burned dwarf and lunged for him. She must help. But the soldier lay dead, a charred husk.

Hands grabbed her and hauled her into a narrow crag.

Boom! More fire slammed into them outside.

"Makwi, I—" Hastra broke the grasp on her and turned, but it wasn't Makwi. A dwarf she recognized nodded, a streak of scorched flesh on his cheek.

"Withling, get down. If fire strikes near, it might reach us." He edged back and squatted.

Hastra knelt as a few more dwarves squirmed into the crag. "Have you seen Makwi?"

"No, Withling, I've not seen him." He drew his dagger with a grimace. "Lost my ax."

Hastra glanced at the others. "Makwi?" They shook their heads.

Boom! Fire slammed their refuge and boiled inside. They fell on the rough stone as heat blasted them. Someone beat on her pack, putting out a fire.

Hastra's arms tingled, and an urgent prayer built in her chest and mind. "Out of the way!" She lunged for the road beyond the entrance.

The dwarves grabbed at her arms. "No, Withling, you'll die!"

"Release me!" Her voice rang in the stony crack, and the dwarves let go. She stumbled onto the road and out of hiding. Fire rolled toward them again. She raised her hands and cried in her prayer language. Wind gusted down the mountainside behind her and into the horseshoe ravine, blowing out the magic attack. She screamed again.

Crack! Light flashed among the Rokans to either side.

Hastra flinched and squeezed her eyes shut at the blinding light. For a few moments, she heard only her own breathing, then the roar of wind in her ears followed by the groans of wounded dwarves. She stumbled back, bracing herself against the rough mountainside, and gasped.

No more fire exploded around them.

Her vision cleared some, and she glimpsed smoke rising among the Rokans at each end of the ravine. Figures in black cloaks struggled to their feet. The two on the left leaned against each other, while the one on the right braced against the wall. Rokan soldiers scrambled to their feet.

The wind roared and splayed Hastra's cloak wide. She swallowed and recovered her balance. *They've been offered mercy. Tell them to flee.* Hastra cleared her throat and whispered to the wind, "Be still." The wind fell silent and still along the mountainside. She spoke, and her words reverberated in the chasm. "You've been offered your mercy. If you won't have it, then flee or die this day."

Rock and snow fell in clumps from higher up at her amplified voice. Her skin tingled, and she raised her arms again.

One of the mages on the left, while holding the other mage upright, raised a hand, and Hastra heard the words of a spell across the distance. Darkness like Magdronu's wings wrapped around the mages and their soldiers. When it cleared, they were gone.

Along the southern arm of the road, the remaining mage hesitated with a cocked head. Hastra's eyes narrowed, prepared to shout her command to the elements, as the mage drew back her hood. It was one of the Beleesh sisters. But which one? Hastra couldn't be sure across the distance, but her gaze locked with that of the fallen Withling across the way.

A Rokan spoke to the fallen Withling, and the Beleesh sister nodded

CHAPTER THIRTEEN

without turning her head away. The words of her spell were lost on the wind and distance. The same tattered darkness like dragon's wings enfolded their foe and whirled them away.

The tingling in Hastra's arms subsided, and the wind roared around her.

Hastra glanced further along the road. Another figure stood there now. Hastra tensed. Nothing was given. She waited and the other person tugged the wide, floppy brim of his hat. She blinked and the stranger no longer stood in the road. Withling or mage? She grunted and shook her head at the question. But the hat was familiar from her past. And likely not Eloch. So maybe another Withling helped her and her friends all those years ago. Best see to the injured. Hastra kneeled beside a groaning dwarf.

Dwarves crawled from the cracks on the road. Hastra touched the wounded dwarf, who tremored from the shock of burns. With a light touch, she followed the unction of Eloch and prayed for the bearded soldier, and his burns subsided into the pink of newly healed skin. She recognized him as one of those saved with Athson, Makwi, and Ralda. "I don't know if you'll bear scars or not," she told him.

The dwarf sighed as his pain subsided. "Life's hard, Withling, and scars are but the marks to prove the tale of them."

"Well said." Hastra stood to tend to others and found Makwi kneeling by a wounded squad member. She knelt beside the champion.

Makwi glanced at her, his face scored with several burns. "Well, can't say as I've seen the like of that before." He dipped his head in deference. "What is needed is given."

"It is indeed." She prayed for the wounded dwarf. Her hands trembled with Eloch's gifting.

When she finished, Hastra found Chertug standing beside her, his arm seared through the leather. "Withling, you've Elokwe's gift and that's no doubt. But they deserved no mercy."

Hastra laid a hand on the dwarf and the other on Makwi. "Eloch would have mercy on them all, if they'd answer his call to leave their master. There's mercy for your wounds always. Would you have that withdrawn from you? It is offered to all, and to withhold from one is to withhold from all." She prayed, and the two dwarves were healed of their wounds. She spoke again. "I wish the lightning had not been required, and I fear that their wounds widen the gulf between them and their former state. But mercy is there for them, even if it is hard at times." She recalled the hesitant sister. Would that one turn back from her evil?

Hastra went to the others and prayed for their healing, several more being among those she'd healed just days earlier. They checked their packs for fire damage as rock and snow trickled from above, loosened from Hastra's booming words.

Chertug ordered the eight dead dwarves laid to rest within the crags of their refuge. "We'll see to them when a relief is sent back."

A sudden crash resounded across the horseshoe ravine. Rock and snow slammed onto the northern arm of the chasm and broke off a chunk of roadway, which fell away into the abyss.

Thefwe motioned to his men and lowered his voice. "Quietly as we can now, lest more tumble on us. Grab what weapons you can, and let's move without speaking." He glanced back at the blocked roadway, where rock and snow still slid down the slope. He snorted and muttered, "That'll be a tough repair come spring."

Makwi slapped the officer's shoulder and winked at Hastra. "'It's the price of Eloch's mercy."

With those final words, they set out again, fewer in number and charred but alive. They passed burnt scores on the road where some Rokans lay dead and tossed the bodies over the side. Two dwarves volunteered to drag the dead dwarven scout back to the cracks while the rest went on.

Hastra walked past the spot where the Beleesh sister had disappeared with her magic. Who knew whether she considered Eloch's offer? Hastra inhaled and exhaled slowly. They were betrayers, and many Withlings had died at their hands. Eloch might forgive it, but could she? Hastra pulled her hood lower over her face as a few tears trickled down her cold cheeks. "What is needed is given." The dwarves around her answered. But she needed mercy for her enemies, it seemed.

~ ~ ~ ~ ~ ~ ~

CHAPTER THIRTEEN

Athson woke to a commotion and sat up in the failing darkness, grazing his head on the upper bunk. He drew his sword. Where was he? The momentary confusion passed. Ezhandun, in the officers' barracks. He cocked his head and listened. No sound of weapons or fighting. He got up with a groan. He'd slept the afternoon away. He shook his head, and beside him, Spark's pointed ears rose.

Limbreth slammed the door open and bounced into the room. "Oops! Did I wake you?"

Athson sheathed his sword. "No. What's going on? Sounds like a party."

"Hastra and Makwi have arrived."

"That's a lot of excitement for just them."

"Just them? You have to understand—Withlings are very important to dwarves, and they haven't seen one in hundreds of years. And Makwi is practically a hero among these people. C'mon, let's greet them." She waved her hand.

Spark rose and trotted her way.

"Humph!" Athson shook his head and followed the mountain hound. "I think Spark likes you. He takes your commands over mine. He's headed for the door now."

Limbreth grinned and brushed her braid over her shoulder. "He's got good taste." She crooked an eyebrow. "Or maybe it's just you."

Athson chuckled. "Yeah, it's me." He leaned close as he walked alongside her. "But let's keep talk of Spark quiet for now."

She nodded and led him out the door, where Spark waited. Along the path between rows of buildings, dwarves crowded around a group entering Duliwe's quarters. Hastra mounted the steps, followed by Makwi amid shouts and cheers. Their packs and clothing bore burn marks. They waved for a moment and then ducked into the door, where Duliwe welcomed them with a wide grin. The dwarf commander paused a moment as his gaze fell on Athson and Limbreth, and he waved them forward with a dwarven salute.

"What's that about?" Athson asked.

Limbreth returned the gesture with a half-bow as she touched her forehead with a finger. She grinned at Athson. "It's a formal acknowledgment. C'mon!" She pushed into the crowd.

Athson and Limbreth passed a dwarf woman at the fringe of the crowd who said, "A Withling, a champion, and an ax-maid with death-grip in the village! Surely our fortunes will change."

They climbed onto the porch. Gweld and Ralda soon followed, and they all entered behind Limbreth, who seemed to go where she wanted in Ezhandun. Spark squeezed past with a low rumble in his throat and trotted past the dwarven guards like he commanded them.

Within Duliwe's quarters, they were beckoned to a backroom by Tordug, whose face beamed his pleasure. As they entered, he hugged Limbreth and muttered in her ear loud enough for Athson to overhear, "Well done! With Makwi and Hastra here, he's ready to name you a queen! Imagine being a dwarven queen and a princess among men."

Athson drew up short in the doorway and snapped his gaze at them. What did Tordug say? He opened his mouth.

Limbreth crooked an eyebrow at him with a flat stare that told him nothing. "Well, go on in." She pushed him into the room and walked in like she owned it.

Athson's breath caught at the sight of Limbreth, all in white that glowed in the fire and lamplight. She exchanged glances with Tordug who gave her the slightest of noncommittal shrugs. Athson would pull the secret out of Limbreth later.

Duliwe cleared his throat after he welcomed Hastra and Makwi in dwarvish. He continued in his tongue, and Athson turned to Limbreth for help. "He says he believes my tale, now that it's confirmed by Hastra and Makwi, and he's prepared to offer us generous assistance." The dwarven leader made an odd gesture toward Tordug. Limbreth smiled broadly. "He's offered Tordug some honor. Perhaps not all that he deserves, but something restored to his name."

Athson bobbed his head in understanding and offered a soft grunt of acknowledgment. But Hastra's gaze caught his attention, her eyes glittered with the question that hung between them from their last words at the guard

CHAPTER THIRTEEN

tower. He offered her a respectful nod before he turned his head to Duliwe, who changed to the common tongue.

"We shall feast tonight, though we've no proper hall for it in Ezhandun. But first, tell us your news of the road." He motioned to Hastra and Makwi.

The Withling deferred to Makwi, who recited their adventure. When he told them that Hastra had called lightning on their enemies' heads, Athson almost choked.

Hastra patted Makwi's leg. "I hardly called lightning. What is needed..." Everyone ended, "...is given."

Duliwe saluted Hastra. "The humility of a true Withling."

As they all left the room, Athson snagged Hastra's arm in his grasp and leaned close to murmur, "We need to talk."

She returned a weary smile. "No greeting? Not pleased to see us arrived whole?"

Heat rose in Athson's face, and he almost answered with the anger that flashed in his thoughts. But she was right. Manners. Concern. What was wrong with him? He cleared his throat. "You're right. I am pleased you both arrived whole."

She answered with another dwarven gesture. "We cannot speak tonight. In the morning, we'll all meet. Right now, we must adhere to dwarven courtesy customs."

Athson released the Withling and followed the crowd over to a barn that had been converted to a gathering hall, where a meal soon arrived with ale. Gweld drank with a grimace, preferring elven wine. There were speeches and gestures given around that Athson didn't understand, but Limbreth often whispered the meanings of honor offered and received according to displayed ranks. He found himself singled out a few times and tried to reply with at least elven courtesy, which was accepted.

Once, Limbreth advised he admire Duliwe's beard knots with specific words, which he did to Duliwe's surprise and acceptance. He whispered to Limbreth, once seated again, "What did I just do?"

Limbreth wiped her chin. "You just acknowledged his rank as leader of the village and as a warrior." She answered a salute to the leader of Ezhandun with her hands. "He's very formal, according to Tordug, but I think tonight he's even more of a stickler to tradition since there are some very auspicious people here. It all boils down to us having lots of honor present while we recognize his generosity—the more correct we are, the more he's willing to sacrifice to gain honor as this community's leader."

"Oh. I'll try to be on my best behavior, then." He remembered Tordug's passing comment from earlier and touched her knee. She jumped a little. She must be ticklish. "We need to talk."

Limbreth arched an eyebrow at him. "Later. Tomorrow, when we have a chance alone."

"Fine." If she wanted to hide information, that was up to her, but he'd tried to be open with her regardless since Marston's Station. He'd wait for her timing. First, the secrets of his family, and now some from Limbreth. What next? He watched his food for a few moments and then continued eating. Best not seem discourteous about the meal. He'd still eaten mostly travel rations while in Ezhandun the last few days, so this was a good change. Limbreth grasped his hand under the table with a squeeze that he returned.

After a while, Hastra excused herself with many a courteous word in dwarvish. Athson almost envied those around him with language and custom knowledge of dwarves. It wasn't long after the Withling left that the feast ended. Limbreth, Makwi, and Tordug followed Duliwe as he left, Limbreth having warned Athson to stay put until the dwarven officers began leaving.

Athson went back to the officers' barracks with Gweld and Ralda. Tordug and Makwi slept elsewhere, and apparently Hastra and Limbreth had their own rooms due to their status among the dwarves.

Athson slept fitfully. Whenever he rolled over one way, the dwarf above interrupted his snoring and groaned. Athson glimpsed Gweld in meditation. At some point, the elf would sleep. But Spark lay right beside his bed. He saw the dog constantly now, along with the inheritance package still in his pack. Athson avoided mentioning either openly unless to Limbreth or Gweld, though the dog less to the elf, since he still believed Athson was hallucinating and needed Soul's Ease.

CHAPTER THIRTEEN

Sleep eventually enfolded him, and he woke early from a forgotten dream, urgency to find his father capturing his waking attention. He lay abed for a few spare minutes while the gray dawn brushed the room with color. Where had Corgren taken his father? The memory of several nights earlier flooded Athson's mind. He should have attacked and saved his father. Why had he done nothing? He imagined stabbing Corgren, the blade running with the wizard's blood, and standing over the dying villain only to finish him off with a slash to the throat. Athson's nostrils flared, and his heart beat in his throat. Such was Corgren's just due, regardless of the return of his father's eye. Athson rose and dressed, the grimness of his anger tight across his face and shoulders, his every move punctuated with rigidity.

He ate in the hall with Gweld and Limbreth. His silence covered them, but his anger boiled across his unspoken thoughts. A rescue needed doing. Corgren needed killing. He needed action. And Hastra wasn't going to remain in his way, no matter what she wanted of him. He chewed roughly and then stirred from his thoughts at Limbreth's touch.

She cocked her head, and her brows knitted together. "Athson? Did you hear me? Are you ill?" She reached for his fist on the table.

He relaxed his hand at her touch.

"Don't mind him." Gweld sipped his water and swallowed. "He's been in a mood since we woke. Hasn't spoken two words together."

Athson glanced at the elf. So, he'd noticed. He shifted his eyes to Limbreth. Based on her expression, his anger hardly went unnoticed no matter whether he spoke or not. "I'm just ready for—" He ran his fingers through his hair with a prolonged sigh. "I need to find him, and I'm tired of waiting, bow or not."

Limbreth started in on her food, speaking around bites. "You'll be glad to know that we'll get started on the business of supplies today. That could take a while, according to Hastra. But she wants to meet with everyone afterward."

Tension like a taut bowstring stretched in Athson. Meetings? His father had suffered all these years, and they did nothing to help? He suppressed a shout. "How long?"

"A while." Limbreth reached for his hand again and squeezed. "It won't be long. We'll get what we need and get our bearings and be off tomorrow."

He lowered his head and his voice, as dwarves sat nearby. "These dwarves waste my time. She wastes my time. I need to find him."

Limbreth stopped eating and glanced at Gweld. "Look, I know it's tough to endure, knowing he's alive. But you must understand that we can only do so much to find your father. You know that, don't you? We all want to help. Right, Gweld?"

Gweld laid a reassuring hand on Athson's shoulder. "Steady there, Athson. We'll get moving in the right direction soon enough."

Athson breathed deeply for what seemed like the first time since he woke. He spoke through a rigid jaw nonetheless. "I suppose." None of them understood his urgency. He'd lived well for years while his father suffered. Now was the time to fix all that.

The supplies took much too long for him. Athson stood away from the others while it was decided how much they were to receive in food, what clothing they needed for the trip, and how many pack animals would be given. There were few enough in the village so, honor or not, the mules were prized. Athson leaned against a wagon in a barn, arms crossed, as he stared at the cluster of people. He noticed nothing of the cold that seeped over his body while the details were discussed and dwarven ritual observed. *Limbreth's right, all these dwarves are crazy. But then, she's almost one of them now.* Limbreth flashed a timely smile at him, and he waved back, then turned his gaze to the weak sunlight thrusting through the narrow cracks between the doors.

They finally finished near noon and ate again. Athson sat silent at the end of a table at the officers' mess, seething about the time.

As the meal wound down, talk drifted to their plans. Athson tapped his foot under the table as Hastra led the discussion.

The Withling sat with her hands hidden in her lap. "I must say something before we talk more of our next destination." All eyes in their group turned to Hastra. "If anything happens to me, if I'm delayed in traveling with you, you must all continue the search for the Bow of Hart."

CHAPTER THIRTEEN

Athson leaned forward and inhaled to speak but Tordug beat him to it. "What do you mean? Are you going somewhere without us?"

Eyes narrowed, Athson watched Hastra closely. Not the question he would have asked. More like, *why are you leaving us?*

Hastra paused but a moment and then spoke. "I cannot say, except that I may not be with you at some point. But you must carry on with the search."

Ralda gaped at Hastra. Gweld's gaze shifted from face to face. The dwarves murmured in dwarvish while Limbreth listened to them with an arched brow. Athson stared at the Withling, who stared back at him.

Athson broke his glare from the Withling and watched his clenched fists. "So you're leaving for what? Another little quest? This one's failed, so you have other strings to pull elsewhere?"

The others sat, wide eyes focused on him, after he'd finished. He shouldn't have yelled. In truth, it just erupted from him. No one else understood.

He cleared his throat and lowered his tone. "I'm sorry, I didn't mean to..." What was wrong with him? "I'm leaving as soon as possible, with or without you."

Limbreth laid her hand on Athson's fist. "No one's saying we won't—"

"I'm merely saying you must go on, with or without me." Hastra's eyes flicked to Athson's hands and back.

He unclenched his fists and took a deep breath.

Hastra turned her head and took in the others. "I've spoken of this to Athson already. Back at the tower, when he was half-senseless, he mentioned his father going to Howart's Cave when Depenburgh was sacked by Corgren's trolls. I then had a vision that the bow was there. That is our destination. That's where it is." She sat back.

Ralda stirred where he hunched on the floor, still looking them in the eye. His hands flicked over his tattoos. "Who Howart?"

Hastra's face twisted for a moment, as if she was remembering something unpleasant. "He was one of the Withlings who escaped with me when our order was mostly destroyed by Corgren, his brother, and some traitors. It's where Howart lives. And likely where Ath took the bow for safekeeping."

Athson released his breath. How long had he been holding it? "How did my father know him? He never mentioned this man to me."

Hastra flipped her hands up with a slight twist of her mouth as she cocked her head. "I don't know. Perhaps Howart made himself known to Ath. Perhaps your grandfather knew him."

Athson sat back and pointed a finger at the Withling. "We've got a lot to discuss about my family." He cleared the hoarseness from his throat. She wasn't telling him everything about his family or her imminent departure. But they would talk when this meeting ended. She wouldn't duck him again. "At any rate, I've decided to go. If nothing else, for the hope of drawing Corgren and my father there." He glanced in turn at Limbreth, who flashed him a brief smile, and Gweld, who offered the barest nod of acknowledgment. "But I don't know where this cave is. We called those fens the Nightmare Marsh because of children's tales of monsters lurking there. Others called it the Long Fen, after the river it drained into."

Makwi stirred and stroked his beard. "I've been there. If Hastra doesn't know it or isn't with us, I can get us there."

It was Tordug's turn to gape now at Makwi. "How do you know of it?"

The dwarf champion shrugged. "You know I've wandered alone in past years. I took council from Howart quite by accident once."

Tordug muttered under his breath.

Athson twitched an eyebrow. Was that tension between father and son? Interesting to note their relationship differently, now that he knew about it. He fixed his gaze on Hastra again. She had likely known it all along and said nothing. He looked out the window. Withholding that tidbit concerned him little in the scheme of things. But what else of import did she withhold? He clenched his jaw and not his fists.

Gweld clasped his own hands. "Now that we have a guide, how do we get back over the mountains?"

Tordug coughed into his fist. "Easy. There's a dwarf road through a sheer pass to the other side. I won't be easy this time of year, but it never is, with all the wind and ice. Still, we can leave up the end of this valley and eventually connect to it easily enough. And with our mules and some luck with the road's condition, we should be out of the heights where snow is

CHAPTER THIRTEEN

likeliest within a few days."

Athson sat back and crossed his arms. "Snow's likely in the mountains any time of year. But if we must, we must." He turned his eyes on Limbreth. "How soon can we leave?"

Tordug clasped his hands together and then flipped them up. "I'd say an early start tomorrow would get us well into the pass by nightfall. Too bad we can't fly."

Gweld chuckled. "Crows and eagles may soar, but they carry none of our troubles." He turned to Athson with a smirk. "I'd fly if I could, though." The others laughed, and so did the elf.

"Well then, we should prepare." Tordug smacked his palms on the table and stood. The others followed his lead.

But Athson stayed seated. Limbreth released her hold on his hand and shot a glance at Hastra before she traipsed after the others. Athson watched her go and suppressed thoughts of her lying on the fur cloak.

"That went better than expected." Hastra's words drew Athson's attention from Limbreth.

He turned his head from the Withling and rubbed his suddenly warm cheeks as he gazed out the window at the snow-capped mountains. Maybe he'd find his father over those peaks. Maybe.

"You wanted to speak?"

"Yes." He waited several moments before he looked Hastra in the face. "I've many questions about all this, now that—"

"Now that you acknowledge all that you know about it? That the bow is yours?"

Athson ground his teeth. Shove his face in his faithful silence, would she? "Yes. Now that I've put all I know on the table. I kept my promises to my father never to speak of these things to anyone, but fate's drawn me in too deep. Fate's as fickle as the wind."

Hastra snorted. "Fate? Eloch's will drew you into this for your own sake—others before you sacrificed much."

Athson leaned forward with his eyes narrowed. "Yes, but you still withhold what I need to know. Since I'm going along with your plans willingly—at least for now—you owe me information."

"I'm sworn to follow Eloch, not you, Athson. If it's given me to speak of something, then I do. Nothing more, nothing less."

"Somehow I doubt that."

"Doubt what you will. But come, put to me the question and let me prove myself how I can. I've never led you astray in all this."

"But I've been astray, is that it?" He half-snarled the question. What was wrong with him today? He wanted to find his father, but this aggression wasn't necessary. "I'm sorry, Withling. I find myself upset today for some reason."

Hastra pursed her lips a moment. "Yes, understandable. But perhaps more than you realize."

"What's that supposed to mean?"

Hastra pointed at him. "You want to know of your family?"

"Yes."

"There's much there to tell."

"I've heard the word *traitor* regarding my family come from that vile wizard's lips." His heart thudded at the memory of the sneering arrogance from Corgren several nights earlier. The knife had lain at his father's throat, or he'd have killed the wizard on the spot. One hand clenched his Rokan dagger hilt at his waist, and the other hand balled into a shaking fist. He forced his hand opened with a grimace, but the other remained locked on his murderous dagger, as if a dwarven death-grip suddenly afflicted him. No. Limbreth struggled with that, no matter how much they honored her.

"There's much to tell from your family history and that of Rok and Hart. I doubt I know the whole of it. But that"—she waved her hand at his own—"that is likely the outcome of it all."

Athson turned his hand over under his doubtful gaze. She was deflecting his questions again. "How does my hand work into all this?"

Hastra chuckled and brought his attention back to her unwavering gaze. "Not your hand, but your emotion in that clenched fist."

He half-laughed and fell silent at Hastra's unchanged expression.

"I don't know everything about Corgren and his brother, Paugren, except that they grew up in southern Rok during a time when the ruling houses of Hart dominated Rok, especially that southerly territory. Somehow, they fell into the worship of Magdronu for the power. They were sent to…remove the threat of Withlings to Magdronu, and afterward they were turned on Hart, gaining influence over each of the great houses over a number of years."

"How did they do that?" The Withlings were another question for later.

Hastra shrugged. "Money or promises or simply seducing them to worship the dragon as they did. However they did it, they soon had power through these thirteen families over the whole country, and Rok took its revenge on the people and those less fortunate of the high families' kin. Yours included."

Athson's eyebrows shot toward his hairline. "My family was one of these thirteen?" He'd never heard even a breath of that in his house growing up.

"There was magic involved, no doubt, probably some vows with curses attached. The houses grew wanton in Hart under that grim influence. But there was one man who sought me out in conflicted guilt. Thayer."

Athson gaped. "He wrote the inheritance note." Finally, a whisper today rather than harsh words, snarls, and shouts.

"Yes, Thayer." Hastra's lips twitched into a smile, and she dabbed her eyes. "A brave man who fought down the base vows of magic he was born into. He fulfilled the prophecy given in front of Corgren well before that time. Thayer made the bow of his own accord, under the unction of Eloch. He—"

The door burst open, and a dwarf entered with Gweld and Tordug in tow. The elder dwarf bowed. "Forgive us, Withling, but there's news. Word has arrived from a messenger that a force of Rokans is close. I fear we must leave ere the evening is old or risk being caught in the fighting, maybe cut off from escape."

Athson stood. Not now. Just when Hastra was opening up to him? "But surely we have time to finish—"

The other dwarf bowed and spoke up, "Forgive me, Withling, but Duliwe requests your service immediately. The messenger was injured and passed out before we could get all the details from him. It's healing he needs, to save lives, if possible."

Hastra addressed Athson. "I'm called for other duty at the moment. Another time, we'll finish this." She turned her head and addressed Athson. "Just remember. Don't give them the bow. It's not for him. Of that I'm certain." She turned to the other dwarf. "Lead on. Eloch's will presses me to your need and this wounded one."

She started for the door with Tordug, Gweld, and the other dwarf following, then paused and laid her hand on Tordug's shoulder. "Remember, you must go with or without me in this. I'll catch up if I'm delayed. None of you worry for me." She turned and cast her gaze at them all, even Athson for a spare moment. She frowned. "Lead on!" Hastra left with the others.

Athson stood by the table. Now? But he needed to find his father. He paced, his breath coming in sudden gasps. She was leaving them all hanging and him the most—and his father. She cared nothing for him or his family. He pounded the table with his fist with such force that it rattled.

With his vision narrowed and his head down, Athson cut a brisk pace to the barracks to gather his things, ready all the while to throw anyone in his way aside. He approached his bed and snatched up his sword. Calm suffused him in moments. Odd, that he should have lost his temper so much today. Athson gazed at the sword. Was there magic or some other influence at work? Hastra mentioned a curse on his family. He suddenly kissed the hilt where the guard crossed it. Perhaps, but perhaps his mood changed with the sudden certainty of action in finding his father. He belted his sword onto his hip and set about packing his belongings.

~ ~ ~ ~ ~ ~ ~

Hastra followed Eftwe from the barracks as the others stirred for a hasty evening flight out of the valley. The dwarf led Hastra across the settlement in the gathering dusk. It was ill news but not unexpected. Eloch had warned her she needed to leave. This was the likely errand. She'd go and return. If they left ahead of her, she'd catch them up. But any delay for her was dangerous. This she knew. Hastra leaned into the wind and trudged through the snow.

Eftwe turned and pointed. "It's just ahead, Withling Hastra."

CHAPTER THIRTEEN

The wind gusted, and Hastra's cloak flapped in her face. She lost sight of the dwarf for a moment as she wrestled with the bothersome wind. "Yes, yes, let me settle this thing." She huffed and followed the dwarf.

Hastra rubbed a hand along each cheek in the cold. What if she fell too far behind the others? She stumbled on a hidden root in her hurry and looked back at it. The barracks lights glimmered, the figures of her companions silhouetted from her vantage point. What if it was tomorrow before she left? Well, let Eloch take care of those details. "What is needed..."

Eftwe heard her mutter and turned with a quizzical arch of an eyebrow. "Is given, Withling. Do you need something before we go in?"

She motioned the dwarf on. They could be so literal sometimes. "Just lead me to the door and then fetch me something warm to drink." Her voice was dry from their meeting and then all of Athson's questions. The Archer wanted everything his way in his anger. A curse that, and he needed to know it now. She'd tell him later.

The dwarf brought her to the door and opened it. "He is here, Withling Hastra." Eftwe stood aside so she could enter.

Inside, Duliwe hastened to her with deep furrows on his brow. "Withling, the scout, he's this way. My thanks for your coming. Your friends are preparing to leave now, yes?"

Hastra unfurled her cloak from her shoulders and turned. "Thank you, Eftwe. Now for that drink, if you please. Lead the way, Duliwe. My companions are gathering our supplies and belongings."

Eftwe saluted her status and shut the door.

Duliwe guided Hastra toward a room. "The scout's in here. I'm sorry to disturb your preparations to leave, but when he arrived in this condition, we closed the lower entrance to the valley until we know more. It's urgent. I fear the Rokans are coming in numbers. It's good that your friends are leaving, as they cannot delay our retreat from this valley."

Hastra brushed a strand of hair from her face and touched Duliwe's shoulder. "It's fine. I'm called for these occasions often. We were leaving with the morning, but this news has set us in motion sooner than that. With luck, I'll join the others as they leave. Otherwise, I'll catch them up soon enough." She entered the room.

Inside, a dwarf lay unconscious, his head bandaged. Blood had been wiped from his face but still stained his beard. Another dwarf attended him, but he moved away from the bed.

The dwarf bowed. "I'm Orstug, Withling."

Hastra nodded. "I remember. You came with Makwi, Athson, and Ralda."

"Yes, Withling." He motioned to the wounded man. "He has a similar wound to Athson's. I thought you might help, since it's likely urgent we receive his report."

She sat on the bed. "What is needed is given. I shall help as I can." Hastra touched the wounded scout's rough hand and bowed her head. She sighed and stilled her thoughts.

Someone knocked softly at the door. Orstug moved past Hastra and opened the door. "Thank you, Eftwe. Stand ready to take Withling Hastra to her friends as soon as she's ready."

Hastra frowned. She would be leaving her friends, and soon. She would miss their departure. Their safety lay in Tordug's leadership until she met them again.

"Withling."

Orstug touched her arm. Hastra stirred. Best have a sip of tea for warmth and to regain her focus. She took the offered cup and drank, then nodded. "Thank you. That's just what I needed." Warm, even if the taste was off from a hasty brewing. She shook her head. Soldiers ignored niceties for little more than necessity.

Hastra drank more before setting the cup aside. She lowered her head again and uttered her prayer. At the moment indicated, she touched the scout's head. Her voice rose and fell as she spoke in Eloch's tongue, following the mystical lead she'd learned.

After some minutes of Hastra's prayer, the scout stirred and mumbled. Hastra drew back, and the dwarf's eyes fluttered and then opened, though not fully. "Where am I?"

She squeezed the dwarf's hand and smiled. "You are safe."

"Rokans." He coughed. "Coming in force."

CHAPTER THIRTEEN

Hastra stood and waved Orstug to the bed to receive the report. She stood aside and listened as she sipped her cooling tea. She frowned as much at the sudden bitterness in the tea as for her impression from Eloch - wariness. She'd better go. Some danger may yet lurk in the valley and she needed to find her companions. Hastra drained the last of the warm drink and found some sweetness yet lingering in the dregs.

Standing, she turned for the door. "I'll leave him to your care, then. I think it best I leave quickly."

The dwarves paused. The scout offered a weak salute, and Orstug stood and bowed his respect again. "Thank you, Withling."

Hastra stepped out the door. In the other room, Eftwe scrambled to his feet. "Lead on, I must hurry," she told him.

"Yes, Withling." Eftwe snatched the door open, and cold flooded into the room.

Hastra stepped out the door. The cold night was bracing, but she needed it. Her eyelids felt heavy. She shook her head as she followed the dwarf. Time for travel, not sleep.

They turned in the fallen darkness among the low buildings. They soon left the settlement and passed into a stand of trees.

Hastra paused and steadied herself. She was so sleepy now. "This—this isn't the same way." Again, the impression—*leaving them*. Confusing thoughts swirled in her head. How long away from them? *Yes, stay wary.*

Eftwe motioned Hastra after him. "Your friends, they were leaving, no? This is quicker to catch them."

She stumbled after the dwarf and tripped over a few roots. Her heavy eyelids blinked. She shook her head amid the puff of her breath. Was Eftwe taller now? That was silly. She must be tired.

A horse whickered in the shadows in the copse. Branches snagged Hastra's cloak. "Why a horse?" Her voice sounded distant.

The dwarf waved his arm. "Come, I have a faster way for you."

Hastra followed. He was taller than she remembered. That was certain. They soon came to where two horses were tied to limbs. This wasn't right—he stood taller than she now. Hastra frowned. "What's going on?"

She swayed.

The dwarf turned, but it wasn't Eftwe who faced her. A familiar smirk flashed across his face beneath glittering eyes. "Stay still there, Hastra."

She straightened. "Paugren!" She should run for help. No! What did Eloch want? No! Run! But her feet were rooted in place among the trees. Her head nodded, and her breathing slowed.

"Now, Hastra, climb up and lay over the saddle. That's right." Paugren's hands pushed her over the horse.

She lay with her hair and hood blocking her vision. Paugren did something with her hands and then moved to the other side of the horse and fiddled with her feet. What was she going to do? *That's it, run and shout.* But she was so tired, and now she was warm.

The horse moved, and she bounced with each step.

"You can sleep now, Hastra." Paugren's voice sounded like he whispered from a distance.

Her head bobbed with the motion of the horse as they slipped into the night. She yawned and closed her eyes. Where was she going? Oh yes, away from her friends for a while. They must be careful with Rokans coming. She yawned again, and sleep engulfed her senses.

Light glimmered around Hastra in blurry scenes of trees and brush. Something snagged her hair repeatedly as the darkness receded. She moaned. Her tongue felt thick with thirst, and she blinked in sleepy slowness.

The clatter of hooves on stone and the jostling woke her further. Her head flopped against the horse's flank, and her mind reeled with vague awareness of her surroundings. Her mind settled on one thought: where was she?

"You're going to my camp." The voice sounded from ahead of her.

It sounded familiar. She tried to brush hair from her face, but her hands were bound. When did that happen? She yawned and sighed, unable to concentrate. The confounded horse wouldn't let her sleep.

She heard laughter. "We'll be there soon enough, and you won't worry about the horse then."

Again, she'd spoken without realizing it. Her brows pinched. "Who did

CHAPTER THIRTEEN

you say you are?" Her voice sounded strange. "Have I been drinking strong ale? No, I was with dwarves who needed my help."

Again, laughter sounded in the wind. "You're not drunk."

"Do you need help in your camp?"

"You are wanted there."

Hastra blinked at the figure ahead, astride a horse. "You've bound me, but I would have come to help if you asked."

"No, you wouldn't."

Hastra muttered and realized she was singing a tune she'd sung with Zelma as children. "I must be drunk, or you wouldn't have bound me over this horse. How long to Withling's Watch?" Of course, she'd been drinking, judging by her slurred speech.

"It won't be long."

"Withling's Watch? We're going there? No one's lived there for centuries. I can't do anything there." She slipped into a hymn to Eloch that she'd not sung for many years.

Feet appeared beside her on the ground. They'd stopped and she hadn't noticed. A hand grabbed her by the hair and another slapped her face. "Ow!" Her cheek stung, but she couldn't rub it with her bound hands.

"Don't sing that song—ever." The familiar voice sounded as cold as the wind.

Hastra nodded. "Don't sing. Right. How long to Withling's Watch?"

The hand shook her head. "We aren't going there."

"Oh right, we're going to...going to...where are we going?"

"You'll see. Now be quiet."

"Hey, am I drunk? My face hurts. Did I fall and hurt myself?"

The stranger sighed. "I didn't want to do this, but—" He grabbed her chin and yanked her mouth open. Bitter drink filled her mouth. She gagged, swallowed some of it, and the rest she spluttered over her cheeks, her dangling hair, and the ground.

Hastra grimaced. "That's awful. What is it? What is needed is given."

The familiar stranger laughed. He bent close with a friendly smile. "It sure is, Hastra. But not from Eloch. He's abandoned you to me and the

Dragon."

"Paugren." She smiled as her head reeled again, and her eyelids grew heavier. "You won't let Corgren stab me in the heart again, will you?"

Paugren let go of her head, and her stinging cheek smacked the horse's flank. Her face hurt. When was she put on this horse, and why this way? Hastra blinked once, and darkness engulfed her senses.

CHAPTER FOURTEEN

Athson gathered his belongings and shoved them into his pack, grinding his teeth. He needed those answers. How could he defeat Corgren without them? Hastra always seemed to avoid providing answers. He felt around inside his pack. There was the inheritance—his inheritance, whatever that meant. His father was in chains and half-blind now, so whatever needed doing was left to Athson.

Limbreth knocked and entered the officer's barracks from a common hall that connected single rooms occupied by Tordug, Makwi, Hastra and Limbreth. She sat beside his pack, crossed her arms, and rubbed them. "Almost ready?"

He fumbled with the clasps and relaxed his jaw with a sigh. "Yeah, I suppose. I hate leaving like this—with night coming on and all."

She shrugged and frowned. "It's better than risking capture by the Rokans."

Athson paused and knitted his brow. There was something on her mind, something she wanted to say. Why couldn't she just say it? "It bothers you, though?"

Limbreth stared at the wall in front of her and fingered a trinket on her braid. "It's, uh, nothing really." She glanced at him sidelong. "It's the Bane. I can feel it out there, far away."

The Bane? Still troubling them? Athson touched her shoulder, and his answer came out in almost a growl. "Stay near. My sword will defend us."

She grasped his hand and held it to her cheek. "Thank you." Her voice lacked her usual bold ring. "It's just that it has marked me, follows me for some reason." Limbreth lifted her gaze to his.

Athson's jaw clenched and unclenched. "You mean it's using you to get at me?"

Limbreth nodded.

He turned to the shuttered window and ran his fingers through his hair. "Does Hastra know?"

"Yes."

Makwi rushed past the opened barracks door, his boots clattering on the floorboards. "I'll be back soon."

Tordug answered from farther along the hall. "Be sure that you are. We must leave soon, regardless."

Athson shared a steady gaze of question with Limbreth as Makwi closed the outside door against the frosty night. Something was wrong.

Limbreth stood and adjusted her clothing and checked her weapons. "It's Hastra. She's not back."

They found Tordug in the hall, stroking his beard. His eyes shifted to them. "All packed? We need to leave soon. We can't risk being caught by the Rokans, and the dwarves will pull out of the valley to other places of refuge."

Athson cleared his throat. "We're ready. But what should we do if Hastra isn't back soon?" He needed more information from her. He squinted at the dwarf. But Tordug didn't order the Withling around. Athson relaxed. Tordug wasn't his problem.

The dwarf frowned. "She said she may be leaving us for a while. We're to go on, and she'll find us. But maybe Makwi will find her."

"So we just leave her here? To the Rokans?" That didn't seem right to Athson. His face flushed at the thought. She had goaded him into this mess, and he needed her around to answer his questions.

"She'll be fine—at least she said so. But we know the way over the mountains, and Makwi has been through the marsh. We'll get there." Tordug turned back to his room.

Limbreth stirred. "Perhaps we should go look for her too."

CHAPTER FOURTEEN

Tordug paused and stroked his beard again, then gave them a glance. "I know it's hard to wait, but better you stay here so we're ready when Makwi returns."

"C'mon." Athson motioned to Limbreth, and they grabbed their gear. Once in the entry-room, they leaned against the wall under the low ceiling.

"They'll come soon, I'm sure of it." Limbreth snuggled close to him and watched out the little windowpane.

Time passed, and they whispered. He wanted to kiss her, but Hastra and Makwi might come in at any moment. By the noise of it, Tordug paced down the hall.

Ralda huffed and hummed as he squeezed out of the hall, red-faced in the crowded home. He motioned and flashed his tattoos. "Ralda better in barn."

Athson chuckled. "Probably so. But we'll all be cold in the night soon enough, if Hastra will get back."

Limbreth whispered in his ear, "Come with me to the barn. I've something to tell you."

Athson took her offered hand and followed her out. He guessed he was about to find out what she'd been hiding.

~ ~ ~ ~ ~ ~ ~

Limbreth led Athson into a quiet corner. She took a deep breath of the hay-tinged air, then looked down at her new boots and frowned. They were so scuffed. When had that happened? She looked Athson in the eye and smiled. Too many miles on the boots to be new. Too many miles with Athson to act so bashful. She opened her mouth. "Uh, that new fur cloak and boots suit you. Looking like a mountain traveler now." She stroked the fur collar of his cloak. "I like it."

"Yeah, the boots are dwarven sized, not quite comfortable. They'll do until we get out of the mountains. The cloak's good and warm too."

Silence stretched between them as Limbreth hesitated. How to begin?

"Well?" He leaned forward.

By the look in his eyes, he expected something. What? A kiss? She wet her lips. If only this were that easy. She kissed him and drew back.

"So that's what you had to say?"

"No." She cleared her throat of the husky sound. If only she could just go on like they were. But she needed to tell him—everything. "I don't know where to start." She flashed him a smile. That usually got him.

Athson scratched the back of his neck. "Look, I know you're from Grendon, and by your horse and tack, from a well-off family or something. Gweld thinks you're—"

"I'm the king's daughter."

He stepped back, eyebrows climbing toward his hairline. "What?"

"I'm a princess of Grendon. My father is the king." She drew her fur cloak tighter in the cold barn. Imagine a princess kissing any young man in a barn.

He exhaled a tuneless whistle. "Uh, that's, I mean—I don't know what I mean. But what are you doing here, away from whoever, whatever?" He motioned vaguely south.

Limbreth raised her chin at the ring of irritation in his voice. "Look, I know things didn't go so well with Hastra, but I need to tell you about me, so if you can just forget about her and—"

"Hastra? What has she got to do with you?" His eyes narrowed. "I got some answers from her, but it's frustrating that she somehow avoids me all the time."

Limbreth frowned at her boots again. "Yeah, I didn't like the way she split us up in Chokkra, but be patient, if you can."

Athson gripped his sword and took a deep breath. "Go on."

His even response lent her courage. "I left because my father kept sending me suitors, and he demanded I marry the last one. We fought. He's chosen someone for me, but I'm not going back." She paced, fists clenched. "Hastra had just left, so I rode after her one night, thinking I'd have some adventures and win the freedom to make my own choices."

Athson ran his fingers through his shaggy hair, his eyes shifting away and back to her. "I saw you."

"What?"

"When I got the inheritance, there were these visions too. Don't tell anyone, because only Hastra knows this. I saw you riding in the night. I

CHAPTER FOURTEEN

kept remembering that image of you, when the fits came before we met, and it helped."

So that explained his surprise when they'd met. He'd seen her before? If he felt trapped by her confessions, then she had every right to be. But she grinned. "That's nice. No wonder you looked like you'd seen a ghost and got all moon-eyed at me. And here, I thought you were stunned by my beauty."

Now he cleared his throat. "Well, you are—that is, I think you're beautiful." His face changed. "But that doesn't explain what you're after. I mean, you left to make a name for yourself. How do I fit in with this? Won't your father send someone after you? Maybe this other man? What happens to me, to us, when all this is, you know…"

She kissed him again. "That's what happens. It doesn't matter what my father wants. I know what I want. I found it. I'm with you no matter what Hastra wanted. It's different now, and I'm doing it for myself. I won't leave if someone comes for me."

He stepped back and his expression hardened. "What do you mean? What does Hastra have to do with us?"

Limbreth reached for his hand, but he pulled it away. "Look, I just took up with her, looking for an adventure."

"So, I'm an adventure, is that it? When it's done, when I find the bow, you're going home and leaving our little adventure behind?"

Limbreth stepped toward him. "No, I'm not. That's what I'm trying to tell you. Hastra had me watch you. She said you needed protection." His face flushed as he frowned. "No, don't get angry, I've not been putting on at all. The kisses are real. And I've hardly spoken to her since Chokkra."

"You've been my bodyguard? So that's why you acted so serious after the banshee. You've been watching me ever since we left?"

Limbreth swallowed and nodded mutely. Back to the Banshee again. She shuddered and wiped a sudden tear away. "I wasn't—it wasn't that way then, hadn't been for weeks." She looked him in the eyes and snatched his hands. "I came for you at Marston's because I couldn't leave you. And then with the Banshee, I failed you. I failed Hastra. I failed me, and I couldn't live with the sudden fear. But don't be angry with me. I've been true all along. It's just that now, I don't like how Hastra is acting, and I want you to know I'm with you. I think we need to finish this and find your father, regardless of what she wants afterward."

He blinked in silence. "How do I believe you?"

She pushed him against a post and kissed him repeatedly, breaking away only long enough to say, "This is how." Then she kissed him again. One of his hands wandered across her backside, pressing her close, while the other slid up her back under the cloak.

Someone coughed. "Athson, you in here?"

It was Gweld. She started to pull away.

"Yeah, we're here. Just a moment." Athson pulled her back and kissed her before letting her go. He stepped along the wall of hay as Gweld came around the far end.

The elf squinted at them. "There you are. Makwi's back. He says no one's seen Hastra. She healed that messenger and left with Eftwe, but they haven't seen either one since. Better come with me. Tordug's ready to leave, and Makwi's ready to go chasing after the Withling."

Limbreth trailed after Athson, their hands still clasped. Her cheeks were flushed. That had gone better than she'd expected. Kissing did the trick. He glanced back at her, his face unreadable as they stepped into the night. At least, she thought it had. She remembered his embrace. If it didn't—well… Her face flushed as she dismissed the stray thought. *Just stay near him, and that Bane wouldn't bother you again.* She could handle Athson, but not the Bane. Not alone.

~ ~ ~ ~ ~ ~ ~

Athson and Limbreth followed Magdronu-as-Gweld out of the barn. Makwi stood outside with Tordug. There was just time enough for Magdronu-as-Gweld to send a message. Snow fell like drifting leaves, and the pack mules snorted misty clouds into the night.

Tordug turned to the three of them. "Are you ready?"

Magdronu-as-Gweld answered with a nod. "I just need my pack." He turned to Athson and resisted laughing in his certain victory. "I can grab

CHAPTER FOURTEEN

yours too, if you're ready." It would be best to have a few moments alone for the message.

Athson shifted his stance and flushed beside Limbreth. "Uh, sure. It's on my bed."

"Good. Be back in a minute." Magdronu-as-Gweld walked away without waiting for any of the replies murmured behind him. Athson had hesitated over the inheritance in his pack. He was still trying to hide it.

"Let me search again. I'm certain I can find her." Makwi's voice rumbled in protest as Magdronu-as-Gweld mounted the steps into the empty barracks.

"No, she said go regardless, and we'll follow the Withling's instruction." Tordug's reply snapped with command.

Magdronu-as-Gweld shut the barracks door on the argument. A quick glance told him none of the dwarven officers lingered in the darkened room. They were all away setting their meaningless defenses when they should be fleeing. He paused at a mirror and smiled, his real eyes reflected, fire rimming vertical pupils. But that was of little consequence. Limbreth's confirmed identity left him with royal blood in addition to a second point of leverage over Athson.

Someone groaned behind him. Magdronu-as-Gweld whirled, a reflexive snarl on his lips that faded as Ralda sat up from the floor where he napped. How had he missed the giant?

Ralda blinked at him with a puzzled expression.

"Catching up on sleep? They are ready outside. I'm just grabbing my things. And Athson's." Had the giant seen his reflection?

Ralda's eyes narrowed, and he wiggled his fingers in that silly speech of his. "Ready. Go pack mule." He stood and gathered his dwarven cloak—several hastily sown together to cover his height and size.

Magdronu-as-Gweld fidgeted with his pack and checked Athson's. The giant scratched his head and mumbled to himself for several moments before he left with his enormous pack. If that oaf had seen... That bore watching, but for now, the message.

He checked Athson's pack and found the inheritance within. Tormenting Athson by applying pressure on Limbreth would be sheer pleasure. Her fear was delectable. Her blood—royal blood—on his hallowed altar would be sweet. He wiped hot saliva from his lips and closed the pack.

Now for the quick message.

~~~~~~~

Corgren answered the summons that flashed from his ring. He bled the hostage too much for his liking. Ath shuffled away under the watchful eyes of his hobgoblin guard, chains rattling. Corgren cared little for the wretch, but they needed him still. He spread his hands over the bowl, paused at a thought, and scratched at his ear. Why had Ath saved him? And now Corgren had given him half his sight.

He shrugged the question away and spoke the spell. Best not keep his master waiting.

In its lurid light, the force of the dragon's presence locked into his mind and vision with the image of the scaled visage that hung over the bowl of traitor's blood. Strong magic, traitor's blood, cursed blood. He bowed. "Master, I answer."

Magdronu purred, a low rumble that shook Corgren's mind. "I have but spare moments. I'll retain the Bane longer and harry or take this Limbreth. I've confirmed she's needed to force Athson to my will. She's royalty in Grendon."

Corgren's eyes twitched. "The king's daughter? Imagine that, my lord."

"She'll make a worthy sacrifice on my hallowed ground with or without the Bow of Hart."

A thought scurried across Corgren's mind. "What if we used her as hostage to gain control of Grendon?"

"Hmm." The pleased rumble shook Corgren. "A pawn for control without drawing a sword. Resources to use elsewhere. It bears merit, Corgren. But the bow first, and she will serve that purpose foremost, along with the ranger's father."

Corgren bowed again. "So it shall be. How shall I proceed?"

"Gather a troop of trolls and bring them across the mountains. We leave for the marshes and Howart's Cave. If the ranger gains possession of the bow, we'll force him to hallowed ground with the hostages and make an

CHAPTER FOURTEEN

end of the prophecy where I'll be strongest. You'll have this princess before or at the cave, so bring all three there however you can. Perhaps we can save her for your idea, perhaps not. I must go now."

Corgren bowed as the spell snapped closed. He stood trembling in the aftermath of the latest message. Not only was she nobility, but that old king's daughter? He smiled as he dabbed cold sweat from his face. Corgren gathered his strength for several moments and called for his troll attendant in trollish.

He strolled out of the room and paused with a squint at his traitorous prisoner. Ath fingered his chains in trembling hands, one bandaged but soaking blood. "Rest now, wretch. You'll need your strength soon." He didn't need the hostage yet. Loathsome creature. "Take him back to his cell."

He strode past in search of his officer. The trap grew tighter. No escaping for the ranger this time, sword or not.

~ ~ ~ ~ ~ ~ ~

Ath's chains clinked in his grasp as he feigned his anxious game. His little makeshift file scraped away at the link. He paused. Was Corgren done with his conversation? He winced at his cut hand. It was hard to hold the file lately with all the cuts. To many cuts slowed his progress, even with half his sight back. He muttered and hushed his voice. They were done. He secreted the file into a tear within his worn boot.

In moments, Corgren marched past in some hurry. "Rest now, wretch. You'll need your strength soon." At Corgren's command, hobgoblins returned him to his cell.

Ath held his breath and rattled his chain as he hid the scored link. Rest indeed. Every stroke prepared his surprise when the chance presented itself. He'd spring his little trap. *Deep breath, deep breath and calm your breathing. No grins.* He hid his smirk until they locked the cell door and left. The right moment was all he needed, and he'd be free with help. After all, he'd saved the wizard just to get a chance at freedom. Too bad he wasn't ready for the last one, with that knife at his throat. Too bad he lacked an eye or he'd have killed Corgren then.

The voice, the sudden sight of his son. Ath's throat constricted with a lump of emotion. It could have been there. *But there'll be another.* He'd not dared speak for the blade at his neck and fear of giving himself away.

Ath curled on the floor to sleep. Rest indeed. He'd be ready. Ready for whatever was needed to save himself and his son. Redemption after all these years. A soft sob escaped his chest through his lips. It echoed in the darkness. He'd be ready. He clenched the chain link with his bloody hand until it shook with the effort and the chains rattled in the silence around him.

CHAPTER FIFTEEN

Hastra recollected little of the ride out of the mountains. She rode like a sack of merchant's wares for several days with only brief moments of enough awareness to be concerned. Otherwise, all was a blur of trees or mountains, but mostly the ground.

She woke in a tent and blinked slowly, her wakefulness dulled. Eloch was a distant awareness. She worked her dry tongue. Something lay in her mouth. Hastra tried to spit, but it refused to move. She reached for her face, but neither hand lifted from behind her. She frowned, tried to stand, and flopped onto hard ground. She grunted.

A face peeked between the tent flaps. The woman smiled.

Someone to help her. Hastra started up and fell back again. She spoke but only uttered muffled mumbles.

"Do you want help?" The woman entered and squatted.

Hastra nodded and tried to answer. She went on a long explanation of who she was, and her thoughts trailed away into silly songs.

The woman laughed. "You don't recognize me?" She unbuttoned Hastra's blouse and ran her finger along the ragged scar at her heart. "You still have this? Eloch leaves you old, wrinkled, and scarred."

Hastra's head flopped over. Scar? What scar? Her eyes closed, and she forced them open.

"I'd dose you, but I don't think you're ready for more yet." The woman's smile turned into a sneer. "You'll never leave us this time, Hastra."

Now she knew this woman. Hastra gasped. If only she remembered those three sisters' names. But she couldn't think now. She blew a wisp of hair from her eyes.

The other woman slapped her. "Where's your crazy sister? Where's that old scarecrow?"

Hastra moaned into the rag in her mouth. Her face stung and her eyes fluttered. Eloch, she needed instruction. She shut her eyes. She felt no presence. She prayed, but her thoughts slipped into fragments.

"You old cow! What's the matter? Can't you remember anything? Can't you hear Eloch?"

Hastra shook her head. It cleared some but not near enough. She spoke. Why was her mouth gagged? She nodded.

The other woman stuck out her lower lip. "Poor thing." She slapped Hastra again.

Tears sprang into Hastra's eyes. Why was she crying? She slumped over and closed her eyes.

Hastra woke later with the gag removed. Hands squeezed her face until her mouth opened. Drink splashed into her mouth and over her chin. She choked on the bitter taste but swallowed. "What are you doing?"

Several voices laughed. A man stood by the tent flap. The women gathered around her, smiling, but their grins left Hastra uncomfortable. She squinted in the dim light at their faces.

The Beleesh sisters. She groaned at the recognition. "How did—" But then memory, vague though it was, washed through her mind. Paugren had taken her.

One of the sisters giggled. "Can't greet old friends?"

The one from earlier nudged the giggler. "Pitiful thing, can't remember us."

Hastra worked her jaw. "You slapped me. You're Esthria."

"Oh, good for you!" Esthria slapped her. "We'll teach you our names, old cow."

Cass snickered. "Neither she nor her sister were much to look at when they were young. But now, Hastra, you're just old and used up. What's wrong? Can't you call lightning on us?"

CHAPTER FIFTEEN

Ahmelia whirled around. "But we're young and glorious still. That was quite nasty hitting us with lightning, Hastra. But we can still use magic. Eloch pays you poorly, old girl. Ask Paugren if he likes having the pretty girls around." She batted her eyes at Paugren, who stood by the tent flap.

He crossed is arms. "Just don't hurt her until Magdronu says he's finished."

Esthria knelt by Hastra. "Really, we could help you if you'd just—"

Hastra shook her head. The dim unction of Eloch remained from days earlier. How long ago? It was something so Hastra clung to that. *Offer them restoration.* "You don't understand. I was sent by Eloch to help you. All of you can still turn back."

Cass threw back her head and laughed. "Either she's still incoherent or she needs more of your brew, Paugren."

He sniffed and cut his eyes at Cass. "It's enough for now. We need her awake enough so she thinks clearly."

Hastra smacked her lips at the bad taste. "What was that? I need something to eat."

"Oh, Hastra, this isn't an inn, and we're not serving girls." Esthria patted her cheeks and then pinched them. "We're going to teach you a few lessons, and if you won't come over to the Dragon…"

Hastra winced and pulled out of Esthria's grasp. "Never. But you can turn back. You can't do me harm unless Eloch wills it."

Paugren leaned into the light. "Really? We've got you this far and completely in our grasp."

Hastra's brow furrowed and she ran her parched tongue over her dry lips. "I have such a bad taste in my mouth."

The sisters laughed and danced around her, calling her, "old cow."

Paugren halted them and knelt by her. "You won't escape us this time, Hastra."

Hastra's thoughts fragmented, but one remained. "I'm only here as long as Eloch wants me here."

Cass clapped her hands. "Perfect, that's forever, then." She drew a Rokan knife. "And we'll have such fun when it's time."

Hastra nodded. "Fun is good, but a little food first?"

The four of them left, gabbing at their success. "Why can't we do her now?"

"How long 'til he gets here?"

Their voices faded, and Hastra lay down and smiled. Such a nice place to rest. Too bad she ached for some reason.

~ ~ ~ ~ ~ ~ ~

Hastra's days of confinement passed like falling leaves. She slept, ate, and slept some more. She remembered more but found her powers of mystic concentration addled. Sometimes she sang but found herself on a different tune than what she'd started. At least they allowed her access to the privy but she never remembered when they put her in a building. She frowned at the door.

A yawn preceded a bout of heavy-lidded blinks. Hastra rubbed her eyes and then propped her forehead in her hands, bracing herself on the table where she sat. She was here for a reason. If only she could figure it out. Eloch was distant in her awareness. But why?

She'd told them she was here for them, for Eloch. But that was habit. What was Eloch's purpose in all this? A gut-ripping knife? Alarm flared at the thought and faded into vague discomfort.

Her stomach rumbled. She hated the food here. At least, she thought she did.

"Well, well, you're still trying to figure it all out, aren't you?" Laughter tinkled in front of her.

Hastra lifted her head. Oh, those women. The sisters. When had they come in? "Come to bring me some food?" Cass, that was who spoke, Hastra thought.

They laughed, and Cass moved a bowl toward her. "Forgot to eat, you old cow."

Another one—Esthria, perhaps—leaned close. "Best eat before it goes cold." She stuck out her lower lip.

Hastra frowned. None of them cared for her. She spooned the pasty mash into her mouth. "It's cold already!"

They laughed, and the third paused in her guffaws. "It's been there for

CHAPTER FIFTEEN

hours. Now eat up!"

Hastra ate. She frowned at the bitterness. "Why am I here?" Maybe they'd help her figure it out. No, they hated her.

Cass pointed and laughed some more. "Look at that ugly face!"

Esthria leaned close again and offered a nice pat on the cheek. "You're here because our Master wants you here."

Hastra shook her head. "No, he has no power. I'm here for—for Eloch's will. To help you, I think."

Esthria's pretty face twisted into a mask of hate. Hastra never saw the slap coming, but it nearly knocked her out of her chair.

The Beleesh sister leaned close with an unfriendly grin. "Eloch has no power here, and we don't need any help from you."

Ahmelia touched Hastra's cheek. "If we weren't ordered to leave you alone, we'd show you that you're the one in need of help." She spat in Hastra's face and shoved her head away, then turned for the door. "Let's go. This is hardly any fun unless we can really make her squeal."

Esthria led Ahmelia out the door. "I swear, sister, we'll have our time with her and laugh our way through it!"

Ahmelia's retort was cut off as the door closed.

Cass whirled and stepped toward the door after a lingering gaze at Hastra. Hastra raised a hand. "Please let me help you."

Cass turned slowly. Her eyes narrowed. "It isn't I who needs it." She pulled her dagger and knelt with the blade at Hastra's cheek. "Perhaps I should ignore my sisters and our commands and start on you now." She let the flat of the blade brush along the Withling's cheek.

"The only harm you can do me is what Eloch wills." Hastra's eyelids fluttered. So heavy, and she should be afraid but felt nothing. Where was Eloch now? So distant.

Cass snickered in the following silence. "I don't think Corgren stabbed you hard enough all those years ago." She raised the dagger, poised to strike.

A hand grabbed Cass's wrist. "You won't do that!" A shadow loomed in the room.

Hastra smiled. "It's Eloch."

A brief struggle ensued. "Let me go. I wasn't going to—"

"You were! And against the Dragon's orders!" Paugren's face appeared from the shadows. He held Cass's arm still.

Cass's lips spread into a grin of hatred. "I'll—"

"You'll what? Kill me? An empty threat!" He yanked Cass away and thrust her out the door. "From now on, you and your sisters stay out of here!"

"Thank you." Hastra sighed. It was hard to focus, but Paugren had saved her. Eloch's will.

Paugren glanced over his shoulder, his expression soft with unexpected compassion. But the look passed into hardness. "Don't thank me. When Magdronu's through with you..." He left without finishing.

CHAPTER SIXTEEN

Athson and the others followed the dim, blue light of their glow-moss lanterns late into the night before they slept under evergreen boughs out of the cold wind. They huddled close as a group for warmth beneath every bit of blankets and cloaks they had. Athson's teeth chattered for a while behind the cloth that covered his mouth and nose until he found a measure of warmth when Limbreth huddled closer. Dawn drew them out of their refuge, and they hurriedly stowed their belongings and set out while eating cold rations. Athson shivered as old markers pointed them higher.

The sensation faded some the next day, and by the end of five days, Athson felt nothing strange. During that time, they traversed snowfields where loud *snaps* echoed above the high pass. The wind uttered a constant moan at a varying volume that sounded more like a dirge. Athson remembered the banshee's wails. He grunted at the thought and quaked for some reason other than cold.

"What?" Limbreth's words puffed through the cloth she wore over her mouth and nose.

He shook his head. "Just tired of the cold." No reason to remind Limbreth of that night. She blamed herself enough for that—wrongly.

By the end of five days, the dwarves led them out of the cracking heights. A chill wind rushed at their back along a road of stone that descended into a shadowed crevasse. After several hours, the deep gash in the mountains spread into a wide valley stretching west. The road wound along the high northern edge of the deep valley. Their path mostly descended but rose at intervals with the terrain, overlooking a sheer drop of thousands of paces. The afternoon sun afforded them a magnificent view of the windswept valley. Birds wove invisible trails on the wind, while below, though the valley lay in shadow much of the morning, the afternoon sun revealed a rushing river that crashed among rocks.

Makwi led them while Tordug and Ralda hung back as a rear guard. Wide steps that led down for long distances jarred Athson's weary legs. At least the mules carried their packs. He doubted they'd have made it without the pack animals. They approached an upward climb, which felt almost like a warm relief from the downward steps. But his lungs burned well before they crested the rise.

Athson looked over his shoulder at Limbreth. Her white leathers gleamed in the sunshine, and the dwarven trinkets fixed in her braid glinted with the sway of her hair. There were new knots in her braid. He made note to ask her about them later. Undoubtedly dwarven-inspired, though. She'd done a lot with her connections. He slowed for her.

Limbreth grinned at him, which was better than her avoidance in the Troll Heaths. She walked alongside him.

He chewed at his cheek. A princess and his protector. Maybe he should suspect her—and Hastra—regardless of her kisses and devotion to him.

She strode closer. "Something on your mind?"

He shook his head. Best not let on that he harbored suspicions. "Nothing, really. It's good to see you smiling in the sun."

"Sun or not, it's still cold. Though it's nice after all the weather on the eastern side."

"Better than the pass too."

"Agreed."

The wind jabbed at them. He turned his face from the blast. Limbreth grunted and leaned into the gust. Snow swirled onto the path, carried from the mountain's flanks above them.

His thoughts turned to Hastra. He was thankful for the Withling's ministrations of healing. He flexed his fingers to prove to himself that he

CHAPTER SIXTEEN

was well. But the Archer had continued suspicions about the old woman's dealings with his family—a noble family of Hart. Had Hastra guided his house for generations? What it all meant still mystified Athson. *I'm not dancing to her lead, though.* He wasn't some child's toy. She probably wasn't returning at all, so he'd get no more answers from her. He should've demanded more when he had the chance.

Athson grunted. The Withling's vision kept him dancing on her string. For now. But her sudden announcement about leaving had seemed a little too convenient to him. He frowned into the wind. Find the Bow of Hart for her, but she was gone. Did Howart still live? Maybe she'd played them all for fools after she'd realized the bow was lost for good. She had her book—what else did she need at this point? But then, they had her pack. He grunted again, this time from the jar of a step on his feet. Tough road.

"You gonna make it?" Limbreth asked, gasping at the frequent descent on the rough road.

He nodded. "Yeah, could be smoother."

"We never finished talking about the Bane back in Ezhandun. What do you think the Bane wants with me?" They reached the end of the series of wide, deep steps.

Athson scratched at his bearded jaw. "Like we discussed before, it's getting at me. You would think it would be after me. Corgren wants the bow for his own ends, so why shouldn't that thing try to use you?"

"Yes." Limbreth's mouth twisted in puzzlement. "That's the only way it makes sense."

Athson grimaced. "He's got my father already. Should be enough. Guess he thinks more influence is better." His eyes narrowed at an idea. They were going for the bow and that was easy to guess. Except for the Bane possibly watching them, why not track down Corgren instead of springing the wizard's trap? Why not turn the tables on Corgren? Instead of getting the Bow of Hart, go after Corgren and his father. At least rescue his father and remove that thorn. Hunt the hunter instead of walking into the trap. But how? Split up? It made sense. Feign going for the bow, draw Corgren close and rescue his father.

"That's an unpleasant thought." She shook for a moment like a limp rabbit in a dog's mouth. "That touch haunts me still. But we'll have to make sure they don't get me."

"You sure the Bane's not close now?"

"I'm sure. That was just the cold and the memory of it."

He leaned close to Limbreth. "I have an idea. I hate how we always get split up, so I want you in this idea of mine."

"Me too. We're not children. What's your idea?"

Athson explained his idea while they walked along a smoother stretch of road. At the end of it, he sighed. "What do you think? Are you in?"

Limbreth paused before she answered. "I want to stay with you, but Hastra said we should go on without her and get the bow." She motioned to Makwi and Gweld ahead of them. "What about the others?"

"Gweld will come. I don't know about Ralda and the dwarves. But three of us can do a lot. We can take the mules and let the others head for Howart's Cave if they wish. It might be better that way. Confuse the Bane, maybe."

Limbreth rubbed her arms under her furred cloak. "I don't know. Maybe we should wait for Hastra. I know Gweld will help you, but I don't like leaving the others."

Athson spread his hands in front of him, palms up. "But we're walking into a trap otherwise. Why not flip this and do something different? Instead of reacting to them, we take the reins of the horse and ride our own path. It'll work, and it gets us out of the trap. Even if there's a bow, Corgren won't get it."

"Let's talk it through it later, maybe. Or even better, why don't you ask Gweld now? See what he thinks."

"I'll ask him later, once we get to a shelter and we can step outside and talk it through. He'll listen to reason. I know he will." Gweld had to listen. But the idea itched on Athson's thoughts all afternoon. Would Gweld agree? The elf wanted him to go after the bow.

Athson sighed and hoped they reached a shelter earlier than they had a day earlier. There were fewer of them on this road, though, and his hopes proved false. They walked until just after the early winter sun fell into a

CHAPTER SIXTEEN

bank of clouds hanging low on the western horizon, and finally Makwi motioned from ahead that he'd sighted the shelter. Athson picked up his pace, ready for a rest.

They found a supply of coal in the shelter but no food.

"Always something in these shelters." Athson settled next to Limbreth while Makwi kindled a fire.

"Other parties will come this way soon enough." Tordug entered with some food from their stores. "There are small mines on this side of the mountains that trade with villages that need it for their forges. They are few now, yet they hold to the old ways such as these. We will leave them what we can as a blessing." The elder dwarf sighed wearily. "But we'll take some coal for later below the mountains, where there are no shelters."

After they ate and the others prepared to sleep, Gweld moved toward the door. Athson stood beside the elf. "Let's check things outside before you settle in for your watch." He leaned closer and whispered, "I need to talk."

Gweld nodded. "Sure, we can check the animals."

They stepped outside into the cold wind and checked the mules. They stood between the pair of pack animals out of the wind.

Gweld laid a hand on Athson's shoulder. "What do you need?"

Athson coughed into his hand. "Just this—we're walking into a trap, you know that?"

Gweld lifted a finger and cocked his head. "But we do so knowingly, so it's not really a trap."

"But why even do that? Why not change it up on Corgren?"

"I'm listening."

"We get out of these mountains and go hunting trolls. We find them, we find Corgren and my father. We can then sneak into their camp and at least free my father. Corgren loses his hostage, and then we don't even need the bow."

Gweld rubbed his chin. "An interesting thought. Let me think this through."

"If you're in, then Limbreth will come too."

"What about the others? What about Hastra? She said to go after the bow and she'll catch us."

Not Hastra again. Always her. Athson looked away and back. "Hastra said we should leave without her if necessary. But we don't even know if she's really coming back. Why do the expected? The others can come or not. Makwi knows where Howart's Cave is. They can get the bow, and we can plan to meet somewhere. We have it all, and Corgren loses. It'll work. Besides, Hastra did tell me not to give it to them. What better way to avoid that than rescuing my father? No hostage, no reason to give up the bow if the others get it."

"If the others agree."

"Well, I'm tired of being Corgren's toy in this. I want to throw him off-balance."

"Let me think about this. I'll let you know, and then we can put it to the others. It's worth considering, though. What about that Bane? It's always watching, coming close."

"Fair enough. Let me take care of the Bane." He half-drew his sword. "This will do the trick. The next time it's at the door, I'll chase it and use this blessed sword to send it back to the dry-lands." If that was where it came from. He trembled at his memories of the Banshee. The Bane needed care, but he'd do it. "I'm sick of this Bane haunting our steps. Good thinking to get rid of it so Corgren won't be alerted."

Gweld spread his hands. "It's a plan. We'll let it lay tonight and see what the others think. Let's get back inside."

~ ~ ~ ~ ~ ~ ~

Magdronu-as-Gweld sat his watch and pondered his reaction to Athson's plans. *Not surprising at all. He's as short-tempered as his father thanks to their curse.* But he needed control. *"Stay away."* His message to the Bane allowed him space to consider all options without disturbing anyone from sleep. At least for now. He smiled. Maybe later.

He tossed coal onto the fire and returned to his seat at the shelter door. Pitiful heat. He settled into his posture of vigilance. He needed Athson. The ranger was his best chance to gain possession of the bow. He'd gotten past Eloch's protections previously, and Hastra made sure of the last move,

CHAPTER SIXTEEN

though she never knew where it went. He'd suspected Howart as the caretaker more than once over the years. But Magdronu needed Athson to hand the bow over willingly, and a hostage proved a winning strategy, and his hallowed ground at the Funnel the best location. The threat of sacrifice and its tension, oh the taste of that he anticipated. Heat rose within Magdronu-as-Gweld, and he suppressed it. Best not heat the room too much. He allowed himself a silent chuckle. Not even Hastra suspected him.

But what of Athson? Magdronu-as-Gweld rubbed his chin. He needed him pointed in the right direction, and more leverage against him than just his father. But other pieces in the game lay at his disposal. Time to put those in motion. He rarely disposed of important pieces too soon. Patience often paid off in the end. Good thing he'd pulled that Withling into his grasp. He'd checked on that more than once with Paugren.

Time to set this little plan in motion and see how Athson liked it. He hid his grin behind his hands lest one of the sleepers stir and notice. Limbreth had at least once. *Be more careful.* He still wanted her royal blood in his claws. *Now to put the brothers in motion.* Magdronu sent his summons so that their rings flashed the urgent color. *"Report for instructions."* Set this plan in motion now, and the Bow of Hart entered his possession sooner. Time was short before Eloch sent the arrow.

~ ~ ~ ~ ~ ~ ~

Limbreth stood her watch and woke Athson. They embraced awhile before she went to her blanket. She yawned and settled in to sleep.

Athson drew his sword and laid it across his knees where he sat against the shelter door.

Sometime later, Limbreth awoke with a start to a familiar chill despite the warmth of the shelter. She breathed in ragged gasps. Her eyes flew wide.

Athson stirred. "What is it?"

She stood. "The Bane. It's near. Very near."

Athson turned toward the possible threat beyond the door, his sword raised. The door rattled as the wind whistled along the pass. He reached for the door.

Limbreth pulled at his tunic. "Athson, don't—"

"Leave us, creature!" He yanked the door open. It banged against the shelter stone. The Bane filled the doorway and reached past Athson. He waved his blade at its cowl. "Back! Or I'll send you to the dry-lands!" He stabbed at the phantom. The Bane slipped away from the attack.

The others stirred with shouts and reached for their weapons. Limbreth took a deep breath as if popping out of water after a dive.

Athson lifted his foot to go after the shade, and she grabbed him. "Athson! You can't fight—"

"Can't I?" He shrugged out of her grasp and leapt after the Bane. The Bane fled, and Athson chased it into the darkness.

Tordug and the others crowded around her. "What's going on? Is it the Bane?"

Limbreth nodded. The chill of the Bane's presence faded. "Athson's after it now."

Tordug turned to the others. "Grab those lanterns! Makwi, take Gweld up the path. Ralda and I will go down. Take care of the road in the night." He paused to glance at Limbreth.

She grabbed her swords. "I'm not staying here alone. I'm going with you."

~ ~ ~ ~ ~ ~ ~

Athson rushed into the night after the Bane. He'd get it this time. *It won't break this blade. Time to end this now.* The shade fled, a presence darker than the night. *Careful. Don't go over the edge.*

Lurid green light blinded Athson. He slid to a halt on the dwarven road. A hook-nosed face sneered at him from the light at least thirty paces away. "Corgren!" He advanced a step. "Now you die!"

Ath stood chained nearby. A hobgoblin held a knife to his throat. The wizard stood with a green ball of magical light beside him.

Athson hesitated, then stepped forward.

Corgren laughed and motioned to the Bane. "Want to go over the side? Besides, there's more you'll want to see."

Athson kept walking toward the wizard. "I can block any of your magic." He always met the wizard without his bow ready. He glanced at the Bane, which stood with the mountainside to its back. Ready to pounce. Athson

CHAPTER SIXTEEN

had his knife. He could throw it. No, no good, he wasn't that accurate. The goblin he'd failed to kill proved that. He took another step and readied for the Bane.

"Look at this." Corgren waved his hands in the green light, and its murky glow cleared to reveal a woman tied to a pole. "Recognize her?"

Athson halted and gaped. His mother? It looked like her. Older, but it was her face. "That can't be! She's dead! Stop taunting me." His chest heaved, and he gripped his sword, ready for his rush past the Bane. "Your spells and illusions won't stop me."

"No? Not even your mother? Tell her, traitorous wretch!" Corgren snapped his fingers at Ath's face.

Ath ground his teeth and nodded slightly, a motion barely seen in the light. "It's true, Athson. She lived when I was captured. When he—when he… I heard her not a month ago, somewhere in Rok, before…" His voice trailed away to silence, but his single eye blinked what he meant. Before Corgren had magically restored his eye.

Athson lowered his sword. "I know what you want. Why show her to me now?" *Rush him. End it before—*

"If I don't give the word soon, she'll be killed. I suggest you take a few steps back." Corgren flicked his fingers at Athson.

Athson ground his teeth and stepped back several paces. "Now what?"

Corgren tapped his chin. "It occurs to me that you might try something foolish. Something like a daring rescue in the night. After all, you know I'm looking for you. So let's set things straight. My brother is in Rok with your pitiful mother as a hostage. I wouldn't try anything like a rescue. However, just so you really understand what I'm saying: Bring the Bow of Hart to the Funnel by the next moon, or both die. If Ath is rescued, your mother dies. You see, you don't have time to save them both, even if you sent your friends and they knew where to go."

Athson almost gaped but caught himself. Corgren had guessed his intentions. Athson glanced at the Bane. Or it had reported his conversation with Gweld. It could have been close enough somehow.

Corgren chuckled. "Oh, and one more thing." He waved his hand at the green display of magic. "Just so you understand that this is real." The view widened, and Hastra appeared, tied like Athson's mother to a post. But the Withling slouched in apparent unconsciousness. "Your Withling cannot help you, either. We'll kill her too if you don't get us the bow in time." He grinned. "I see by the look on your face that you understand. The full moon is still some weeks off, so I should think you've got time to find the bow and get to the Funnel."

Corgren spoke a word of his spell, and darkness enfolded him, the hobgoblin, his father, and even the Bane.

Athson stood alone in the darkness with the wind ruffling his cloak.

"Athson!" The blue light of glow-moss shined in his face as his companions ran toward him. Tordug held the light high, and the others stood with weapons ready. "Did you get it? Where is it?"

Athson shook his head and squinted at the light.

Tordug stepped forward. "That was foolish, lad. Let us help you!"

Athson swallowed and found words. "My mother. She's alive. They have her in Rok." He nearly dropped the blessed sword.

CHAPTER SEVENTEEN

A thson stared at Limbreth's stunned face in the available light.
"What?" Ralda's hands flashed confused signs like moths in the lantern light.

"Corgren. He was here." Athson leaned against the rock opposite the roadside wall. "They have my mother in Rok. Hastra too. They're hostages."

They all gasped at the news.

"That can't be." Tordug tugged his beard. "We shouldn't have listened to her."

Tordug motioned toward the shelter up the road. "Come back. Tell us what happened."

Athson shambled after the others. He trailed the blessed sword's tip along the road surface and then sheathed the blade. Captive. What was he going to do? First his father, now his mother. What of Hastra?

They soon returned to the shelter. Tordug signaled to Makwi farther up the path. The other dwarf returned with Gweld, and they all crowded into the shelter and gathered at the fire. Athson leaned against Limbreth, and she hugged him as he recounted his encounter with Corgren.

"So they have everyone, and there's nothing I can do. I've got until the next full moon to get the Bow of Hart to the Funnel if I have any hope of saving any of them."

Tordug slapped his knees. "Well, that settles all our hesitation about Hastra coming. I suppose some of us can go back for her."

Athson shook his head. "Corgren said none of you have time for that or even know where my mother and Hastra are held. The Bane can likely alert them anyway." He slouched against Limbreth, and the deep emptiness of his old losses opened. That numbness was familiar. Leering troll faces loomed out of his memory. *His mother whirling after she pushed him out of the window.* Not a fit. He grasped the sword hilt, and it all faded—except his sense of loss. He sighed. "She saved me that night. Now I can do nothing for her. Again."

Ralda's hands flashed in the firelight. "We go cave. Take bow. See what happen. Eloch work for Hastra. We do what can."

Tordug exhaled and pursed his lips between mustache and beard. "I think you're right, Ralda. Hastra said we should go with or without her. She has a sense of Eloch having a plan for her. We'll trust the Withling to Eloch and do what we can with the bow." He raised his hands, palms up. "Nothing else we can do. Maybe we can save your father, lad."

"You think they'll let Hastra and my mother go if I give them the bow?"

Makwi frowned. "You forget your father and mother sacrificed themselves to keep it from Magdronu. When you thought them dead, it didn't matter. They know the consequences. It'll be worse if you give it up, lad."

Athson shook his head at Makwi. "Not your losses to deal with! They're mine, and I can't just let them die!"

"Easy, Athson." Tordug squeezed Athson's shoulder. "Let's just get the bow and see what happens. Maybe we'll work something out by then. Maybe we can pull a trick on them somehow."

Makwi tugged his beard. "Perhaps we'll find Howart and he can help."

Athson stood, pounded a fist on the shelter door and leaned against it. "And what will a Withling do? Pray them out of Rok?" Corgren had outmaneuvered him again. The wizard held all the pieces in his hand, and Athson danced to his pleasure.

Makwi shrugged. "I don't know. Withlings have done amazing things in old tales. But we can't just give up the bow."

Athson stared at Makwi. "*You* can't. But it's not yours." His heart thumped in his ears. "How long do I have? How many days?"

Tordug wiggled his fingers.

CHAPTER SEVENTEEN

Gweld rose and laid a sympathetic hand on Athson's arm. "You have almost three weeks. We'll make it. We'll figure something out."

Athson turned to the others. "I've no choice but to get the bow, it seems. All of you get some rest if you're coming and keep up."

Gweld, Ralda, and Makwi checked the animals outside and returned with Spark at their heels. No one slept well the rest of the night, fearing the Bane's return. Athson slept between Limbreth and the door with his sword unsheathed in his hand.

The sun rose hours later as they set out. That day passed without incident, though a cold rain passed over them and thunder rolled in the heights behind them. Four more days passed as they descended from the mountains with naught but the distant sight of mountain goats or birds sailing overhead for news. Athson eschewed scouting forays for Limbreth's company, his unspoken protection. They wouldn't get her too. But he pushed them all, often trotting well ahead with Limbreth in tow. They wouldn't slow him down. If he had to, he'd take a mule and go.

At the end of those four days, the old road descended toward low hills and wound among them into sprawling grassland. The morning after they left the pass, the travelers waded through high grass standing dormant in the early winter. Athson cast glances toward the hills and the pass. Nothing there. The Bane was out there, watching. And so were Corgren and his father. He cleared his throat. "How far to the river?" Ambush at a ford was possible. *Look for what you hunt near water.*

Makwi halted and scanned the horizon. "Several days." He looked to Tordug.

They ate near midday under a rare stretch of blue sky. But dusk arrived early under an ashen sky, so they tethered the mules with haste and built pit-fires in the soft soil, using what fuel they found at hand and coal scrounged from shelters on the dwarf-road. Athson shadowed Limbreth as night deepened, and they foraged for any fuel more substantive than grass.

Limbreth ate her ration of jerky and hard biscuit at their meager fire later. "What do we do after we reach the river?"

"We cross the ford and head for the marshes." Makwi's breath plumed in the chill as he spoke.

Athson shifted his glance between Limbreth and the Chokkran champion. Makwi hadn't called her "ax-maid". He must be tired or bothered. Athson considered which. He pulled his hood lower. He watched Spark watch him. Something for thought as they proceeded.

Gweld brushed crumbs from his clothing. "It's been many years since I traveled this region, but I think we'll reach the river day after next, midday."

Makwi grunted. "About right, I think."

Gweld took his usual watch as talk faded to weary silence. Athson bedded down next to Limbreth, his sword drawn for action should the Bane assail them. Limbreth clasped his hand and squeezed, but she too grasped a sword in her other.

Later, they shared time during their watches as they walked a circuit of their camp. Spark trailed them.

"Let's just leave and go ourselves. They're slowing us down. They'll keep me from doing what I have to do." Athson stared into the silent night, his tone hushed. Time was wasting. Each night the moon phase progressed. His gut clenched. "It's not their decision."

"Athson, they mean well and understand your feelings." She paused, hefting a sword. "But there are the bigger issues of the prophecy. Hastra knew her risks and has for years."

The paused by the mules, and Athson patted one on its side. "But I can't abandon my father and mother again." He turned to Limbreth and grasped her shoulders. "I've lived well with the elves while they've suffered. I can't just run off and forget them."

She leaned forward, her forehead touching his. "I know. It's not easy. Maybe an answer will present itself."

His voice rose in challenge, and he stepped back. "Like what? I'm trapped. They are trapped in Corgren's clutches."

Limbreth gazed toward their sleeping companions and back to Athson. "Quiet, you'll wake the others. I don't know what will happen, and neither do you. But I'll go through it with you." She took his hand and came closer. "I'm here now. For you. So are the others."

CHAPTER SEVENTEEN

Athson shrugged. Was her support just words? She had a suitor waiting for her. Somewhere. "What if the others scout out Corgren? I find the bow while they sneak my father away. Then, then…" Then what? His mother died?

Limbreth lowered her face. "What about your mother?" She sighed. "Tough questions and no answers. Yet."

Athson paced away and back. "Well, just get some sleep. We push on before the moon."

A falling star streaked across the sky. Athson remembered a similar sight in his vision at Eagle's Aerie. The arrow Eloch prepared. He frowned at the sparkling sky. The inheritance lay in his pack. The same words written on the will. He needed an arrow?

"That was beautiful."

"Yes." Athson managed. "There's supposed to be an arrow."

Still watching the sky, Limbreth frowned. "What arrow?"

"It's in the prophecy." He thumbed over his shoulder toward camp. "It's in that will I got. I don't know where that is. I remember something. A falling star like a smoking arrow from back at Eagle's Aerie. But if it's not with the Bow of Hart I don't know what to do to find it. But if I did, I'd have something to fight back with. Maybe."

"Perhaps, but at least we'll know if it's there, and maybe we can ask Howart, if he's there…" She lifted her arms to his shoulders and stepped closer, her eyes still to the sky. "Then we'll decide. You know we'll do something based on all that information. There's an answer, Athson. It's not hopeless."

He scowled a moment then realized her tone held encouragement. "Thanks." He held her a while under the stars as the time slipped past him.

They pushed their pace throughout the next day and into the night before they came to the Long Run River. With their lanterns, they crossed the shoals and camped for the remainder of the night and dried themselves by a fire. In the morning, they found troll-spoor around the crossing, all signs that they were being scouted.

Athson read the troll-spoor with Gweld. "I just wish I knew where he was."

Gweld slapped his back. "We do. With Corgren, and the wizard wants the Bow of Hart. Best we go, eh?"

Spark stood beside Athson, hackles up. He squinted into along the river. Maybe trolls hid nearby. But he followed Gweld back to the others, Spark trailing him.

Makwi pointed northwest. "This will be the driest we get for a while, but it will be warmer in those fens, yonder."

Athson lifted his head. Tall grass stretched into the distance, broken only by occasional thickets and twisted trees until the edge of the wooded swamp. Birds soared and dove into the water farther west. There was probably a lake that way. He frowned. "Lots of mud means lots of footprints left behind. Ralda will leave deep ones." This was foolish with the threat of trolls or worse. He shook his head.

Makwi shrugged. "Nothin' for it. But we can stay in their prints as long as we can."

When they left, Limbreth offered her hand and pulled Athson to his feet. "Cheer up. We'll know soon enough." She held onto his hand and led him behind Makwi.

Their way turned wet soon afterward, and their pace slowed. Makwi sought the driest paths leading northeast among the fens. Often enough they retreated at one dead-end or another, but by sunset they entered the tree line and found a dry—more or less—patch of ground among the thick trees that stood on exposed roots.

"Watch for snakes." Makwi found dry enough fuel for a fire, so they soon had a meal cooking. "Boil any water you collect."

Ralda kept fidgeting and muttering about snakes.

Tordug hunched over the fire and watched for the water to boil. "How far now?"

Makwi shrugged. "Two days, maybe three."

Ralda groaned.

Gweld smacked his arm and flicked a dead bug away. "You're sure of the way? We shifted direction often this afternoon."

CHAPTER SEVENTEEN

Makwi blew out his mustache and tugged his beard. "We'll find the rim of the swamp where land rises out of the bottom-land. It's drier there, and we can follow that to the Withling's hole in a big rock formation." The dwarf held his hands apart to emphasize the size of the rock formation.

Athson tossed a stick into the fire. "Who is this other Withling?"

"Howart?" Makwi chuckled and shook his head with a grin. "He's a hermit and an oddity. He's lived here so long, he may not even know just how long it's been."

"I never heard much of him. Just the name of the cave." Athson motioned to Gweld. "How about you?" He would know, if anyone else did.

Gweld glanced away with a shrug. "One hears rumor of Withlings throughout the years. If they want to be found, they are—like Hastra."

Athson opened his mouth to complain about the old woman but shut it. No sense in discussing her again. She was hostage and nothing he did would change it. Either the bow was in the cave or not. He touched his sword. Spark sat across the fire, tongue out and panting.

Water plopped in pools all around them. Frogs croaked, and other creatures uttered their calls near and far. Night closed quickly in the swamp. Ralda stirred at some movement and wiggled his hands. Gweld rose and paced around their camp. Tordug hummed a tune with his eyes closed and leaned against a tree, its writhing limbs festooned with hanging vine and moss. Makwi muttered over the kettle while the fire gleamed in his eyes. And Limbreth watched Athson.

He lay on his back and stared at the swamp's canopy. It smelled, and he just wanted to leave. He clenched his jaw. He might be done with the rangers after this fruitless search. Nothing held him to Auguron. Tattered swamp mist drifted through the trees. Patches of sky appeared through rents in the cloud cover. Stars winked at him here and there.

A shadow moved among the branches. That was not mist or cloud. Athson tensed, sat up, and reached for his sword. Spark stared in the same direction. Shadows flitted across the starlight. He cleared his throat. "Limbreth, do you sense the Bane nearby?"

She cocked her head. "Not at all. Why?"

"Something of shadow watches from the trees. There…" He pointed.

Limbreth lifted her chin with her mouth slightly agape and spread her hands. "Where?"

"They won't hurt you." Makwi stirred the soup. "Howart calls them Lurks. They watch but don't cause physical harm. But they are deceptive and corrupt the land here. That's what he says, at least."

Athson's eyes narrowed. The dwarf talked like a Withling. "How do you know so much?"

Makwi paused and fixed Athson with an indefinite expression. "I've been here in years past, as I said. I saw these creatures then and, after meeting Howart, asked about them. He also told me this place was not a swamp when he arrived here long ago."

"How long ago? What is he doing here?"

Makwi stirred the soup again but shrugged as he did. "You can ask Howart whatever you want—if he's here. I only know he arrived sometime after whatever happened to the Withling's Order over in the Grey Spires centuries ago."

Athson gripped his sword. "Can they be killed? Shot?"

"Lurks? Perhaps, if you've a mind to track them in this mess. Now let me finish this if you want to eat." Makwi ended with a dismissive wave of his hand.

"I don't like something evil watching me."

Tordug cracked one eye open. "Relax. If Makwi thought them threatening, we'd do something."

Ralda wiggled his hands and spread them palms down over the ground. "Snakes more seen this place."

Makwi chuckled. "You're right there, giant."

Athson cocked an eyebrow at Gweld and flicked his gaze toward the branches.

The elf watched the shadows for a moment. "Best not waste arrows in the dark. If they can't be shot, then we'd be out good arrows when we have short supply."

Athson sat cross-legged and folded his arms across his chest. Things were

CHAPTER SEVENTEEN

only getting worse, and no one seemed alarmed. He scratched his neck. But Gweld was probably right.

Makwi tapped his spoon on the kettle. "Soup's ready. I'll boil enough water. Then, I'll put the fire out soon, lest we draw flies and such, so best eat while you can see."

They ate, set their watch, and slept. Athson slept well on either side of his middle watch. They passed the night without incident and rose before sunrise. Makwi guided them with a lantern of glow-moss until sunrise. Thereafter, they slogged through mud and followed what game trails were to be found, headed for the northern slope of the swamp.

Athson never caught direct sight of a Lurk, but movement among branches overhead kept his head turning. He was as jumpy as Ralda about the snakes. Even Limbreth wasn't troubled. Spark watched but didn't raise his hackles. Athson eventually stopped bothering with the Lurks since no one else did.

By late afternoon they had climbed out of the mud and onto a gentle, wooded slope that swept west around the lower fens. The stench slackened, and they hiked with ease until almost sunset. They halted and set a hasty camp with a pit fire.

Athson yawned as they ate. "How long until we reach this rock formation and this other Withling?"

Makwi ate with his head lowered but arched a bushy brow to stare at Athson while he chewed. "I don't know. Maybe tomorrow. Maybe the day after."

"Lost your bearings?" Athson frowned. Just what they needed. The Withling gone, and they were lost in the wilderness.

"It's not my bearings. Howart is hidden. When he's to be found, he is."

Limbreth wiped her face. "How's that?"

Tordug belched. "What is needed is given. When Howart's presence is needed, it will be given."

Athson groaned in his best imitation of Ralda.

Makwi grinned. "But I think we shall find what we need soon, if what we need is there at all."

The next morning, the slate sky grew darker with the threat of rain. Mist rose from the swamp in thick billows and carried the stronger scent of decay. The wind gusted, and dead leaves rattled among the trees or along the ground.

Athson muttered about when they would find what they "needed." He kicked some dead limbs.

Limbreth nudged him. "Are you there?"

"What?"

"Gweld's been motioning to you. I think he wants you to quit that racket."

"Sorry." He nodded to Gweld and Makwi when he caught their gazes. His noise didn't matter. The noise of the wind covered it. But he'd been foolish. He should have been more attentive. The Bane or some trolls might show up. Movement among tree limbs caught his attention again. Those Lurks might draw attention to them.

By mid-morning, thunder rumbled in the distance. The swamp mist swirled in the rising wind.

Athson wrestled with his hood and leaned against the gusts. "I wish we'd find Howart and shelter from this storm."

Limbreth raised her voice over the rustle of wind. "I don't like the thought of being washed into the swamp."

Athson replied with a vigorous nod.

They halted, their mouths opened as they stared. Ahead, the mist parted, and in the growing gloom, a massive bulk of stone loomed among the trees. It rose perhaps ten spans high where the slope slanted sharper. Its summit climbed from higher on the slope like a construction ramp. From there it fell with cracks and crevices, where large oaks rose around it. The mist lingered at the base of the formation.

Makwi waved them forward. "Just what we needed."

Tordug spread his arms and lifted his face. "And it was given."

Rain pelted on the carpet of leaves. Ralda trotted ahead, and soon they all followed his lead against the storm. They found shelter under an outcropping as the storm released a torrent of rain. They drank water and dried themselves.

CHAPTER SEVENTEEN

Athson put away his water-skin and wiped his chin. "Now what?" They'd found what they needed, but where was Howart?

Makwi motioned with both hands toward an unnoticed crevice. "Howart's palace awaits."

Athson peered into the darkness. He sighed and shrugged his pack off his shoulders. "I suppose I must go. No time like now."

Makwi lifted his lantern. "I've been there, so I'll guide you."

Gweld dropped his pack. "And I'll go with you."

Limbreth followed Athson. "I'm coming too." She kissed him. "I'm with you this time."

Athson hugged her. "Thanks." He needed her with him. Maybe always, if they survived this at all. If she was as true as her word. But there was that suitor back in Grendon for her to deal with…

Makwi paused. "Someone must watch."

Tordug sat on a rock. "Ralda and I will stay as guards."

With their numbers divided, Athson and his companions squirmed into the crevice in search of Howart and the Bow of Hart.

CHAPTER EIGHTEEN

"Wake up." Someone shook Hastra.

She stirred. Her mouth tasted bitter "Hmmm?" It was light outside. Someone wearing a wide-brimmed hat knelt beside her. She narrowed her eyes. Something familiar about him. Her eyes fluttered, and the thought drifted away. She laid her head down again.

He shook her again. "Wake up. It's time to go."

She peeked at him. "So tired. Where am I?"

"Where you have been for several weeks now."

"Oh yes, there." She frowned. "I'm not sure where that is."

"Let's get you up." He took Hastra by the shoulders and brought her to her feet.

She wobbled when she stood. "Who are you? Do you have water?" She noticed a cup on the table and reached for it.

The man offered her a water-skin instead. "I don't think you should drink that brew."

She drank, and some spilled from her mouth and chin. It was sweeter than what she remembered having in a while. She gulped and gulped.

The man pulled it away. "I think that's enough for now. You need to get going. You can have more later."

"Yes, I suppose you're right." Her head felt clearer than it had in a long time, but not enough. "I'm hungry."

Her helper took her hand and pulled her to the door. "You'll need to wait a while for that." He stopped her and began working with her feet.

CHAPTER EIGHTEEN

Hastra chuckled. "That tickles."

"You need your boots to travel. There's snow, and it's cold."

She wiggled her toes on the wooden floor. "Well, I don't recall what happened to my boots."

"I have them, let me help you with them." He soon had her boots on and then he led her out the door.

Hastra wobbled as she walked. They walked past other people—Rokans by their dress—and soldiers. "What is this place? Where are we going?" Mountains loomed in the distance ahead of them.

"You're in Rok as a prisoner. You need to go over the mountains. But you need to leave now. The Dragon has had His way long enough. You've done what you can for now. Almost." He pulled her along.

Hastra stumbled after him. "But I'm so tired. Can't think clearly. I need to rest."

"That will get better. I'll help you. You need to help when you get over the mountains."

"But that's so far."

"Just trust me."

That sounded familiar, and she was out of her captivity. She leaned against her benefactor as they walked among the rows of buildings. Rokan guardsmen marched past them. They turned between buildings and found a woman crouched and sobbing softly.

They paused, and Hastra touched her. "Do you need help?"

The woman gasped and raised a hand to her throat. Her tear-stained face revealed weathered lines on a middle-aged woman. "Uh, no. Don't tell them I'm here or I'll be whipped." Her eyes narrowed. "Wait. I recognize you when they tied us up. But he's a stranger here. Who are you?"

The man on whom Hastra leaned never hesitated. "If you want help, it has come. There will be confusion soon. Come with us."

The woman clenched her hand still at her throat. "But I cannot. My hand, it's marked with magic so they can follow me."

"Show me."

She extended her hand. A mark like the visage of a dragon glowed red on her skin.

Hastra touched the mark. "If only I had my wits, I'd remove it. But I've barely the concentration to talk." Her head dropped.

The man touched the woman's hand. "It is done."

The Rokan slave looked at her hand. The mark remained. "But it's still here. You've done nothing."

The man's hat brim brushed Hastra's cheek. "Haven't I? Just trust that it is done. For now, no one will notice a difference on your hand. Gather what you will and follow up there." He pointed to a short ridge covered with trees and stone.

"Yes." The woman rubbed her cheeks clear of tears and slipped away.

The man tugged his hat brim with a nod and moved with Hastra down the alley. "Come quickly." He hauled her into a quick step.

She struggled with her helper out of the encampment and into a stand of trees. The wind picked up, and the chill stirred her wits. They climbed amid new-fallen snow out of the vale and onto a pine-covered ridge studded with gray humps of rock decorated with snow as well.

The Withling's eyes lifted to the afternoon sky. That woman, her eyes were familiar. Hastra looked over her shoulder at the encampment.

"Don't look back. Hurry!"

She turned her head forward and pushed her pace. But her legs were so heavy still. She must keep moving.

Horns and shouts echoed up the vale below them.

The man pushed his water-skin into Hastra's hands. "Take this and drink it all. At the rise, kneel. You'll know what to do then."

The Rokan slave followed quickly and began the climb. Their rescuer helped the slave as far as where Hastra stood.

"Thank you, Eloch. I'm so thirsty." She drank.

The man beside her chuckled. "I've been many places and gone by many names but I'm hardly that."

"You're who?" She frowned. Must still be confused. Hastra hugged the water-skin and then drank. When she lowered it, she was alone with the Rokan slave-woman. She staggered in a circle. "Where'd he go?"

CHAPTER EIGHTEEN

The Rokan slave stood slack-jawed and stammered, "He, he was here and then he, he wasn't here. Who is he?"

Hastra scratched her cheek. "I don't know." What was she to do? Go on to the top. Drink it all. Yes, that was it. Hastra stumbled and bent into the slope as she climbed higher. Every few steps, she paused and drank from the water-skin. It tasted so good. "Help me." She offered her arm to the other woman, who half dragged Hastra up the hill. "Who are you? Your face looks familiar."

Behind her, the noise of pursuit mounted. Men shouted among the trees. Horns sounded and dogs bayed.

"My name is Danilla. I've been a slave for years. Step here. Yes, that's better footing. Hurry or they'll catch us!"

Hastra touched her head. "They must not catch us. He said, climb and drink." She took another deep swig and lifted her foot. She found more energy and climbed in earnest. The baying grew closer, but her head felt much clearer. Hastra pressed her pace and scrambled to the edge of the ridge beside Danilla.

She drank the remainder of the water-skin's contents and wiped her chin. The ridge afforded her a view. Men and dogs covered the slope below her, sweeping over the snow among the trees, looking in every hollow. It was so good to be able to think again.

Danilla glanced along the ridge at the pursuit. "What now? How are we to escape?"

Hastra fell to her knees. "This way." She uttered her prayer as Danilla dropped to her knees beside her.

The wind roared around her, and the sound of pursuit faded in it. Rain fell around them. When she opened her eyes, she was no longer in Rok, but a storm raged around her. A massive wall of darkness and rain boiled toward her and Danilla. Trees were uprooted in its path, and limbs flew past them. Hastra stood, raised her hands, and cried out in the wordless prayer long familiar to her.

The whirlwind lifted away. Hastra laughed. "That water sure was tasty." She shook the skin and got a few more drops from it. Now to find out where she was. "Come with me, Danilla, and taste your freedom. It's as sweet as that water was!"

CHAPTER NINETEEN

Makwi led the way between solid walls of jagged, natural stone. The dwarf held his lantern aloft as they squirmed into the darkness. The echoes of thunder and rain from back down the cave faded.

Athson followed everyone with Tordug's lantern. He touched his sword and cast one last glance outside. Spark sat waiting. The mountain hound waited? It must be safe. Somehow it wasn't comforting.

The crag was closer than the approach to the Well of the trolls. Just not that horrid spell. Uneven stone challenged Athson's footing. He and Limbreth stumbled more than once. They often scrambled sideways, hugged by both darkness and stone.

Water dribbled on Athson. He raised the lantern and dried his face. "How far is it? Will it be safe from water?"

"Safe enough. Can't you swim?" Makwi's grim chuckle echoed.

Limbreth smirked and rolled her eyes. "Dwarf humor."

"Yeah."

Makwi laughed louder. "I heard that!"

They squirmed and writhed deeper into the earth. Sweat rose on Athson's forehead in the close quarters. If only it were cooler here. "I understand how worms feel."

Limbreth made a face like she tasted something bitter. "Thanks for that picture."

The crack opened into a small chamber of scattered rocks half buried in dirt. The air blew cool in their faces.

Athson nudged Limbreth. "Found something you don't like."

She lowered her chin in the dim light and her lips narrowed. "And what of it?"

Gweld dabbed his face. "Why's it so hot back there."

Makwi tugged his beard. "Hot? It's gotten cooler all the way in."

"Well it's been hot to the rest of us." Limbreth wiped her face and showed her sleeve to the dwarf.

Athson nodded.

"That's really odd. There's not hot spring near here that I can tell." Makwi shrugged. "You three must be hot-natured."

Gweld frowned. "I guess so, maybe."

Athson cocked his head. Gweld didn't seem very sure of that answer. Why were they hot?

"Howart's cave is this way." Makwi pointed into a deeper recess.

"Beautiful place for a hermit to live." Athson shuffled after the dwarf and the others.

Makwi scrambled into a space little more than a hole. "You'd have never found him, ranger."

Athson ducked into the deeper cave. All this crawling underground. He hoped they got something out of it. His throat went dry. Maybe if he found nothing it would be better. What would he do with the bow once he found it—if it was real. What would he say if there was nothing? What about his father, mother and Hastra? His heart twisted in his chest. It had to be there. He didn't know where else to look for it.

Makwi squirmed deeper and the uneven ceiling rose. The dwarf turned sideways as the cave narrowed. He fell back against Gweld and grunted. The lantern clanged against stone. Gweld stumbled back and knocked Limbreth into Athson. He caught her under the arms and his fingers touched something soft.

Limbreth's brows knitted and her lips squeezed tightly. "Careful, there."

Heat rose on Athson's cheeks. "Sorry." He considered the softness a moment. Best pay attention. The bow and all that. Still. He exhaled.

CHAPTER NINETEEN

Makwi held the light aloft where he sat. "Something pushed me back."

Gweld offered a hand to the dwarf. "You're getting clumsy."

"No really. Something pushed me. Try it yourself."

Gweld stepped forward. *Pop!* Green light blinded Athson for several moments. The others gasped and covered their eyes. Gweld flew back, arms and legs flailing, and slammed into the rock wall. The elf slid onto the stone and dirt with thud and a grunt. They helped the stunned elf to his feet.

Athson brushed off his back. "What was that? You alright?"

Gweld winced and rubbed his head with one hand and his side with the other. "Hit my head and a rock gouged my side. I don't know what the light was."

"That'll leave a bruise." Makwi peered ahead with his lantern held forward. "I don't see anything."

"Now what?" Athson leaned against the cave wall. "No way through so no Bow of Hart?"

Makwi scowled. "There's a way. I've been there with Howart."

"Wait you went in with Howart last time you were here?" Limbreth peered ahead and then at the dwarf.

"Well, yes, that's right."

Athson sighed and rested his head on his forearm where it was on the rock. "So, we just wait for Howart to come along—if he's still alive—and then we get in?" He rolled his head along his forearm. What a waste of effort. He was stuck with no bow. He knew it all along. Hastra was so wrong and his parents would suffer along with her. His heart sank into emptiness in his belly.

"Wait." Makwi squinted at Athson. "The bow is meant for you. If your father came with it then maybe you can go on too."

"Really, that simple?"

"Just try." Makwi glanced at Gweld who still rubbed his side. "Gently."

Athson shuffled past Limbreth and leaned close with a smile. "Catch me. And then we all have that talk."

She punched his arm. "Just try it."

231

Athson's boots scrapped on the stone as he stooped and edged ahead. He leaned back and waited with jaws clenched. Whatever power lay here would throw him back like Gweld. He kept moving. Nothing happened.

"Ah, just go." Makwi pushed him.

Athson lunged forward. He grunted but caught his balance after a few steps. He was past whatever barrier stopped Gweld and Makwi.

"I guess you go on alone from here." Makwi motioned Athson along. "It's not far and there are no other passages. Even a dwarf baby could do it."

Athson clenched his jaws. "Whatever!" He whirled and stumbled away. There was a time he'd hoped Hastra was wrong. Not any longer, not for his parents' sake.

~ ~ ~ ~ ~ ~ ~

Tordug turned from the crack as the others scrambled into the dark with only a glow-moss lantern for light. "I guess we'll know if it's here soon enough. No telling how long it'll be, though."

Ralda peered into the crevice where the others were looking for Howart. He scratched the nape of his neck. "Too small there, me go." He shrugged and wiggled his fingers. Rain fell in sheets beyond the overhang of rock.

"C'mon, let's set these packs in order and eat." Tordug worked the pack off his shoulders and set it under the overhang.

Ralda snagged Athson's pack and put it near the crevice. They moved the packs discarded by Limbreth and Gweld as well before they settled for a rest out of the rain. Thunder rumbled, and the rain fell so thick that the trees were almost obscured. Lightning flashed in frequent succession.

They ate, and Ralda nearly dozed. He stood and stretched. A sleeping guard wouldn't do. He motioned with his hands. "Sleepy."

Tordug closed his pack. "Let's set our guard. I'll warrant those Lurks are troublesome."

Ralda wiggled his hand, thumb up. "Snake." But no telling if the Lurks might stir up trouble for them or not.

Tordug laughed. "You take the left, and I'll watch this side."

Ralda nodded and shook his head. He took up a position at the edge of the overhang with his staff in hand.

CHAPTER NINETEEN

The rain dropped to a slight shower after a while. Though he propped his chin on the end of his staff and gripped it two-handed, his eyes drooped. "Rain sing sleep me."

The putrid smell of the swamp rose as the rain slackened. Ralda scrunched his face. He would be too glad to leave the snakes and the stench. The wind shifted and rustled through the trees. That was better. But Ralda heard a different sound. Footfalls. He sniffed again. A sour smell drifted under his nose. He squinted through the trees along the slope. Shapes shifted in the undergrowth. "Trolls!"

Trolls sprang from among tree trunks. Grunts, roars and hisses announced their arrival.

"More from the other side." Tordug backed away, his ax held ready.

Ralda glanced over his shoulder and his chest tightened at the sight of more trolls. They snarled and brandished weapons. There were so many. More than three double-fists! "We trap. Too many." He backed close to Tordug with his staff raised.

Many of the trolls drew arrows and aimed at them.

Ralda's shoulders slumped. There was no chance. He groaned.

The trolls split, and Corgren stepped from among them. Behind him, the Bane loomed, leading a one-eyed man on a chain. Ralda's eyes widened. Athson's father. He lived indeed. But little good it did them. He shuddered at the sight of the Bane.

Corgren stood with feet apart and hands on his hips. "I think surrender would be wise."

Tordug spat and raised his ax again. "We'll take a few with us, Ralda."

"I think not. I can use a spell." Corgren chuckled.

Ralda sighed and dropped his staff. Tordug grumbled in dwarvish but laid his ax on the ground.

"That's better." Corgren strode past them toward the cave. "You both might survive."

Ralda doubted the wizard's words. Beside him, Tordug clenched his fists.

"Tie them." Corgren then motioned to the cave. "I presume the others went this way?"

Ralda remained silent, as did Tordug.

"I see that is the case." Corgren motioned to the Bane. "Follow me but leave that vile slave here." Corgren and the Bane squirmed into the cave, followed by a few hobgoblins.

Trolls came forward and tied Ralda and the dwarf hand and foot, then left them lying beside one another and forced Ath to the ground near them.

After a moment, Ralda cleared his throat. "I Ralda. Giant of plains. You Ath?"

Ath shifted toward him. "You know me?"

Tordug kept his voice at a hoarse whisper. "We've traveled with your son. We're after the bow."

Ath snorted. "You needed an army."

"Ralda, here, is an army himself. Eats like one too."

They all chuckled while the trolls watched them and quarreled with each other. Humor while facing death was a good. There was no hope, so why not laugh?

~ ~ ~ ~ ~ ~ ~

Limbreth's shoe scuffed on the rock. She should have gone with Athson. Gweld still rubbed his side where he'd landed after being repelled forcibly. Maybe if she'd held Athson's hand she could have gotten through with him. She sighed. "Want some help there?"

Gweld shook his head. "Nah, it'll be fine. Feels like Ralda punched me though."

"You can go back out with the others." Makwi sat, leaning against the stone like it was his home.

"How far is it?" Limbreth quit tapping her book. Hiking no longer hurt her feet. She'd never noticed when it stopped.

Makwi adjusted his beard. "Far enough, but not hours."

She cocked her head and frowned at the dwarf. "Thanks for the sarcasm. How long has it been since Athson left?"

The dwarf arched an eyebrow. "Not that long."

Limbreth glanced at Gweld.

The elf shrugged. "How would I know in here? But he's right, it's not

CHAPTER NINETEEN

been long."

Silence lengthened between them. Funny how they'd traveled so far and had so little to say. She guessed they were tired. Limbreth yawned. Not enough sleep the last few days. She sighed. It was too little room to pace, so she settled for crossing her arms. "I hope he finds it."

Gweld patted her arm. "If it's there, he will."

Makwi nodded.

Sounds of movement reached them. Makwi stood, his face tense.

Limbreth pushed away from the rock at her back. "Something wrong?"

He shifted his eyes to her and then back into the darkness that crowded their lantern light. "Probably just Tordug come to check on us." He touched his ax.

A quiver ran along Limbreth's spine. "It's so cold now, I—the Bane! It's here!" She reached for a sword and whirled.

Gweld grunted and collapsed. He stared at nothing and quivered.

A black-cloaked shape entered the light, which dimmed.

Makwi jabbed with his ax haft, but the Bane flowed around the attack. Misty hands touched the dwarf. He dropped and stared just like Gweld, shivering as frost formed on his beard.

Limbreth backed away, sword extended. "No! Stay away."

The Bane struck. The cloak flapped as it flowed around her. Limbreth whirled. Hands grasped from behind. One clasped her mouth and the other her sword arm. Trolls! The hobgoblin squeezed her wrist, and she dropped her sword.

"Well, we have a princess, a worthless dwarf, and a useless elf. What a menagerie!"

The hobgoblin wrenched Limbreth around with a hiss. She trembled. Where was the Bane? A whimper escaped her.

A hook-nosed man stepped into the light. He caressed her face with the back of his hand. "My master likes blood such as yours." He drew back. "Allow me to introduce myself. I'm Corgren Vanthai. And you are my prisoner."

Limbreth writhed but couldn't break the grip on her. Athson needed a

235

warning. But how? There was no way to enter. Did the barrier block sound? No, he had talked to them. She bit the hobgoblin. "Aths—"

Corgren slapped her. Stars hung in her vision. The hobgoblin clapped its scaly hand over her mouth again and held her jaw closed.

Corgren leaned close. "None of that."

The wizard stepped away. He motioned toward the narrowed cave, and two hobgoblins tried to go forward. The first was thrown back. It bounced off the rock and fell in a writhing heap of pain. The second paused.

Corgren squeezed past it. "So Eloch keeps unwanted visitors away from Howart and the bow. Then we'll just set a little trap. Move that dwarf just there." Corgren directed the scene and poses. When the trolls finished their work, the wizard motioned them back into the darkness. "Now we wait. Gag her for now. We'll let her talk when the time comes."

The trolls knotted a piece of sour cloth tightly around Limbreth's head and bound her arms.

Through tears, she saw the Bane meld into cave shadows, waiting for Athson.

CHAPTER TWENTY

The further he went, the wetter Athson found his surroundings. He slipped and caught his balance more than once on the slick stone. It was cooler. The passage yawned away into darkness, and the path lay smoother. Someone had moved the loose rock from underfoot. That alone confirmed someone had lived here at some point. He jumped at the sound of drips into hidden pools. He swung the lantern around, but darkness crowded close. He hunched his shoulders and took the path.

After a short trek, he halted. Did he see a light ahead? He shuttered the glow-moss. A soft glow shone in the darkness. Perhaps this other Withling waited ahead. He shook his head. "No, couldn't be. It's just an exit."

Athson opened the shutter on the lantern and followed the path toward the light. He jerked to a stop. "That was close. Glad I opened the lantern." The path took a sharp turn, and below his feet lay of pool of water that stretched to his left into darkness. *No telling how deep that is.* Or how cold. Or whether he could have crawled out of it. The path led him to the right and skirted the edge of the water until he was forced to climb over rocks and follow the path as it continued on the other side.

The light grew quickly as he approached the far end of the natural chamber. He gasped and stood still. He'd seen this before. "That dream outside Chokkra." The light reached for him from the darkness then—and now. The vision was identical to what he had witnessed back outside Chokkra. Athson groaned. If only there was escape from these visions.

He recovered from his surprise and strode toward the light. It didn't flicker or vary in intensity. Athson drew his sword. He wasn't entering the next chamber off his guard. He shuttered the lantern and set it beside the path.

He glimpsed footprints in the light. Larger than a dwarf's. A man was here. He pressed his lips close and tread lightly as he approached. Athson made the turn and found another chamber opening beneath steady light, but not from an outside source. This was no exit.

With his sword held ready, Athson checked for traps or anyone hiding in the shadows. The chamber roof vaulted high, but light shone on it. A few rough shelves stood against the rock. A few rough chairs sat empty. Athson took stealthy steps into the little cavern. "What is this place?"

"And who might you be?"

Athson whirled. A man of indefinite age sat on a carpet. He tilted his head but never moved otherwise. "Howart? Are you Howart? The Withling?"

The man shook his head, and wisps of gray hair fell in his eyes. "I'll gift my name for yours. Who might you be, to pass Eloch's Gate and come to his hidden chamber?"

"I'm Athson." Eloch's Gate? He must mean the barrier that repelled the others. Athson stepped closer. "My father was Ath of Depenburgh. Did you know him?" He pulled out the ring and necklace. "These were his. I've been told you have something for me, though I don't know why."

"I am Howart of the Withlings, such as we still are." The old man unfolded his gaunt body from his cross-legged pose on the threadbare carpet. He moved closer, and his eyes narrowed. "But I do see the father in the son before me." He examined the heirlooms Athson held and motioned farther into the chamber. "Come, I have some bread and wine you can eat. We'll talk." Howart put his hand on Athson's shoulder and led him to a table where bread lay on a wooden platter. Howart retrieved a bottle from a shelf.

Athson groaned. The table was just like his dream. Athson sat and waited while his host poured. He glanced all around. "Where does the light come from? You have no fire."

"For you." Howart offered a cracked cup, which Athson took. "It is Eloch's gift for me. I have all that I need. I've been fed by penniless widows and

CHAPTER TWENTY

birds, among many other ways, over my long years."

"My thanks. The lives of Withlings are strange indeed." Athson chewed some bread, surprised it wasn't stale, and sipped the red wine. If Hastra was right, then—

He choked, coughed, and set the cup down. Wine sloshed on his hands, and he looked at his stained palms. An image flashed in his mind of actual blood on them. He slowly shook his head. Whose was it? No, it wasn't real. The bow was likely here too. He wiped his hands on his dark breeches.

"It's not that bad, is it? Gone to vinegar?" The Withling slapped Athson on the back.

Athson coughed until his throat cleared, but his voice was hoarse when he answered. "No, it's fine. I just realized something surprising." It was very dry wine, though. He wiped tears from his eyes.

"And what is that?"

"If you knew my father and Hastra is right, then the Bow of Hart is here, isn't it?" His breath caught. His father did have it. He toyed with the cup.

"It is, left in my safekeeping, since no one enters here without Eloch's leave but me." Howart sat.

Athson lifted his cup again and tapped his fingernails on it. "Then everything else is real. The bowstring, the visions, the inheritance, everything."

"Of course it's real." The Withling stood and reached for a natural shelf of stone. He twitched a cloth away and retrieved an unstrung bow of gray color.

Athson rose from the table, the cup forgotten in his grasp. "And I thought it was all just my…" Best not tell all his secrets. "So they sacked my home for that. It looks brittle, at best."

Howart shrugged. "What is needed is given." He offered the bow to Athson, who set down the cup and accepted it.

His throat constricted. His vision blurred. Athson's father had born this bow. Everyone else from Depenburgh was dead because of it. All his friends. All the children. He dropped it like it seared his hands and whirled away, wiping his eyes. "Why? What's it all for?"

"I only know that it is not for Magdronu."

Athson's sudden laughter sounded bitter even to his ears. "So I've heard from Hastra."

"Why isn't she with you?"

"She never made it over the mountains. Corgren, or somebody, captured her. Probably won't see her again." He turned back to the table and found Howart had set the bow on it.

"Captured? Only by Eloch's will though." He looked like he knew something but said nothing else. Howart motioned to the chair. "Please sit, we'll talk awhile."

Athson stood with his hands in his pockets. "What's to say? I've suffered for this bow that's supposed to destroy Magdronu. But I don't even want it. I don't care what it's for."

"Sit. You can tell me."

Athson tucked his chin and ground his teeth. There was no trusting a Withling. "I have friends waiting." *Yes, waiting to see me with the bow.* He was wrong. Everything was wrong and so confusing. But there was no leaving now, not without the Bow of Hart. "I just need to know what it's for."

Howart patted the bow. "Eloch has given a task and the means to do it. He will reveal more, but you must discover that for yourself, if you will." He pushed the bow across the table. "The choice is yours, like it has been for others over the ages." His gaze lifted to Athson. "Me, Hastra, Zelma, Thayer, your father. We all made a choice, and so must you."

The Bow of Hart lay before him. The desire of enemies he never chose within his reach. He stretched out his hand. Could he be the destroyer of his foes? The bow wasn't his destroyer. His enemies needed death. No, that was revenge! He snatched back his hand. But his father had hidden it, perhaps hoped in Athson once he was taken.

Athson took the bow. He cradled it in his arm. "I'll take it up for my father's sake." *Dead or alive.*

Howart arched one brow. "Your motivations are your own choice. Only be careful of them, or they will sift you like flour in a bakery."

"Withling riddles." Athson shook his head with a frown. "I'll take it and

CHAPTER TWENTY

do what's needed if someone will just let me know what the task is."

Howart burst to his feet and loomed over the table like a skeleton. "Have a care, Athson of Auguron, son of Thatanath, of friend and foe, but mostly of yourself."

"I'll take this and my leave then." Athson stood tall and squared his shoulders. He remembered his manners and saluted to his host elven-style. With his silent farewell, Athson whirled and left Howart's cavern. He turned into the cave, and all went dark. He knelt and felt in the sandy dirt for his lantern. "Confound that Withling. Playing tricks on me."

The lantern clattered in his grasp. He opened the shutters and it cast thin glow-moss light in the cave. Then he snatched the Bow of Hart and stomped back into the cavern with curt words on his tongue. But in the light of his lantern, Howart's cavern lay empty of everything. There were no chairs, tables, or shelves. No wine, cups, or bread.

No Withling.

Athson left after a few moments and scurried away from the chamber. Time to get on with whatever his task may be. He skirted the pool and strode the smooth path in haste.

The faint glow of the other lantern glimmered ahead of him. The narrow way. It must be Eloch's Gate, as Howart named it. It required that Athson go through hunched.

He stopped. There were no voices. Maybe two of them went back and left someone to watch for him.

Athson shuttered the lantern. Those Lurks might draw attention. He leaned lower and glimpsed the way ahead. Makwi's lantern sat balanced on a rock but nothing moved. He edged as far over as possible. The tips of a pair of boots—toes pointed up—were the only indication someone was there. Those were Makwi's, by the style. Was he asleep? Athson doubted it. Not Makwi.

He waited. Sweat beaded on his brow in the cool cave. Athson slid his sword free.

At the whisper of his movement, something fluttered past the lantern. The boots never moved.

Was it a Lurk? Athson held his sword out. If only he knew who—or what—waited for him beyond Eloch's Gate. It waited there, unable to enter. He was safe, but not his friends.

His eyes narrowed. A black cloak fit what had rustled past the lantern. The Bane was there. And where that thing lurked...

He swallowed. "Makwi? You there?"

Silence answered his call. The boots remained still.

He waited.

Few choices presented themselves to Athson. Either he charged through a narrow way and fought the Bane and whatever—or whoever—else there may be, including Corgren, or he stayed in safety. But the others were in danger. If only he knew their condition. He was safe for the moment, but they might all be dead. His jaw clenched. Not Gweld! Not Limbreth! Not again...

Energy filled his limbs for a mad charge. He had to help if he could. If he failed, then—

"Athson, are you there? Can you hear me?"

The voice and situation echoed from Athson's childhood. Corgren was here. His breath caught and his heart thudded in his throat. Thank Eloch for the sword, or he might have had a fit. He waited, though he wanted to rush the wizard.

"Either you won't talk, or it's nothing but threats. I just want the bow. You do have it, don't you?"

The voice coaxed, but Athson withstood the temptation. "You can't reach me here."

"And that means you have it, or Eloch wouldn't be protecting it. Remember the deal. Now it's the girl, your father, your mother, and Hastra for the Bow of Hart."

"Murderous bastard. I'll kill you." Athson's chest heaved. He'd dive through and attack. Corgren's magic would deflect off his blessed sword.

The wizard laughed. "Come here, wench!"

Feet scuffled, and Limbreth fell hard into view. Terror painted her face. She gasped and sobbed. "Athson, don't let him have it."

CHAPTER TWENTY

A boot stepped on her neck. Limbreth screamed.

"She's special to you, no? I know the feeling. It's not unfamiliar to me, though it was long ago."

"I'll kill you if you hurt her. Any of them."

Corgren's laughter echoed. "She's more special than you know. Royal blood. My master likes that."

"You wouldn't dare."

Limbreth's eyes rolled. She whimpered and sobbed. "The Bane has my legs."

A hand touched her cheek. "Wouldn't I? Poor thing. You see, Athson, she's a princess of Grendon. My master likes that kind of blood. It's got more kick."

"I'll kill you."

Corgren knelt and showed his face beside Limbreth's. "You threaten a lot." He laughed. "I don't like Grendon's power, have I ever told you that? No? Well, I don't." He smiled. His hooked nose cast a menacing shadow in the light of the glow-moss. "But I understand. It's hard to think here." He waved his hand at the surrounding rock. "It's cramped. You need a breath of fresh air." The smile faded. "Meet me at the Funnel. You know where. Bring the bow, or she meets the Hidden Dragon. There's one week until the full moon."

Corgren stood.

Limbreth was dragged away. "No, Athson! They'll just kill you when they have the bow!"

The noise of slapped flesh echoed. Limbreth grunted.

"Shut up. Follow me and make the trade, Athson, or else. I'm killing the others so you get the message when you leave the cave. Gag her. I'm sick of her screeching."

Athson gripped his sword. He groaned as his chest heaved. He almost charged. But his father had attacked rashly.

Limbreth's muffled cries and her boots scraping on the stone faded.

A troll kicked Makwi's lantern aside and dragged the dwarf away. He groaned. An eye twinkled in the torchlight and winked.

"I'll kill you!" Athson's shout echoed in the cave. It was an empty threat from his position. He clenched his teeth and paced in the narrow space. Makwi was alert, and that was something. Maybe the others were too. He should charge out and help them into the cave so they could defend the narrow space.

That was his father. Rash. That was Athson all too often as well. He'd wait just long enough and then go help. If he could. But not in an angry charge. He swallowed his rage just this once and grasped his blessed sword.

~ ~ ~ ~ ~ ~ ~

Corgren ducked out of the cave and inhaled. Fresh air at last. Good, there was less rain now, so he could set out.

The Bane rippled out of crevice, followed by the trolls leading the woman and carrying the dwarf. They passed with the elf.

Corgren smiled. His master still played his ruse. But Magdronu would make his appearance when necessary, resplendent and victorious. Just a few short days now. He motioned toward the other captives. "Put the dwarf and elf with the others. Tie the woman with a leash and give it to the Bane. Bring that wretch along too, I'll need him."

The trolls lay the unconscious dwarf by the other captives along with Corgren's unbound master. Hobgoblins bound the young woman, whose eyes rolled when they put her in the Bane's care with a respectful bow.

Corgren laughed. *The fool is a craven before true power.* "Hurry up! I wish to escape the storm while the rain has slackened!"

A bugbear hastened to the Bane with the slave's leash and retreated with fearful bows. Ath stumbled over rocks, struggling still with one eye.

Corgren motioned to the remaining four captives. "Kill them. They are not needed. But leave the elf and bring him later. Take what time you want but follow when you are finished. Eat the mules if you want." The trolls would obey in a day or so. But they had served their purpose. He didn't need them for his next task. He stood straight and squared his shoulders. "Now for my triumphant march. Bring these two."

The Bane followed Corgren as he climbed the slope. Rain still pattered around them. The woman and the half-blind man slipped more than once,

CHAPTER TWENTY

scrambling to their feet behind their uncaring warden.

Atop the slope, Corgren mounted his horse and turned north. The Bane motioned the reluctant captives to mount a horse while it too mounted another. Both of the captives' hands were bound, so they couldn't guide the horse, and the leads were taken by the Bane before they set out for the Funnel.

They covered perhaps a furlong before the rain ceased. Behind, thunder rolled a wall of rain over Howart's home, and the wind roared like a nest of hungry dragons.

~ ~ ~ ~ ~ ~ ~

Limbreth groaned at the chill of the Bane's touch as she rode bareback behind Athson's father. It had to be him, chained as he was. The Bane had her. She'd feared it for weeks, since the mountains. If only Athson could help. But he wasn't there. It was up to her. She had to do something. She clenched her left fist and took a deep breath. *Slide off.*

Corgren pushed the pace across the grassland and away from the storm. The implacable Bane would stop for nothing as long as Corgren's horse moved forward.

Limbreth shoved into Ath's back with the horse's shifting gait.

Ath grunted. "Who are you?" He turned a bit in the saddle.

"I'm Limbreth, a companion of your son. We've traveled in search of the Bow of Hart with a Withling named Hastra."

"So Athson was in there? Did he see Howart? I'm Ath, by the way."

"I guessed you were him. I don't know about Howart. And pleased to meet you, though not like this." She'd wait for the pace to slow. Then she'd try, just try.

"Then he's found it. Why are they taking you?"

The Bane yanked Ath's chain, Limbreth's rope, and the reins. She almost fell off but grabbed Ath in time to regain her balance.

She trembled. A pit widened in her belly. Adventure wasn't being roped and stolen from her friends and love. "I'm a hostage for the bow. Corgren will kill me otherwise."

Ath clenched his jaw. "He will likely come for us. But it may be best if doesn't. He can't give Corgren the bow."

Now Limbreth almost fell off on her own. Athson leave them to die? It was a weighty choice. All was lost without the bow, according to Hastra. "My friends can't help. I think they were killed." Her throat constricted at the thought. A rotten end for them. Her heart twisted with pain. Dead? Tordug? He'd taught her much, like a father. Sudden tears brimmed in her eyes. What of the others? She swallowed her sob. "If, if only Hastra could help—or Howart." She'd traveled and camped with her lost friends for months and now they were gone…

"Where are they?"

"I don't know about Howart. Maybe Athson is still with him. Hastra was captured. They're holding her hostage in Rok with your wife. Maybe Howart can help us and steer Athson from this choice."

Ath sat up straight. "Danilla hostage with Hastra. I knew she was there but I thought they'd forgotten her." He shook his head. "They held her all this time, just in case they needed her too." Ath cleared his throat. "Only Eloch knows what will happen. My rash decisions brought us to this. I should have hidden Athson instead of seeking revenge."

The Bane yanked their leads, but the pace slowed.

Limbreth tensed. *Just a little slower.* She waited, and the horses slowed more. "Let me see if I can even the odds."

Ath uttered a hoarse whisper. "Don't. I've got a plan."

Too late! Limbreth half-slid off the horse. She landed awkwardly, and it jarred her breath. She clenched her jaw. Just a punch. Then that dagger in her death-grip. She feigned anger. "You pulled me off, you…" She got to her knees

The Bane dismounted and loomed over her. It reached for her bound wrists.

The chill of fear gripped Limbreth's spine. *Do it anyway.* Her snarl erupted as a whimper. She lunged at the Bane's cowl, fists doubled.

The Bane dodged back and caught her wrists. It lifted her off her feet, its magic sucking at her resistance.

"Uh." A weak gasp. Nothing to grab. The feeling left her arms. *Spit! Kick!*

CHAPTER TWENTY

Do anything. Her mind numbed. Limbreth's vision failed. She slumped and twitched in the Bane's grasp.

~ ~ ~ ~ ~ ~ ~

Ralda waited for a chance to break his bonds. He needed a shift in the odds. Any change that favored him breaking the thin cords and attempting the same with the dwarves.

The trolls snarled to each other in their gruff language, and several drew knives and stepped toward their captives. They cringed as thick rain whipped under the wide overhang and the moaning wind rose to a rumble.

One of the mules brayed and kicked at the trolls. Several of them dropped, and the others backed away while they laughed. They cut the other mule's throat. It squealed as its blood spurted onto the ground. One troll slashed wildly as it scrambled away from the kicking mule, cutting the animal's lead. The mule reared and charged through the throng. The trolls whooped. The mule trampled a few in its passing and knocked several others from their feet. The animal dashed for freedom up the rise amid a rising scatter of leaves on the wind.

The trolls milled and snarled in confusion. Ralda tensed his muscles, poised to break his bonds.

The wind rumbled and vibrated through him. Rain swirled. Trolls standing in the downpour disappeared. One bugbear looked Ralda in the eye, knife raised. The troll's eyes bulged as the wind lifted him. The gale snatched the other trolls like dolls into the blinding wall of rain.

"Wind-beast." The roar swallowed Ralda's yell. The air pulled him from the overhang and lifted him from the dirt. Tordug rolled past, and Makwi writhed in his bonds.

Ralda floated low to the ground. A branch smacked his head, and he shielded himself with his arms. A troll-mace whirled past him, followed by a shield. Other debris pelted his body. He yelled without words, and the wind swallowed it. He shut his mouth.

Ralda passed someone standing on the ground. He wore a floppy hat. How was that possible?

Tordug and Makwi no longer floated near him. He twisted his head for a view between his arms. Where were they?

The wind-beast weakened, and Ralda hit the ground hard. He slid across mud into a tree. Branches, leaves, and other debris piled over him. The tree quivered, all but its thickest branches stripped away.

Blood trickled into Ralda's eyes. Pain shot through him in multiple spots. The wind-beast's roar dwindled in the distance. He groaned. His voice sounded raw, but he could hear it in the sudden quiet. His clothing was in tatters.

Everything went black.

Ralda jerked awake. Boots squished through the mud and stopped close to him where he lay under the cover of branches. He moved his hands. His bonds were gone. The wind had torn them away.

The pair of boots squished closer.

Ralda clenched his fists and poised to burst from the pile of limbs.

~ ~ ~ ~ ~ ~ ~

Athson set the bow aside inside Eloch's Gate.

His opened lantern shutter revealed the way. He crept through the narrow. There was nothing there. No waiting Bane. He retrieved the Bow of Hart and then set out to attempt a rescue. He stepped with care and silence through the natural passage.

Eloch had left him to fend for himself as usual. He held his sword ready to attack.

Shouts echoed in the cave. Athson took a quick step. A wail roared in the confined space, and he halted with furrowed brow. What was that?

Air burst past him.

Then silence lingered.

Athson shuffled forward. That noise and wind weren't normal. Had Corgren killed his friends with a spell?

Something glimmered ahead. It jerked toward him. Athson opened the shutters wider, and the lantern shined brighter. "Spark!" His loud whisper echoed around him.

The mountain hound tugged Athson's pack into the cave. He scurried

CHAPTER TWENTY

toward his faithful companion. "I don't know what you are, but you've brought my pack, so you must be real." Wait, this meant he had the bowstring. He rummaged through his belongings and found the inheritance.

Athson strung the Bow of Hart with the inherited bowstring. String and bow proved stronger than his expectation. He secured the bow across one shoulder and moved forward with Spark. His other bow was outside, but now he had two.

Daylight glimmered ahead. He dimmed the lantern and proceeded with what light there was. No sense giving away his presence. Best surprise the trolls if he could.

Spark exited the crevice. Athson scrambled out, sword ready. There was nothing to attack. He gaped and lowered his sword.

Trees lay toppled like straw in a wide swath. In some places whole trees, roots and all, had been torn from the earth and cast into others, revealing root systems and gaping maws of earth. Beyond the immediate wreckage, trees still stood but had been stripped so that only large limbs remained.

The swamp lay still. There were no trolls. Corgren and the Bane were nowhere in sight.

Athson rubbed his forehead.

The dwarves weren't there. Ralda too. Gweld—where was he? There was no sign of Limbreth.

They were gone. All of them.

CHAPTER TWENTY-ONE

Footprints and other marks riddled the ground outside the cave. Athson read what remained, but abrupt endings led him nowhere. Only a great storm toppled trees like that. His friends—and the trolls—had certainly been swept away.

But the tracks that led away from area proved promising. Athson followed them, with Spark trailing him. One of the mules had run away and covered some tracks from two men and smaller boots that he recognized as Limbreth's. Amid these signs, he spotted the trail of the Bane, similar to what he'd followed before in Auguron. The trail led him around the rock outcrop and up the rise to the edge of trees at the grassland that swept north toward the Trolls Heaths. He found where his quarry had mounted three horses and ridden away. Four sets of prints. His father must be with them, but no trolls. Corgren left his trolls behind with the prisoners?

Athson stood atop the rock outcropping. The storm's devastation stretched into the distance. If his other friends lived, finding them seemed impossible. No cry for help rose from the destruction. Who could survive that? His throat tightened. Gweld might be dead.

Athson turned away and went back to Corgren's trail, which led northeast. Toward the Funnel.

But the mule's tracks veered north. He couldn't hope to catch Corgren afoot, but the mule might give him a chance.

Athson crossed his arms. He hesitated between his choices. The others may be injured or dead. Limbreth lived and needed help. Searching for

CHAPTER TWENTY-ONE

the dead seemed fruitless if she were alive and captive. His time was short anyway. And then there was his father, half-blind and haggard. His chest heaved with sudden anger. His father needed him. This was Athson's chance to free him at last.

He ran back for his pack.

Spark sat while Athson readied himself for travel. Few supplies remained in the storm's wake, but some were strewn about the foot of the rock overhang. He gathered enough for himself and left the rest piled by the cave should his friends make it back. He never found his old bow, but he still wore his quiver. The Bow of Hart would have to do for now, old or not. The others needed to know his location. He laid an arrow in the direction he intended to travel. He also scratched an elvish rune for his name on a piece of wood and set it beside the arrow.

He glanced at Spark sitting nearby and panting. "The others can help each other. There's no one to help Limbreth or my father." The mountain hound stood and wagged his tail.

Athson set out and called Spark to follow. There were hours of sunlight left. Even with a horse, Corgren could only travel so far. Athson might catch the wizard well before he reached the Funnel, but first he needed the mule, and that would delay him further. But when he caught the wizard, Athson would give Corgren a taste of what he sought

~ ~ ~ ~ ~ ~ ~

Ralda gritted his teeth.

Someone—not a troll—knelt beside him. Tordug's face appeared, blood smeared along his cheek. "You'd think a giant would be easier to find." The dwarf-lord grinned through his beard and turned away. "He's over here. And alive."

Other voices answered. Ralda's ears rang, and he blinked. What did they say?

Tordug cupped his hands around his mouth. "Yes, he's got blood on his head and arms." The dwarf squatted. "Don't worry, she's coming. You look like you might pass out."

Ralda blinked again. "Who come?" Why were his fists still clenched?

"Hastra's back. She'll help you."

"Hastra?"

"Yes, and she's got a tale. Brought Athson's mother!"

Ralda pushed through the branches while Tordug pulled them away from the pile. "We ride wind-beast. Save from trolls."

"Yes, amazing we're alive." Tordug helped him lean against the tree.

Ralda was weak. Bright specks twinkled in his vision. He couldn't have fought a troll. He shut his eyes. "Need sleep."

"No, stay awake. Your head's injured. Inside."

"Inside?" Inside what? Where was his head? Nothing made sense.

Someone else knelt beside Ralda. He squinted. Hastra's face frowned at him. Why was her face surrounded by streaks of light and dark? "Hastra! Ralda's head, inside something. Maybe tree?" His hands fumbled for the proper signs.

"Here, let me look. Tordug, go see to Gweld's leg. Makwi's on his feet now, though wobbly." Hastra motioned for the dwarf-lord to go.

Ralda frowned.

Hastra touched him and spoke, her voice low. She said something, and everything went dark.

When he opened his eyes again, Hastra smiled.

"Better?" She dabbed his face with a cloth.

"What? Where you go?"

Hastra sat back. "Ralda, your head was injured. Eloch placed me here, or you would have been injured for days. You made less sense than usual. Can you stand?"

Ralda got to his feet with slow effort. He was steady now. "My thanks. Many blessing, you." His hands made more sense now. "Where others? Who this?" He motioned to the woman with a familiar face and graying hair.

Hastra jerked her head toward the rise behind her. "They went in search of Athson. There's been no sign of trolls, though I've heard them further down in the swamp. This is Athson's mother, Danilla. She came from Rok with me."

CHAPTER TWENTY-ONE

Ralda greeted Danilla with a bow. "Good meeting, Danilla. Have Athson eyes." He indicated color and features with his flicks of his hands. Danilla blinked at his movements and size.

"Well met, Ralda. My son has many friends, I see." She cast her frowning gaze at the surrounding wreckage of trees.

Ralda pointed in the direction of the whirlwind's path where the tip of Howart's Cave was just visible. "We go see." It carried them this far away?

The Withling gathered her belongings and went with Ralda and Danilla. Strength returned to his limbs as he walked, but his stomach rumbled.

Tordug shouted, and troll snarls answered him. Weapons clashed and echoed across the muddy devastation.

Ralda, Danilla and Hastra hurried through the maze of uprooted trees. Ahead, Tordug, Makwi, and Gweld fought several trolls. Ralda rushed ahead of the Withling and scrambled halfway up the rise toward the rock outcrop.

"Ralda!"

He whirled. A hobgoblin and several lesser trolls leapt from among the trees littering the ground. Ralda needed a weapon. He grasped a broken limb dangling from a tree trunk and tore it lose. Hastra snatched her belt-knife free. Danilla grabbed a small branch. The two women waved their meager weapons and backed away from the attackers.

Ralda charged the trolls. He slid in the mud but smashed a goblin into a tree trunk with his makeshift club. The remaining trolls leapt off the downed trees at Ralda.

He regained his footing and swung at his attackers. His longer weapon slapped the goblins and kobolds away. One jumped on his back and bit him.

A hobgoblin slashed at Ralda with a tulwar. He parried the blow with the branch, but the blade bit deeply and caught. The troll held tightly to its weapon.

Hastra shouted from behind, and the kobold snarled and flailed at his shoulder. Ralda yanked the creature around in a tugging match. He whirled and slung the hobgoblin into exposed, broken roots. Danilla dodged out of the way. Dark blood spurted from the impaled hobgoblin.

Ralda reached over his shoulder. The kobold on his back snapped at his fingers, but Ralda's huge hands grabbed the lesser troll and tore it away. His clothing ripped with the motion.

The kobold stabbed his hand. Ralda threw it at the same clump of broken roots. A jagged point burst through the lesser troll's chest. It twitched a few moments, then slumped. Ralda whirled but found no more trolls moving. He'd beaten the others. No more surprise attacks from them.

"That was close." Hastra wiped her bloody knife on one of the goblins and sheathed it. "I stabbed that one on your back, or he would have stabbed you in the neck."

"Many thanks, Withling!" Ralda reached for his back. Now he felt the pain where he'd been bitten. He forgot to add proper hand signals when he found his wounded hand covered in blood.

Danilla stood with her branch held ready and watched among the toppled trees for more trolls.

Ralda pointed to Danilla's arm tattoo. "You go to Dragon?"

"No, never!" Danilla yanked a sleeve over Magdronu's symbol. "They marked me years ago, in their camp. It was magical so we prisoners couldn't escape without being found."

"Here, sit down." Hastra motioned to a tree. "Your hand is in bad shape. I'll work on that shoulder bite too."

"You okay over there?" Tordug stood with his hands cupped at his mouth. They no longer fought trolls.

Hastra waved Gweld and Tordug to her. They half-slid, half-walked along the slope of the swamp's rim. The elf leapt atop a fallen tree and scanned the area for more trolls.

"That's a nasty wound, Ralda." Tordug motioned for his hand. "May the scar be just as ugly for the tale you'll tell your children."

Ralda grinned and then cocked his head. "Where Makwi?"

Tordug waved back to the rock overhang. "He's gone ahead to check the cave for Athson."

"Too much to do." Hastra sighed. "You're all too impatient. I need to go in there. Be still and let me pray for Ralda's wounds first."

The men and Danilla bowed their heads while Hastra chanted in her

CHAPTER TWENTY-ONE

unknown tongue. The pain faded from Ralda's hand and shoulder, and she stopped her prayer.

"Let's get out of this mess and up on the slope so we can walk faster. Between my other adventures, being brought here, a whirlwind, and fighting, I'm getting tired." Danilla came beside Hastra and helped her through the mass of wrecked trees.

Ralda assisted Hastra as they climbed the slope. "My thanks." Ralda remembered to add polite hand signals. "What you go Rok?"

"Oh, that." Hastra waved her hand with a frown. "Did I worry you all?"

"We wondered, Withling." Tordug tugged his beard. "Athson encountered Corgren one night and we found out you were their prisoner and hostage." He nodded to Danilla. "Along with her."

Gweld wheeled around, looking for more trolls, an arrow nocked. "I know Athson thought you weren't coming back."

"Humph. Well, I'm back." Hastra squeezed Ralda's arm. "Sorry if you were worried. Magdronu set a trap to kidnap me, but Eloch had other plans." She grabbed Danilla's hand. "And for her too."

Danilla offered Hastra a thin smile. "My thanks to you. But where is Athson?"

Gweld shrugged. "We don't know yet. Last we saw, he was in the cave."

Ralda flicked his hands. "We look Ath, too. Come with wizard."

Danilla halted and her raised a hand to her mouth. "My husband? Alive? Here?"

Tordug nodded and Ralda remembered to use the same motion instead of shaking his head like among his people. "Yes."

Hastra continued toward Howart's Cave. "We'd best see what happened."

They others followed, but Tordug's pace faltered. "How did they hold you prisoner, Hastra?"

"Well, they drugged me first, so I couldn't sense Eloch's instructions."

"Drugged!" Tordug tugged his beard hard and his face flushed.

"That's a story for when we have a chance, Eloch permitting. Let's have a look in Howart's Cave first."

Makwi emerged from the cave as they approached the overhang. Bugbears and hobgoblins lay where they fell. The dwarf shook his head with frown on his pale face. "I fought these trolls off when I got here. I still can't get back there, but Athson doesn't answer." His face was pale and his breath labored.

Gweld cast his gaze around the mess. "Here's one of Athson's arrows." He searched further and pointed. "And here's something with Athson's elven rune. I think Athson left this, but it's been scattered. There are plenty of footprints leading this way around and up the hill."

"I still need to check Howart's grotto." Hastra moved toward the entrance. "Is there a light?"

"There's nothing there." Makwi handed her a lantern.

"And we need to get moving." Gweld pointed at a broken arrow. "Look, Athson's prints go that way. It's the same way Corgren went with Limbreth, the Bane, and Athson's father. We need to go now. Limbreth and Athson need our help!"

Danilla hugged herself and sucked her trembling lower lip as tears brimmed in her eyes. "Yes. Please. Let's go search for them. I, I never believed this chance would come."

Hastra paused with an arched brow. "I won't be long, Gweld."

"But we've delayed too long already. Athson can't fight the Bane and Corgren while rescuing Limbreth and Ath."

"As I said, I won't be long. But who—"

Gweld turned to follow Corgren's trail. "I'm going to scout at least." He left without another word.

Ralda shifted his feet and motioned with his hands. "Strange." The elf never got upset.

Tordug stroked his beard. "Yes, it is, Ralda. But then, we've had a strange day." He turned to Hastra. "If you're going, then hurry. We've lost a lot of time, and there may be more trolls that survived."

Makwi leaned against the rock. "Another person to rescue. At least we have the chance Athson wanted in Chokkra. But hurry, Withling. I don't feel so strong, even after your prayer revived me. That Bane…" The younger dwarf shuddered.

CHAPTER TWENTY-ONE

Hastra touched Makwi's arm. "I'll pray again when I return." Makwi shook his head. "No, there won't be time. I'll get along until we camp. But I don't think I can fight more trolls if we linger."

Hastra responded a nod to Tordug and stepped into the cave.

Tordug, Danilla and Ralda retrieved their packs, weapons, and other belongings while they waited for the Withling. More than fortune smiled on them. The storm had done nothing to that stranger, whoever he was. Elosha, maybe? And Hastra had arrived when needed. And with Athson's mother, no less. It wasn't luck that they had survived. Ralda went in search of a straight branch for his lost staff and soon found one. While they waited, Ralda retrieved spare clothing in his pack and changed out of his torn things out of Danilla's sight.

He returned to the others and Tordug spoke while Ralda stowed his things, "I guess our dwarven armor and helms kept us safe in that storm. Never thought of that."

When Hastra returned, she paused and pinched her lower lip between a finger and thumb. "There's no one in there." She pointed along the path of the whirlwind. "That's not normal."

Tordug hefted his pack. "But it was fortuitous."

"Perhaps, but such storms travel northeast and they don't happen in winter, let along in this region. I've seen these before in the south only and never like this."

Ralda signed with his hands. "What mean, then."

Hastra gathered her belongings and checked for her book. "Just that I was brought here for a purpose, not chance. If I was sent to stop the storm then magic caused it. The question is whose? Corgren's?"

Makwi exhaled and wiped his pale face. "I doubt he'd kill his own trolls." He leaned against the natural wall of rock. "But we're here, alive and need to go on if we're to help."

Hastra hefted her pack with a grunt. "That was powerful magic and uncontrolled for some reason. It saved you but something far larger was at work here, and not intended, I'll wager. And not of Eloch's doing. Come, lead us on the trail."

They wasted no further time departing. Ralda hoisted Makwi's pack.

"I'll carry it." But the dwarf sounded weak.

Ralda patted the dwarf's shoulder. "No pack, you go better. Take ax." He could carry the dwarf, but Makwi would be offended.

Makwi nodded and led them away.

Ralda followed last. *Makwi put up no argument. He must be worse than he lets on.* Ralda followed his companions as they scrambled upslope around the outcrop.

Atop the rise, Makwi found the tracks that led northeast. But Athson's led north, following mule tracks. Gweld was gone, his tracks leading the same way. "Either he's gone on alone, or he's scouting like he said. We'll follow Gweld anyway. Looks like Athson went after one of the mules so he can travel faster. Otherwise he won't catch Corgren, since they're mounted."

Tordug stroked his beard. "We certainly won't catch Athson or Corgren. But we must follow as best we can."

Hastra started forward. "Well enough. We'll follow after dark with a lantern to make up lost time. But tell me all that has happened."

Tordug launched into the tale with Ralda and Makwi adding what details they knew. Makwi soon fell behind even Hastra. After a while, they found where mule tracks joined those of Corgren's horses. Tordug pointed it out. "Looks like Athson caught the mule. Maybe he has a chance that we won't."

Ralda paused and turned to Makwi. *He's ten strides back now.* "We stop? Wait? Go slow?"

The dwarf waved them on when everyone stopped. "No, don't mind me. Go on. I'll catch you."

At nightfall, they opened the shutters on the lantern and followed the tracks while eating a quick meal. They stopped well into the night and set a hasty camp. Makwi arrived, having followed their light, and lay down with a grunt. Ralda refrained from helping him. *Stubborn, proud dwarves. But he made it.*

Makwi lay still and muttered about the Bane and being weak-kneed. Hastra touched his brow and blessed him. Ralda found food and gave it to the dwarf and then shared more with Danilla.

CHAPTER TWENTY-ONE

The younger dwarf chewed and swallowed. "Where's Gweld?"

Ralda cleared his throat. "No come." Where was the elf?

Hastra settled onto her blanket. "He'll be along tonight or tomorrow. That elf can take care of himself. We'll set our watch and rest." She removed her book from her pack. "But for now, I've other concerns to ponder. For one, who is helping us? And for another, if that storm was magically spawned then it could only mean the Dragon was near. But where?"

Ralda signaled with his hands in the firelight. "See no others than we speak of."

With a frown and a nod, Hastra wagged her finger at Ralda. "It makes sense that Magdronu would be near but if we never saw him then where and why the uncontrolled magic?"

Tordug grunted and got to his feet. "Well, I don't have an answer, Withling. But, I'll take first watch without Gweld here." He found a blanket for Danilla. "Use this tonight. I see you have a cloak already but this will help in the cold too."

The next morning, they rose early and sought their friends on the trail. Ralda followed last while Makwi led. The younger dwarf never complained, but he wasn't himself. He hesitated before he lifted his pack. Their way soon led them off the plain of tall grass and wound into the southern Troll Heaths.

At midmorning, they found Gweld waiting by the trail. The elf frowned when Tordug hailed him. "We were slowed, since Makwi wasn't hale until this morning. Did you ever see Athson?"

Gweld rubbed his neck and stood. "No, so I made camp and hoped you'd find me. I fell asleep and dreamed a shadow stood over me, and I woke and called out. I didn't sleep after that."

Hastra took the elf's hand. "Did it touch you? Any symptoms?" The Withling peered into his eyes.

Gweld pulled his hand away. "No, I feel fine. But I'm worried about Athson alone on Corgren's trail."

Tordug visored his eyes as he scanned their surroundings. "Corgren hasn't turned for the river."

Makwi snorted and spit. "No, he's headed for the Funnel."

Danilla gasped. "The Funnel! Yes, it's where he took me and the other survivors."

Hastra frowned and shook her head.

"What wrong?" Ralda shifted his gaze between his companions. They knew the region better than he did.

Makwi shifted his pack. "Trolls gather there."

Gweld shouldered his own gear. "It's where Athson's father was captured."

"Let's move along." Hastra motioned to Gweld. "If you weren't harmed, then please scout ahead." She frowned at the sun. "It's a long way, but maybe we can catch them if we keep our travel longer than theirs. Corgren took hostages after Depenburgh, and he's done it again. But this time, he knows he can lay his hands on the bow since Athson has it."

Ralda groaned. All their travel and struggle, and Corgren might get the bow. Should he just run ahead? He might catch them all. No, he'd save that for later if necessary. He'd best wait. They might find Athson and catch Corgren yet. Better if Hastra was with him. But he wasn't about to leave his friends, not like he'd cut Kralda loose.

~ ~ ~ ~ ~ ~ ~

The Bane yanked the rope, and Limbreth almost fell off the horse. With her bound hands pulled forward, she had to constantly adjust her perch on the horse lest she tumble off. Her thighs ached from the constant work on the horse's bare back behind the saddle.

The rope cut her wrists as the Bane dragged her and the reins together. She grunted and pulled back on the rope. The Bane pulled her harder into Ath's back.

Limbreth fought for slack. "Stop yanking me around, you vile—"

The Bane reined its horse to a stop and let the one carrying her and Ath draw close. It loomed over Limbreth. She leaned away with a tremble and almost slid off. She grabbed Ath.

"Enough!" Corgren turned his head. "You can toy with them later, but we must ride now."

The Bane kicked its horse after Corgren but left slack for Limbreth.

CHAPTER TWENTY-ONE

A small win. For the moment. She balanced herself to the horse's gait. She cowered. Her heart seized. Still too close to that thing. But that failed last time. She needed a weapon though. Her left hand might lock on something. Show it the death-grip, as strong as its own. She locked her fingers together, but her hands trembled. What would she find there? Her legs quivered. She feared that. Limbreth lowered her head and gasped a whisper. "If I get my hands—"

Ath turned his head toward her and uttered the barest whisper, "Just wait." His chain clinked as he patted her leg once, twice. He gave her leg a hard nudge.

Limbreth glanced at Ath's hand. His fingers wiggled. She felt his hand for reassurance.

Ath's fingers forced a link into her hand. Her fingers passed over a groove. She forestalled a gasp and cast a quick glance at the link. Almost cut through.

He turned his head again. "Soon."

She patted his hand, and he moved the link away.

Corgren drifted back near their horse. "Now, now, princess, you don't want to fight the Bane again." He flashed a winning smile. "Be nice, and I might let a troll lead your horse when they get here, wherever those cursed beasts are."

The Bane never turned back in its hood.

"I don't think Athson will trade the bow for us." She avoided looking at the wizard.

"You'll find out soon enough." Corgren twisted in the saddle. "You'd better hope your new traitorous friend's son makes it in time."

She almost slid off the horse again. "Or what? Without us, you get nothing."

Corgren laughed. "I can wait for that. But he doesn't have to get you unharmed." He glanced at her and then Ath. "Does he, traitor?"

Ath tucked his chin and ground his teeth. "Just leave her out of this. It's between my family and Rok. Not her."

Corgren laughed again and offered a mocking sneer. "It's between whoever it needs to be where Magdronu and I are concerned, traitor!"

The wizard kicked his horse's sides and rode into the lead again.

Limbreth leaned close to Ath. "The Funnel, isn't that where they captured you?"

"Yes." He grunted as he shifted in the saddle.

"What's so special about it?

"It's where Corgren and his trolls sacrifice captives to Magdronu."

Limbreth's breath caught in her throat. The Bane's cold slithered along her spine. Surely Athson was coming. Not Hastra. This was in Athson's hands if anyone.

They'd do something. But there was also the weakened chain link and her death-grip. Slim chances, but something. Her body trembled as the Bane drifted near.

~ ~ ~ ~ ~ ~ ~

When they camped later, Corgren left the Bane to guard the hostages by the fire. The summons of his master flickered on his ring's stone. He carried the blood from Ath and knelt in the wet grass out of earshot of the prisoners. He spoke the words, and the crushing weight of Magdronu entered his mind. The dragon's visage filled the small window of magical viewing that radiated his master's heated nature. "My master, I have the princess well in hand."

"As expected." The deep rumble of anger stretched through the dragon's magic. "However, news has come to me. Eloch has rescued the Withling and the mother. Your prisoners are our only leverage. Paugren cannot be blamed, as Eloch's glamors are beyond his abilities. I worried this might happen, but Athson knows nothing of it. Make sure the father finds nothing out."

"I've left this spell small and walked out of earshot. The traitor will not know of this news." Corgren's face trembled with effort.

"Good. Make all the speed you can and save your magic, as my powers are lessened with fewer sacrifices in the mountains of late. Athson rides one of the mules, so be wary of delay. This is the second time Eloch has intervened and that's not like him. He works through the faith of his underlings. Have you seen anyone else?"

CHAPTER TWENTY-ONE

"My master, I obey. But I've seen no one else. Who might it be?"

"Perhaps another Withling we don't know about."

"I killed them all but the three who remain when we took Withling's Watch centuries ago."

The communication spell throbbed as Magdronu fell silent a moment. "You're sure of that?"

"There is only one from the legends of Withlings I remember whose faith could defy you but he's long dead. Apeth Stellin."

"This isn't Eloch's way so it must be someone. Leave it to me. But I must investigate the shrine in the mountains. My ability to share magic has waned since that encounter and I suspect more happened than I guessed. Also, you will have no trolls following. They were swept away by a whirlwind."

Corgren almost fell over under the strain of the spell. "What? How could that happen unless it was Eloch."

Little pressure oozed along the spell. Magdronu grunted. "I tried rashly to pass Eloch's Gate and uncontrolled magic escaped me. It warred with Eloch's presence which set off the whirlwind. Watch your heels for Athson. I shall come for the bow when you sacrifice."

The spell closed without the usual power display from Magdronu. Corgren sighed. Then Paugren couldn't supply more sacrifices. Were the dwarves disrupting their guards? Or was it Eloch's doing some other way? And his master seemed embarrassed about the whirlwind. He chuckled. Saved our enemies with that mistake, it seems.

The wizard stood with a groan and returned to his camp. He lay on his blanket by the fire and spoke to the Bane. "Wake me after two watches. We travel early." He'd wear Athson thin before he'd let the ranger catch him.

~~~~~~~

Ath lay with his back to the fire away from Corgren and the Bane. Limbreth lay under his blanket and writhed in her restless dream. He needed to take care, since her foolish display almost revealed his secret. He lay as still as possible while he worked his little file over each side of the link. It was dulled now, but he kept at it. For Athson, and for Limbreth now. So much closer but still so far to cut through the link. He needed to be careful lest he break it soon. He often gripped the link now. Best not let it be seen by Corgren. No trolls for now, though. Good time for a surprise with even numbers. He wiggled the file. Gently, not too much motion...

CHAPTER TWENTY-TWO

Days of bouncing on the skittish horse followed by nights of nipping wind by Corgren's spare fire blended into one long nightmare. Next to the Bane, Limbreth's boldness shriveled. She slept little, and when she did, her dreams flowed with shadows of fear.

Their winding course through the hills left her weary. She never felt comfortable on the fearful horse. She leaned toward Ath. "We have to do something." Their time grew shorter.

"I may have my surprise ready if—" The Bane yanked their horse forward.

Limbreth almost fell off, having no stirrups for her feet. "Later. I'll shout when I make my move." Something had to be done. If Athson brought the Bow of Hart, then any effort from her might help. But the chill wiggled along her spine. The Bane's fearsome essence siphoned her resolve. But she'd try. Doing nothing was unacceptable.

She slipped toward the horse's rear and snatched at the saddle. She kicked for purchase. *Focus on the moment, not the past. Ignore the Bane. Ignore the fear. And don't fall off.* But the fear gnawed at her mind. She stifled the rising lump of a sob in her throat.

Bleak light shone through slate clouds. They turned east between two hills, the wind whistling between the crumbling crests. She slid forward into the saddle when they crossed the height on a rough trail. The horse swayed on the downward traverse, nickered, and lashed his tail.

Limbreth blinked at the sight spread before them. A flat shelf of rock spread north and south but ended in a sheer cliff perhaps forty paces from the slopes. A few boulders lay tumbled from craggy heights on the shelf. But it was the large flat stone by the cliff's edge that caught Limbreth's eye.

They were here. The Funnel. Where Corgren sacrificed. She swallowed hard at the rising need to retch.

She almost slid off the horse but found purchase with her bound hands. If Athson didn't come, Corgren would— She avoided the rest of that thought and stared at Ath's unkempt hair on his bowed shoulders.

Wind screamed along the shelf of rock and threatened to toss Limbreth from the horse in its constantly shifting gusts. If the wind whistled in the little pass they'd come through, here it moaned and shrieked like dying victims offered to Magdronu. But beyond the cliff's edge, it howled down the gorge of the Funnel. She shifted into the variable currents and struggled to stay on the horse. Why? She needed to do something. What? Numbness throttled her resolve, her every mustered intention.

Corgren led them into a sort of alcove in the steep wall of broken rock rising to one hill's crest above the shelf. The wizard and the Bane hobbled the horses. The Bane led Limbreth around and made her gather wood fallen from the spindly trees that balanced on the heights above them. Limbreth forced herself to drop the wood once. The Bane grasped her shoulder in a painful pinch. Her legs wobbled, and she sobbed. She didn't drop the wood again after that.

Later, once a fire was lit, she sat out of the wind and waited for what came next. She hoped for the trade and a chance to escape. At least the Bane hadn't staked her to the ground, since it was all stone. She ached all the worse on the hard surface. Or was that fear.

Limbreth stood and added more wood the fire with her hands still bound. She paused a moment and warmed her fingers as the fire danced.

Corgren stirred. "It's time. He's near." He stood and peered into the surrounding shelf.

Ath scrambled away from Limbreth. He strained at the end of his leash. "Athson! Don't do it! He won't kill us without the bow!"

The Bane moved to quiet the distraught blind man.

Limbreth leapt the other way. She snatched Corgren's dagger from his

CHAPTER TWENTY-TWO

belt and held it two-handed. "Let us go! Now!"

The wizard whirled. He smiled and advanced on Limbreth. "You'll die trying!"

She lunged. Her legs wobbled under her from pain. Corgren dodged her like a dancer. Then the Bane loomed over her. Limbreth's hands wavered, and she re-doubled her grip on the hilt. She'd do it. She'd stand her ground. The chill ran along her spine.

The Bane moved closer, arm extended.

Limbreth swallowed the lump rising in her throat. "No! You won't beat me, demon." Her arms wavered. She poised to lunge at her nemesis. She would do it. She'd help Athson regardless of the cost.

Corgren stepped closer and waved his hand. "Nasht ag tun."

Limbreth blinked. Heaviness forced her to her knees. The dagger slipped from her grasp, and she fumbled for the weapon. She opened her mouth to speak, but her words were unintelligible, and she groaned. What had Corgren done? She slumped onto the rock and rolled onto her back.

Corgren and the Bane watched from the top of a well of darkness. The wind roared in her ears. Darkness closed in on her. No! She'd failed Athson again. At least she tried. Emptiness covered Limbreth like a blanket.

~ ~ ~ ~ ~ ~ ~

Days of pursuit slipped past Athson like a dream of eating, sleeping, and tracking. The trail into the Troll Heaths led him unerringly after Corgren and the Bane. Spark trailed him throughout the days of cold and lay near him in the dark, keeping him warm, just as the dog had cared for him since he first escaped the Funnel. And now Athson stalked his enemy willingly back to the place of his losses, a journey of years for which he sought an end.

He climbed into the hills of the southern Troll Heaths, riding the mule. Thank Eloch, he'd found the animal. It had saved him time. Perhaps the sure-footed mule would gain on Corgren's horses.

Athson recognized parts of the trip, memories from his father's failed rescue years earlier. Now he was doing the rescuing. He shuddered at the memories and often held the hilt of his blessed sword to ward his fits away.

He didn't need Soul's Ease, even if he'd had it. When he approached the Funnel, Athson hobbled the mule for use later. If he survived.

The wind roared and buffeted Athson like attacking trolls when he crept through the pass above the Funnel. He crouched behind a screen of boulders with Spark. Below, the flat shelf of rock stretched to the sheer edge above the river. Corgren directed the Bane toward the Altar of the Trolls, that hated stone where Corgren sacrificed to Magdronu. Limbreth lay limp in the Bane's hold. She must be alive. Athson shifted his gaze. Ath lay in a disheveled heap near the wizard.

Spark panted in silence within Athson's reach. "I'll use it now." It must have the necessary power to do what he needed, just like his sword. The mountain hound's ears rose to a point in expectation.

Athson peered out of his hiding place again. The worn path wandered on the wide rock shelf below him. That was no good. Corgren would see him. The rocky slope bent away south and turned toward the edge of the Funnel, cutting off the shelf. If only he could scramble among the boulders and attack at the closest point to Corgren.

He motioned Spark to follow and worked his way among the rocks along the slope, his cloak pulled close for concealment. The high wind stood in his way of a long shot. Athson spotted a tall boulder near enough to the wizard. He might release an arrow from there with good result. This bow of prophecy must do the job. He had nothing else at hand to even his odds. He was the only one left to help Limbreth and his father. His stomach fluttered. The only one left.

Athson worked his way with care among the rocks. The constant rush of wind along the gorge covered any noise he caused. He crept down to the boulder close to Corgren. Ath lay twenty paces way. He might be asleep. Athson nocked an arrow. He peeked around first one side of the boulder and then the other.

Corgren whirled and gazed along the slope. "Come out, ranger. I know you're here." The wizard motioned to Limbreth where she lay on the altar by the Bane. "I have your woman. She'll die unless you give me the Bow of Hart."

CHAPTER TWENTY-TWO

Athson peered at Limbreth. The Bane brandished a wolf-head dagger. Athson gritted his teeth. It was like the one he carried, the one with which the Bane had murdered Heth and Cireena. A choice lay before him—the Bane or Corgren. If anything could kill that creature, it was this bow. Surely it bore some virtue like his sword. Either shot was a risk, but taking down the Bane secured Limbreth. Athson ran his fingers along a feathered vane.

He rose in shadow from behind the boulder, drew the arrow, and aimed for the Bane.

"Reveal yourself and turn it over. You have no choice, unless you want her to die. Like your mother on that very rock." Corgren laughed.

Athson suppressed a scream. Heat flooded his veins. His heart pounded. He shifted his aim and released. At Corgren.

~ ~ ~ ~ ~ ~ ~

The arrow sprang away from The Bow of Hart. The heat of Athson's rage fell into an emptiness that opened in his belly. What had he done? Limbreth! The Bane would have her! He groaned.

But the arrow faltered in the gusting wind like his regrets. Even as it left the bowstring, Corgren's head rose, and he wheeled at its approach. He uttered a spell, eyes wide. The arrow slowed, and the wizard snatched it out of the air.

Athson gasped. He dropped the bow. It had failed him, failed the promise of prophecy as a weapon against evil.

The wizard staggered, and a look of confusion covered his face. He turned his gaze on the Altar of the Trolls. "Kill her! Do it! Now!"

Limbreth's arms flailed against the Bane.

Athson drew his sword and started for the Bane. His blessed steel would work where the Bow of Hart had failed.

But Corgren ripped his dagger free of its sheath and charged Athson. "You die now, ranger!" The wizard leapt at Athson and slashed at his stomach with his wolf-head dagger.

Athson scurried back and then parried a thrust from Corgren. Blue and red flashed against green.

The struggle continued at the Altar. Limbreth held the Bane at bay somehow. Then Spark charged the Bane.

Corgren lunged, and Athson barely sidestepped. The wizard was good with a knife.

The wizard stepped back, his eyes narrowed. He grinned and circled Athson. "I'll have the bow, and your blessed sword won't help you." He raised a hand. "Auf-cusal!"

Athson's sword rang and quivered in his grip. He stared at the blade as light flared on its edges. *The blessing resists his magic.* He lifted his gaze and found surprise on Corgren's face. "Yes, it's blessed, and you can't break it again like you did when my father wielded it!"

~ ~ ~ ~ ~ ~ ~

Ath lay as if exhausted, his chain secured by Corgren's magic. The chain was too short to reach them. With Limbreth carried away by the Bane, Ath sawed crazily at the link. Corgren shouted for Athson. It was time to help. Was the chain weak enough?

Sound of a struggle reached his ears. Ath rolled over. Athson was attacking Corgren with his sword. Corgren uttered a spell, and the blade sang in complaint. The wizard hesitated. He spoke another word, and the sword flew from Athson's hand.

Now! It had to be now! Ath scrambled to the full length of the chain. Still too far! He clenched his jaw and yanked once with all his might. Nothing. Again. Nothing. The third time, the link snapped. Ath rolled over backwards. He'd done it! At last! His eye flew wide at the sight before him.

~ ~ ~ ~ ~ ~ ~

Ath stirred in Athson's peripheral vision and scrambled toward the struggle. Spark snarled as he bit and yanked on the Bane's arm.

Corgren reached for Athson. "Mestu-amusa quei!" The wizard made a yanking motion, and the sword ripped free of Athson's grip. The blade clanged on the stone ground and slid past the wizard. Corgren took a step toward Athson, who whipped his own wolf-head dagger out of its sheath.

Athson feinted at the wizard. At least he had another weapon. "You won't

CHAPTER TWENTY-TWO

get the bow or me today, wizard!" Memories past flashed to his mind. Not now!

Corgren grinned. "So, we trade knives! I was once a fighter in the Hartian rings with these."

Spark snarled. Limbreth wrestled with the Bane.

The wizard stood straight and smiled. "But I've no time for these games, ranger." He repeated his spell, and the dagger flew from Athson's grip. It skittered on the stone and stopped near Ath.

Corgren made a move at Athson and the bow behind him. Athson blocked him, dodging a thrust from the knife.

Suddenly Ath stood behind Corgren. The wizard went stiff and howled, eyes wide.

In the same moment, Limbreth screamed, and blood flowed on the Altar.

Athson staggered toward Limbreth. Her scream was like an eagle's. *From the dream after Chokkra. The eagle's scream.* He ran for her. "Limbreth!"

~ ~ ~ ~ ~ ~ ~

Limbreth's awareness crawled with sluggish reluctance from the well of darkness. The wind roared like a wild bear. She quivered and blinked her eyes. Where was she? Her vision cleared and distilled into the Bane looming over her. She gasped. Not that nightmare again!

"Kill her!" Corgren's shout carried on the wind.

The Bane raised a knife over her.

The familiar chill ran along her spine—the chill that froze her will. Her throat constricted, and she lay gasping on the stone altar. They were sacrificing her!

The knife blade descended.

Limbreth grabbed for the Bane's wrist with her bound hands. She caught the creature's arm somehow. but the knife lowered with inexorable force. Limbreth ground her teeth. Her grip tightened. And then her left arm locked. The death-grip!

The Bane struggled against Limbreth's grip. It couldn't force her hand loose or her arm away. She flailed on the altar. She turned her head away from the Bane, and her eyes went wide. The Funnel yawned beside her. She rolled away from the chasm and tried to tear the knife from the Bane.

Voices carried on the wind, and weapons clattered. "Athson!" Her shout died at her tightly pressed lips. Her face twitched, and her heart thundered in her chest. Now was her chance to help Athson.

A snarl erupted and the Bane turned to fight something with its free arm. It sounded like a dog. Was it Spark? She kicked at the Bane but missed, then tried to wrest the knife away.

The Bane freed its other arm and snatched the knife beyond her grip. The snarling continued as its arm rose with the knife. The Bane stumbled back and fought free of the other attacker.

The knife plunged toward Limbreth. She twisted her body into the Bane and attempted to block the blow with her right arm. She missed. The blade sank into her right side. Someone screamed, and Limbreth realized it had erupted from her. Her limbs went weak as pain shot across her torso. Her grip on the Bane broke, and the Bane pushed her.

Limbreth fell into the chasm, flailing in the wind.

~ ~ ~ ~ ~ ~ ~

Makwi recovered over the following days, but Ralda kept track of the dwarf anyway as their way wound higher into the Troll Heaths. Hastra drove them hard after Athson and Limbreth. The Withling often muttered about the bow slipping from their grasp. Ralda saw it by the puffs of Hastra's breath in the chilly air.

Gweld almost never stayed with them, sometimes returning early in the morning as they broke camp. Hastra tried to ease the elf's worry, but he ignored her as often as not and outdistanced them, saying he hunted trolls.

Ralda remained with the Withling and the dwarves. The grassland north of the marsh melted into the southern heaths after several days. Always they found the trail of the wizard's small party and of Athson's mule, but they gained little on either, by the age of the tracks.

One morning Gweld sat in their midst when they awoke. "We're near the Altar of the Trolls. We must make haste or lose all. It's a much higher climb." He pointed toward craggy hills rising higher above them.

Hastra rolled out of her blankets at the news as they set to work on food

CHAPTER TWENTY-TWO

and breaking camp. "Gweld, you must stay with us today. I feel we'll need your help."

The elf cut his eyes at the Withling. "Why? I should scout ahead and look for trolls."

Ralda wiggled his fingers and flashed his tattoos. "We stay close. If many troll attack, we have need of all." There was no sense in risking trouble when they were close.

Gweld sighed, but he narrowed his eyes. "Well enough. I hope you know what you're doing, Hastra."

Ralda cocked his head and rubbed his chin. Gweld wasn't himself. He never went against Hastra. He must be worried for Athson. Danilla said nothing but helped break camp and stayed near Hastra as usual.

Tordug spit in the fire and kicked dirt over it. "Ralda's right, we need our numbers against any trolls and when we get there."

"I said I'd stay." Gweld got up and stood some paces away, shifting his weight from one foot to the other.

They gathered their packs and weapons and set out in the predawn light. Ralda gripped his staff as the hills rose in jagged heaps before them. The moaning wind helped them little in detecting trolls. He tied his cloak tighter about him, thankful for the winter provision from the dwarves' kin. He gazed ahead at the craggy hills. Hours of climbing lay ahead. If only they could reach their friends in time to help save them and keep the bow from Corgren.

Near mid-morning, Hastra stopped. The Withling cocked her head and furrowed her brow, while Tordug called a halt.

Makwi approached the old woman. "Are you ill, Withling? We must hurry if not."

Hastra meandered away from the trail. She stopped and turned in a circle.

Gweld crossed his arms and then waved them above his head. "If you're going to delay longer, at least let me try to catch them."

"No, we go another way now." Hastra shook her head and motioned them after her as she scrambled toward a nearby crevice.

Gweld scowled. "What are you doing? It's this way!"

Danilla peered into shadowy descent. "Are you sure? We need to find Athson and my husband like Gweld said."

Ralda scratched his neck. Gweld never lost his temper, especially with Hastra. "Withling Hastra, why we go not on trail?" He finished his sign with a motion in the direction they had been going. He supposed Danilla was right, though.

"Quickly, we have little time. I'll need you all in this." Hastra waved them after her once more and turned into the narrow cleft.

Ralda shrugged at Gweld before the two of them followed.

"The ways of Withlings are often a mystery." Tordug slapped his thighs and followed.

The Withling disappeared into the cleft, but her voice echoed out of it. "What is needed is given."

Ralda squeezed into the narrow between towering rock walls that scraped against him. It went on for a while until the way opened into a hidden chamber of stone. Gray clouds rolled overhead. They were well below the hilltops in this cleft.

The wind rushed up a steep ravine that plunged toward the rushing water well below their position. The way down lay strewn with loose stone, rough natural steps, and sudden stretches of a dry gully.

Hastra pointed to Makwi. "Stay here, gather firewood and bring it down. Danilla, you too."

The dwarf spread his hands. "Why? There's only a few old pieces of wood lying washed in here."

Hastra started into the ravine but paused long enough to look over her shoulder. "I see more scattered below and down at the river. Tordug and Gweld can fetch more. What is needed is given. Everyone else, come." She turned away without further words.

Makwi gathered the scant wood and handed loads to Tordug and scowling Gweld.

Ralda followed the Withling. Hastra knew something. If only he knew they were helping. The wind whistled past him, yanking his cloak, and then fell away.

CHAPTER TWENTY-TWO

Gweld hung back. "Now we make a hidden camp? I'm fetching firewood? Athson needs us! I'm going after them. Come on, Danilla."

Athson's mother paused and shifted her hazel-eyed gaze between Hastra and Gweld, an arm-load of wood clutched to her chest.

Tordug wheeled on Gweld and motioned to Makwi. "I think you should help like the Withling asked."

The elf crossed his arms and squinted as Makwi blocked his way out from farther up. "You heard her. She needs us doing this. It's a sending from Eloch."

Gweld clenched his jaw and then followed after a glance at Danilla

Athson's mother shrugged and carried the wood toward Hastra. "She and Eloch saved me from that prison camp. If she says we are needed here then who can say what will happen. She stopped a whirlwind with a prayer!"

Ralda followed the Withling, who took care with her steps in the descending wash. He turned back to the others, whose faces were set. That wasn't a confrontation soon forgotten. Gweld glanced at Ralda and pushed past him.

Tordug stopped by Ralda and gathered more wood. "What's gotten into him? We're all worried for them."

Ralda shrugged. "No see what needed. Ralda no see. But big if Hastra know it."

"Ralda, I sometimes think you are the wisest of us all. Lead on." Tordug dipped his head to Ralda.

The giant proceeded along the gully. Water rushed past in the river at the end of the defile. If only they were sure Hastra knew what she was doing. There was only water at the end of this trail of hers.

Hastra whirled to all of them. "Here, lay the fire here. Quickly!" She motioned to a patch of river-sand well above the water, washed up when the water ran higher.

Gweld frowned. "I don't understand, we should be climbing up to the Funnel to help the others."

"Just kindle the fire, now!" Hastra stared at the river rushing past their little cover of rock, sand, gravel and dead-wood.

Ralda dragged wood close and Makwi came with more as Gweld kindled the fire into a smoking blaze. The fire soon crackled with dancing flames.

Hastra grabbed Ralda's arm. "Come with me." She led him close to the water along the sheer wall of rock. "Stick out your hand, close to the water!" She yelled over the noise of the rushing river.

Ralda edged as close as possible to the river. He grabbed a crevice and leaned low. If he fell in, he risked being swept away without help from the others. He reached with his hand, fingers splayed wide. He gasped as something wet grabbed his fingers.

~ ~ ~ ~ ~ ~ ~

Athson winced as the echo from his dream slid into real life. "No!" The wind forced his shout back on his lips. Spark leapt over the edge after Limbreth, glowing with many colors. But she was gone, no matter what Spark did.

As Athson ran toward Limbreth, he saw Ath reel away from Corgren, holding Athson's bloodstained dagger. Corgren whirled and stabbed Ath high in the chest. Athson's father yelled and fell onto the rock shelf. Corgren stumbled away, fumbling for the wound in his lower back, which gushed blood.

Athson froze in mid-stride. "Father!" He turned back to the altar, torn between helping Limbreth or his father.

Corgren groaned and staggered toward the Bane.

There was something Athson could do. He leapt for his sword, but as he snatched it up and turned to the wizard, Corgren spoke a spell. Green light flashed, and Athson fell back, covering his eyes. When he blinked away the light's effects, the wizard and the Bane were gone.

Ath groaned. "Athson?"

Athson rushed to his father. Blood spilled over his torso and soaked his ragged shirt. Athson pressed on the wound with his hands, but blood coursed between his fingers. "It's me, here to help."

His father reached with weak hands to touch Athson's face. His one eye rolled with a shudder of his body. "Grown now. So proud. All my fault."

Tears welled in Athson's eyes, and he shook his head. "No, I should have

CHAPTER TWENTY-TWO

searched for you. I—I dreamed of you pulling Corgren in the dark by this chain." He lifted the links attached to his father's arm. "I tried after that, but I didn't know where you were."

Ath's lips trembled, and his face paled. "Yes, saved him. For chance to get to you. We—are—at—altar?" His voice faltered amid a gurgle of blood in his throat.

Athson pressed harder. "Yes."

"So—many—died—here. Limbreth?"

Athson sniffed. "Gone. The Bane pushed her over the edge. Corgren spelled himself away. Thank you, Father."

Ath gave him a weak smile. "Least…could do. Listen. Limbreth—good woman. Too bad." He gripped Athson's arm with a suddenly strong grip. "Your mother—Danilla—must save her. Rok."

Athson almost released the wound. "I know but where? I still have the bow, so they'll hold her and bargain. We'll go together. You and me. I'll get you patched up. We'll find her."

Ath coughed frothy blood and shook his head. "Dying." His body trembled beneath Athson's hands.

Athson's tears fell on Ath as his father released him and fell back. He needed Hastra. Athson shook his head. "No! I just found you! Stay!"

Ath gasped more blood. His chest rose and fell twice, then ceased. Athson fell on his father's body and wept. After a time, he stood and wiped his face, smearing blood on his cheeks. He was alone again, just like when he was a boy. And now he'd lost Limbreth. That was his fault. He should've shot the Bane. Athson eyed the Bow of Hart. It was only a bow after all, and it had failed him against Corgren.

He buried his father under stone as the wind scoured his cheeks dry and tore at his cloak. He stood for a while, head lowered. Then his head shot up at a sudden thought. His mother lived, and Corgren was gone. The wizard would find her and use her, maybe kill her too. Athson gathered his things—even the Bow of Hart, since his old one had been blown away by the storm. He'd bargain for her with it, though.

Before he left, Athson stood on the edge of the Funnel and watched the river churn below him. There was no way she could have survived that fall and the river. Limbreth was gone. Everyone close to him died, and it was his fault.

He would find his mother.

Athson set loose Corgren's horses and retrieved the mule. It was a better climber for these hills and the mountains he'd cross. He left the Funnel and headed north for the old road that led into the passes through the Drelkhaz and into Rok beyond them. Danilla was there—somewhere—and he would find her.

EPILOGUE

Sarneth entered the receiving room from his office. He couldn't see why it was so urgent a message as to be given in person. His ears only? All the way from Grendon? He closed the door. "I'm sorry to keep you waiting. Perhaps there was some error made by…" His voice faded along with his polite smile. This was no messenger.

A slender man, taller than Sarneth, stood and stared out the window. His expensive cloak of black and red draped down his back but did not hide his expensive cavalry boots. He turned to Sarneth, his house sigil displayed on the wide collar of his cloak. "Error? I'm afraid not. Didn't they tell you who I am?" A ready but practiced formal smile spread over his long face, which displayed a hint of command. He slowly blinked his dark eyes and produced a sealed scroll from a hidden pocket.

Sarneth cocked his head. An emissary of standing in Grendon. Not worn from travel, so plenty of men and servants in his retinue. He cleared his throat. "I'm Captain Sarneth. You are…?" The seal flashed into view. Sarneth's eyes narrowed slightly. The royal seal?

"Dareth of Tinnewell, commissioned by His Royal Highness, Hamgas, King of Grendon as his emissary and betrothed to his youngest daughter." He offered the scroll. "I'm here to collect the princess and return her to Grendon." He cleared his throat. "Wedding, you know."

Sarneth slipped his finger around the wax to break it. "I'm sure I don't know of such a person being in the city. Who is she?"

"Limbreth. I believe she traveled in the company of the Withling Hastra."

The scroll almost slipped from Sarneth's hands. "Limbreth is the king's daughter?"

"You know her, then?"

"Indeed, I do, though she's not in Auguron at this time." Sarneth unrolled the scroll and scanned the contents but found nothing more than already shared by Dareth. The king requested his daughter be returned immediately under Dareth's official escort. Didn't sound good for Limbreth.

"Not here?" The smile faded from the emissary's face. "I don't understand. She sent word that she was here, though that was some months ago."

"Have a seat, please. Shall I call for refreshments?" Sarneth sat after his visitor unfurled his cloak from his shoulders and settled into a chair.

"Uh, no." Dareth crossed one leg over the other and cocked his head with an expression of expectation.

"I was unaware that Limbreth was a daughter of the king. She passed herself off as an adventurer in service to Hastra."

Dareth's eyebrows shot up, and he inhaled a deep breath, then forced a smile. "An indulgence of the king for some years that she act the adventurer. I'm afraid she's taken it to heart. Do you expect her to return this way, or shall I seek her elsewhere?"

Sarneth forced a smile in turn. "I do expect them to return with a Rokan fugitive, but I've heard no word from them in weeks. That was last from our eastern borders."

"Troll country, I believe?" Dareth fidgeted in his chair.

"Indeed, it is. I can offer you letters to a certain elf named Marston, should you wish to investigate further." *Doubt he's much interested in trolls. But best to offer anyway.* Sarneth tapped the scroll against his leg.

Dareth squinted at him. "You say you expect this party of adventurers back?"

"Two of my own rangers travel with them on additional business to bring this fugitive back, should they lay hands on him."

"Then they may be on their way here now?"

"It is possible. My communication has been sporadic from that direction of late." Sarneth regretted admitting that last bit of information. A puzzle,

EPILOGUE

that. And worrisome. Marston acted as his agent and passed news of all kinds to him aside from more official messages.

"Would you have suitable accommodations for myself, my officers, and three hundred horsemen?" Dareth offered a slight smile, but he left his eyes fixed steadily on Sarneth's.

"It can be found." Sarneth rang a bell for the runner on duty. No belly for trolls, wife or not? "If I'd been aware of your impending arrival, I'd have prepared to receive you. I shall have rooms booked at the best inn."

Dareth stood abruptly and offered his hand. "My apologies. An oversight I shall have investigated by my second."

Sarneth shook Dareth's hand with his best gracious smile. Entertaining a rather large force so far from their home? He doubted it was an oversight. Dareth had hoped to surprise Limbreth, and now he'd squat in the city and spend as little of his own money as possible. Limbreth was in for a surprise when she returned. He'd best not send a bird with this news. She might not come back, and he didn't want that on his hands, given she was a princess. Hastra had some explaining to do as well, Withling or not.

~ ~ ~ ~ ~ ~ ~

Within a few days, snow whipped on the wind in Athson's face. He stumbled over stones and snags under the gathering drifts as he led the mule. These blasted heaths were a curse on his life. Everyone missing from his life had some attachment here, and they might be the death of him if he didn't find shelter. A cough surged from his chest. Weakness dragged at his limbs. He squinted into the snow, found nothing, and plodded into the gust and swirl of white.

His teeth chattered. After a while, a dog's bark brought him to a halt. "Spark?"

The mountain hound waded through the gathering snow behind him. And beyond the dog, a figure in a cloak followed. The Bane! Athson flexed his trembling hands. He couldn't use his bow—*the* bow—in this wind. If it was even accurate.

He tramped on, redoubling his effort. His sword would do the job. He just needed a place to hide. He swung his head from side to side, searching as he went. A boulder, a crag, anything!

As Athson sought concealment, his shivering stopped. Warmth grew in his limbs. He should take off his cloak. He stopped as snow beat at his eyes. No, it was the cold, but he was in danger from more than the cold. He moved on and almost fell. A cough wracked his body, and cold sank deep in his chest.

Behind him, Spark was closer—along with the Bane. If only the dog would do something. He had at the altar when—when Athson failed. He wouldn't now. He'd get Limbreth's killer.

Athson staggered away. In minutes, the dog and the Bane closed on him. Athson's knees wobbled, but he kept moving, kept searching. For what? He'd forgotten what he was looking for.

Spark barked just behind him. The wind gusted, and Athson rocked with it. He fell to his hands and knees. He half-rose and grabbed for his sword, but missed and fell flat, sputtering in the wind.

The Bane stooped over him. Spark sat nearby, merely watching! Athson fumbled for his sword, but the Bane pushed his hands away. The creature lifted him and started walking. Spark followed. Athson reached for the dog, his arms going limp. "Help me, Spark." Only the howling wind answered as Athson closed his eyes, unable to retain awareness. They had him—and the bow.

Athson struggled to open his eyes and glimpsed the folded brim of a hat beneath the hood. He raised a hand and blocked the wind and snow from his eyes, peering into the hood. Instead of darkness, a weathered face loomed into view. "You!"

"Me." The trader from his travels lifted Athson onto the mule. "You look like you could use some help." He gathered the Bow of Hart into his arms and led the mule forward into the storm.

Spark bounded away.

Athson bowed beneath his cough and weakness until he hugged the mule's neck and let the trader lead the way, his eyes barely open.

His mother. He needed to find her.

After the storm.

EPILOGUE

The End

Dear Reader, I hope you enjoyed The Bow of Destiny, Book One of The Bow of Hart Saga. I have to tell you, I really love the all characters but especially Athson, Limbreth and Spark. Many readers have written me asking, "What's next for Athson?" Well, be sure to stay tuned, because the saga of isn't quite over. Athson will be back in book 2. Will he find the Bow of Hart? I sure hope so. When I wrote The Bow of Destiny, I got many wonderful reviews and ratings from fans thanking me for the book. Some had opinions about all the events in the book and asked what would happen next. As an author, I love feedback. Candidly, you're the reason I've been able to finish the series. So, tell me what you liked, what you loved, even what you hated. I'd love to hear from you. You can write me at ph@phsolomon.com and visit me on the web at www.phsolomon.com. Finally, I need to ask a favor. If you're so inclined, I'd love it if you would post a review of The Bow of Destiny. Loved it, hated it— I'd just like to hear your feedback. Reviews can be tough to come by these days, and you, the reader, have the power to make or break a book. If you have the time, here's a link to the book page where you can leave your thoughts. Thank you so much for reading An Arrow Against the Wind and for spending time with me.

In gratitude,

P. H. Solomon

P. S. As an added bonus, click this link to request an Authorgraph autograph from me and I'll respond with one you can insert into your e-reader.

Keep scrolling for a preview from the next book, *The White Arrow*, and information about joining my social circle.

EPILOGUE

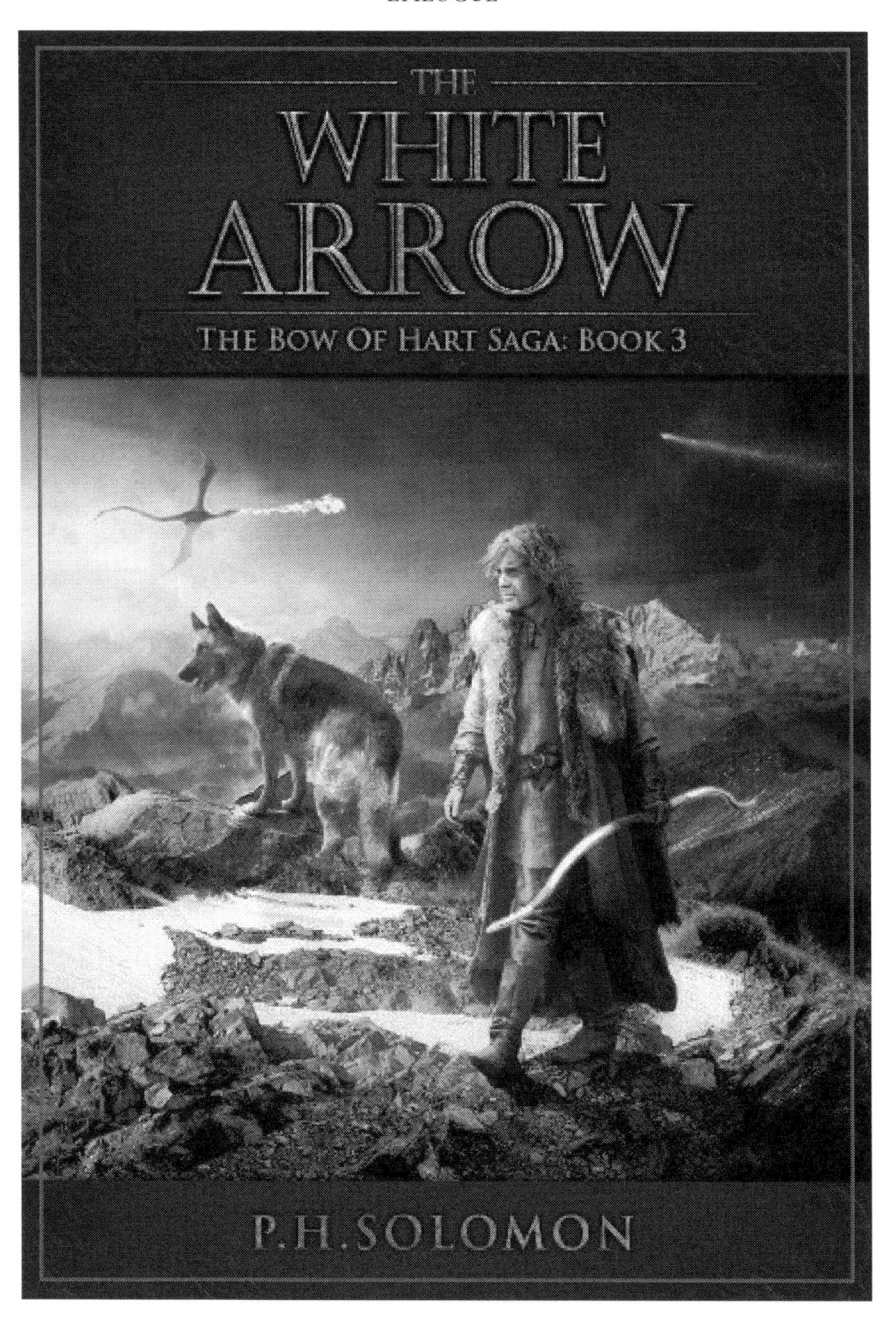

Now Available on Amazon

The White Arrow

Apeth pushed himself to his feet, stepped around the fire and knelt before Athson. He touched Athson's head and whispered a word Athson never heard clearly though it echoed across his mind in a moment that passed like hours.

Wellness covered Athson in an instant like a raincoat donned in a sudden downpour of rain. The cascade of sickness rolled from him and the fever fell away. His dizziness ceased and his vision snapped into clarity along with his thoughts. Weariness clattered from his limbs like loosened manacles from a prisoner. He gasped in delayed reaction to the Withling's healing.

Apeth Stellin withdrew across the fire and rolled his bedding. "I was wondering why I was withheld from healing you immediately. And now it's clear."

Athson stood and inhaled deeply. "Thanks for that but I don't follow your meaning."

"We need to move." Apeth pointed toward the cave entrance past the mule. "That wandering star is a sign. We aren't the only ones to have seen it. You can bet Magdronu is seeking the arrow because of the sign. North is our way but choices lie ahead for you."

Athson shoved the last of his venison in his mouth and chewed. In his mind, there was but one choice. "I see one way ahead."

Apeth tugged at the brim of his hat and his blue-eyed gaze twinkled at Athson. "Oh, you have choices. What to do with the bow. Whether to finish this quest and find the arrow."

With his arms spread wide, Athson lifted his gaze to the darkened cave roof rising above them. "Don't you see? There's no need for choices. Everyone's dead that matters to me. My father. Limbreth. My companions. I can only see my way to one thing now and that's bartering for my mother's freedom."

"That's a choice to let the curse on you continue to grasp your life, Athson, continue to let Magdronu's evil control you. You have a choice to stop it." Apeth stepped close again, his gaze intense but not threatening. "As for Limbreth, by your dream, I wouldn't assume anything about her fate. But

EPILOGUE

there are choices ahead. Will you go as far as Marston's Station with me before you make your final choice about the bow?"

Athson nodded. "I'll go that far. I need supplies. But there's no other choice for me."

"Oh, but there is. Your dreams indicate something you must face." Apeth gathered his things and paused in front of Athson.

Athson crossed his arms. "What must I face?"

"That you are gifted to be a Withling, asked to serve Eloch with everything you've been given." The Withling strode toward the mule.

Athson's head spun anew but not from fever. Light from the wandering star glimmered in the entrance of the cave and lit the Bow of Hart where he'd left it near the mule. His anger burst in a sudden bellow, "No!"

Find The White Arrow on Amazon
&
Finish The Bow of Hart Saga

About the Author

P. H. Solomon lives in the greater Birmingham, AL area where he strongly dislikes yard work and sanding the deck rail. However, he performs these duties to maintain a nice home for his loved ones as well as the family's German Shepherds. In his spare time, P. H. rides herd as a Computer Whisperer on large computers called servers (harmonica not required). Additionally, he enjoys reading, running, most sports and fantasy football. Having a degree in Anthropology, he also has a wide array of more "serious" interests in addition to working regularly to hone his writing. His first novel, The Bow of Destiny was named 2016 Book of the Year by Fantasia Reviews and is the first book of The Bow of Hart Saga. The sequel novel, An Arrow Against the Wind, was released in April of 2017. The third book of the series, The White Arrow, is due to be released during the Fall of 2017. P. H. Solomon also authored the award winning short story, The Black Bag, which won best published short story at SCWC 2012. P. H. is also a member of Science Fiction and Fantasy Writers of America (SFWA).

If you enjoyed reading my work, you can subscribe to my newsletter for more information about my other books, fun updates about the series and news about upcoming releases. Click here to subscribe and receive a gift. Read on about the next book in the series.

Join P. H. Solomon's social circle.

Website/Author Blog | Twitter | Facebook | Pinterest | Email | Google+ Goodreads | Wattpad | Amazon Author Page

About the Author

Multiple Retailer Bestselling Author, Fantasia Reviews Book of the Year Author 2017 & 2018.

U. S. author, P. H. Solomon grew up with a love of books including fantasy. Always interested in odd details, history and the world around him, P. H. has found an outlet in writing where he mixes a wide range of interests from the regular world, history, and anthropology into his fantasy books.

His epic fantasy series, The Bow of Hart Saga, brought a fresh viewpoint to the genre where magic, myth and mysticism mingle. Described by readers as a "mixture of the classic fantasy past with new ideas."

Trading Knives (0.1)

What is Needed (0.2)

The Bow of Destiny #1

An Arrow Against the Wind #2

The White Arrow #3

The latest series, The Cursed Mage Case Files is a mash-up of classic Sherlock Holmes, The Dresden Files and Harry Potter into a unique fantasy world where magic is both the arcane and technology to be used. Join

Mandlefred Mandeheim and Wishton Ackford as they team up to investigate magical mysteries.

The Order of the Dark Rose #1

The Unseen Hand #2 (upcoming)

The Nine Jewel Heist #3 (upcoming)

More books:

Curses Dark and Foul

The Black Bag

Connect with the P. H. Solomon via the following links:

Twitter | Facebook | Goodreads | Website | Pinterest | BookBub | Amazon Author Page | Archer's Aim Store | Text

Subscribe to my newsletter:

✉ https://landing.mailerlite.com/webforms/landing/z4b8h8

Also by P. H. Solomon

The White Arrow, The Bow of Hart Saga, Book 3
"Twists and turns" with "stop in your tracks kind of moments." ★★★★★

Bound to prophecy, his destiny balanced on an arrow's tip.

With the Bow of Hart in hand, Athson is hunted by his enemies. His mistakes haunt him as much as his past.

Magdronu plots to thwart the prophecy as his trolls attack Auguron City.

Hastra the Withling reveals Eloch will send an arrow for the bow. But when the arrow arrives, it is from an unexpected source and lands in unforeseen hands. Events twist like an arrow in flight…

Can Athson overcome his past and use the Bow of Hart as intended?

The archer and the bow await the coming arrow…

The Order of the Dark Rose, Volume 1 of The Cursed Mage Case Files

"Magical world-building, brilliant characters, amazing, leaves you craving more, sleight of hand story" - Reviews from Readers Favorite

An arch-mage can handle anything. Unless he's cursed, lost his job and facing an unknown enemy.

Arch-mage Manny Mandeheim fell under a curse, watched his fiancé die, and then lost his job as a spy. What's an unemployed arch-mage to do? Start his own magical investigation service while he works to clear his good name and avenge his lost love.

With his very un-magical partner, Wish Ackford, Manny discovers the menace of a conspiracy looming behind his curse. But the limitations from the hex leave him at a distinct disadvantage as he and Wish investigate.

Assassins lurk at every corner or in every tram car. The threat of an unknown mastermind with murky intentions lingers just out of sight. A questionable source offers the hint of a secret order hounding Manny's footsteps. A murder leads to wrenching discoveries.

Nothing an arch-mage can't handle…

Unless the curse limits how much magic he can use or kills him outright.

A mixture of gaslamp fantasy and Sherlock Holmes-like cases, The Order of the Dark Rose is a sleuth private detective mystery set in an alternate fantasy world where magic is both commonplace and dangerous. Mysteries abound in this original, new fantasy from P. H. Solomon, author of the award-winning, best-selling epic fantasy series, The Bow of Hart Saga.

Can Manny survive long enough to break his curse? Or will the arch-mage's hidden foe escape him?

The Unseen Hand, Volume 2 of The Cursed Mage Case Files
This book is pending release during 2022

Trading Knives, The Bow of Hard Saga, Book 0.1
Trading a knife costs a life. The offer of help may cost more.

Corgren more than holds his own in the prize fighting rings where skill with a knife is the only mercy he'll find. While an old enemy haunts his memory, new ones gather with each victory gained.

Corgren's choices narrow.

A stranger offers Corgren power for his service, tempting him with revenge for past wrongs. He considers the offer with doubt. Demands for a cut of his winnings squeezes his independence until a foe possibly more skilled and cunning than him enters the ring.

Will he accept the offer at the cost of himself?

What Is Needed, The Bow of Hart Saga, Book 0.2
Hastra begins having visions of the destruction the mystic Withling order of which she is a member. Without any guidance, she investigates who the source of the danger may be. But how much time does she have and who should she trust with her visions? This is the second prequel short story to the novel, The Bow of Destiny, by P. H. Solomon.

Curses Dark and Foul

Grim words spoken. Foul intentions invoked. Curses never offer surrender.

Three tales of fantasy in Curses Dark an Foul from Amazon bestselling author, P. H. Solomon

The Black Bag: Coryss finds herself alone against three powerful witches. Young and foolhardy, she confronts her foes and challenges them to a simple contest. Hopeless, Coryss finds help from an unlikely source. But the dark and foul curses fly without mercy. Can Coryss save herself?

Shadow of the Beast: Sa'hatap serves the Seddessan Empire faithfully as a foreign conscript, his people merged into the political scenery of merciless overlords. An enemy tasks the warrior and holy-man with ending a curse upon the missing empress. Unwilling, yet with his people under threat of annihilation, Sa-hatap sets out to accomplish the impossible and kill an accursed beast that cannot be defeated. Will his sword and his faith save him?

For No Reason: Dax is haunted by the curse upon his village as the living emblem of the revenge of a witch. No one can kill him and his touch is death. But the curse will take Dax's mind and transform him into a beast of retribution. His only hope is helping the village, but they hate him. How will he ever save himself, and them?

If you like short fantasy with a mix of sword and sorcery and dark fantasy, then you'll like Curses Dark and Foul. Bestselling fantasy author, P. H. Solomon, presents three short stories of curses both dark and foul, where characters never had a chance. Yet in the darkness, the glimmer of hope, the slimmest of chance against overwhelming odds exists.

Dire curses threaten these characters with inescapable fate. Will each hero make a choice and take a stand regardless of hope or chances of success?

The Black Bag

Coryss finds herself alone against three powerful witches. Young and foolhardy, she confronts her foes and challenges them to a simple contest. Hopeless, Coryss finds help from an unlikely source. But the dark and foul curses fly without mercy. Can Coryss save herself?

Archer's Aim Press Store

Find a range of items based on the artwork from books by P. H. Solomon

https://www.archersaimpress.store

Made in the USA
Columbia, SC
28 January 2025

a4be7225-d6cf-4227-becd-c1600979a168R01